The
B
Word

Bisexuality in
Contemporary
Film and
Television

The
B
Word

Maria San Filippo

INDIANA UNIVERSITY PRESS *Bloomington & Indianapolis*

This book is a publication of

INDIANA UNIVERSITY PRESS
601 North Morton Street
Bloomington, Indiana 47404–3797 USA

iupress.indiana.edu

Telephone orders 800-842-6796
Fax orders 812-855-7931

© 2013 by Maria San Filippo

Manufactured in the
United States of America

Library of Congress
Cataloging-in-Publication Data

San Filippo, Maria.
    The B word : bisexuality in contem-
porary film and television / Maria San
Filippo.
    pages cm
    Based on the author's dissertation
(doctoral) – University of California, Los
Angeles.
    Includes bibliographical references and
index.
    ISBN 978-0-253-00879-4 (cl : alk.
paper) – ISBN 978-0-253-00885-5 (pb :
alk. paper) – ISBN 978-0-253-00892-3
(eb) 1. Bisexuality in motion pictures.
2. Bisexuality on television.
I. Title.
    PN1995.9.B57S36 2013
    791.43086'63 – dc23

2012042177

1 2 3 4 5   18 17 16 15 14 13

In memory of

MADELINE CRIVELLO (1952–2011)

and of

ALEXANDER DOTY (1954–2012)

and

ROBIN WOOD (1931–2009)

Contents

Acknowledgments

DURING THE LONG GESTATION OF THIS PROJECT, I HAVE benefitted from the insights and support of many advisers, colleagues, friends, and family. I especially wish to thank my UCLA dissertation committee, Denise Mann, Kathleen McHugh, Jim Schultz, and especially my chair, Janet Bergstrom, as well as the other mentors who have guided and advocated for me and become friends in the process: Laura Mulvey, Vivian Sobchack, Wini Wood, and the warm, wise women of WGS at Harvard. My gratitude goes out to Tania Modleski for offering her assurance of my project's potential, and to Jane Behnken for first showing interest in my manuscript and for shepherding it along. Jane's colleagues at Indiana University Press, especially Peter Froehlich, Darja Malcolm-Clarke, Raina Polivka, Sarah Wyatt Swanson, and Jenna Whittaker, have provided invaluable support along the way, and Eric Levy proved an outstanding copyeditor in the final act. My undergraduate alma mater and postgraduate home, Wellesley College, and its passionate, talented teachers and students, are an ongoing source of creative revelation and intellectual stimulation for me. My UCLA classmates and friends Ross Melnick, Jennifer Moorman, Maya Montañez Smukler, and Laurel Westrup have contributed a decade's worth of personal and professional celebration and commiseration, for which I'm eternally grateful. Candace Moore has been an inspiration as a thinker and writer, and in so many other ways. My parents Frank and D San Filippo, my sister Kristina San Filippo, and my "sister" Ivey Doyal Rucket are all immeasurably part of who I am and what I've done, for which I'm forever in their debt. Above all, I wish to thank Vernon Shetley – my unflagging mentor, my most discerning editor, my favorite fellow cinéaste, and "the best and loyalist friend a girl ever had."

The
B
Word

The way the world is, how seldom it is that you meet that one person who just gets you. . . . It's so rare. And to cut oneself off from finding that person, to immediately halve your options . . .

CHASING AMY (KEVIN SMITH, 1997)

Chasing Amy and Bisexual (In)visibility

WHEN ASKED ABOUT THIS BOOK'S TOPIC, I TYPICALLY RESPOND that it deals with bisexuality in film and television. The most frequent response, offered up by people from diverse areas of my life, is, "You mean like *Chasing Amy*?" This American independent film about a self-proclaimed lesbian who is forced to question her sexual identity after meeting and falling for a man clearly occupies a prominent place in cultural consciousness around bisexuality. (The other steadfastly recurring response has been, "You mean like *Basic Instinct* [Paul Verhoeven, 1992]?" I address this film in chapter 2.) In thinking about why *Chasing Amy* should leap to mind when the topic turns to bisexuality onscreen, I recognized several ways in which this film provides an apt entry into the concerns of this book. *Chasing Amy*'s female lead, Alyssa Jones (played by petite, blonde, Minnie Mouse–voiced Joey Lauren Adams), adheres to mainstream culture's preference for safely gender-conforming images of queer women, at the same time that Alyssa's femme appearance also contradicts prevailing assumptions about what queer women look like. Indeed, it is Alyssa's *not* being visibly queer that allows for the film's first-act revelation on the part of male lead Holden (Ben Affleck) and presumably a substantial number of spectators who would not have surmised Alyssa's sexual preference from the coy hints given in the film's trailer ("She just needs the right guy") and tagline ("It's not who you love. It's how"). In this way, Alyssa's visual imperceptibility serves to foreground the recurring issue, both in queer media representation and in the everyday experiences of many bisexual/queer women, of bisexual invisibility.

3

Yet I would immediately revise this to read *(in)visibility,* to signal the spectral presence that bisexuality occupies, both onscreen and within the broader landscape of sexual identity. Bisexuality is both visible *and* invisible, as my parenthetical designation indicates, due to the slippage between its representational pervasiveness and the alternating measures of tacit acceptance, disidentification, or disavowal that render bisexuality discursively un(der)spoken. Bisexuality's (in)visibility belies its ubiquity within our culture, and indeed constitutes a disavowal of the twinned fascination and anxiety bisexuality provokes. For there are traces throughout the contemporary screen mediascape that suggest the degree to which bisexuality serves as a driving force in the production, marketing, and consumption of screen media and technology. Not just in queer cinema or on cable channels targeted at "the gay community," but on network shows and in Hollywood movies playing at the local multiplex. The presence of bisexuality is not limited to bisexual characters and plot lines involving bisexual relationships; bisexuality is also a crucial component in the strategies and processes involved in selling and experiencing screen media. Yet this key presence goes almost entirely unacknowledged and undiscussed. Media scholars and critics occasionally appear to notice it, but they call it by other names: gay, lesbian, homoerotic, homosocial, queer . . . To a surprising extent, bisexuality remains the orientation that dares not speak its name. Into this discursive gap falls a good deal of knowledge that it is essential we retrieve in order to grasp with precision how sexuality works – not just within film and television, but with regard to everyday desires, behaviors, and subjectivities.

Chasing Amy's boy-meets-lesbian plotline sets into motion such a retrieval, through its explicit appraisal of bisexual (in)visibility and the related cultural attitudes about bisexuality it confronts: namely, the belief that bisexuality is "just a phase" or "the easy way out," bi-phobia on the part of both straight- and gay-identified individuals ("Another one bites the dust," Alyssa's lesbian friends say upon hearing she is dating a man), and the stereotype of the promiscuous, commitment-phobic bisexual. As a film aimed at and embraced by a young straight *and* queer viewership, *Chasing Amy* is an example of what the television industry calls *dual-casting:* a media text strategically designed to cross demographic boundaries to appeal to two (or more) niche audiences. The third installment

P.1. To look or not to look? Holden (Ben Affleck) and Banky (Jason Lee) negotiate uncomfortable visual pleasure.

in Kevin Smith's "New Jersey Trilogy" – it aims considerably higher than its predecessors *Clerks* (1994) and *Mallrats* (1995) – *Chasing Amy* owes more to Richard Linklater and Quentin Tarantino than to New Queer Cinema. Its hyperarticulate, endlessly referential dialogue and slacker mien targets, and flatters, an alternative subculture of clever-yet-disillusioned (and primarily heterosexual) young adults much like the ones that populate Smith's films. Geographically, *Chasing Amy* straddles the heternormativity of Smith's world – Holden shares an apartment in Hoboken, New Jersey, with his best friend Banky (Jason Lee) – and the big-city bohemia of downtown Manhattan, where Alyssa lives. When these worlds collide, straight guys Holden and Banky are our guides for a touristic venture into the Lower East Side lesbian scene circa 1997, complete with insider references for in-the-know spectators, such as a scene at now-defunct girl bar Meow Mix featuring a cameo by *Go Fish* (Rose Troche, 1994) scribe and prominent lesbian Guinevere Turner. Touristic observation never develops into outright voyeuristic leering, however; *Chasing Amy* acknowledges that female same-sex desire fig-ures prominently in heterosexual male fantasy, but largely abstains from gratifying a prurient desire for "girl-on-girl action" (to borrow the porn industry's term for women's "gay for pay" scenes). In the one instance in which Alyssa is seen making out with a woman, the shot quickly widens to include the uncomfortable Holden (downcast as he realizes his crush is unrequited) and the leering Banky. Rather than indulge complacently or reject entirely the accustomed visual pleasure in femme lesbian eroticism, the scene unsettles and complicates our enjoyment by exaggerating how these images overwhelmingly emanate from, and are dictated by, a heterosexual male perspective.

In addition to literally peering into queer spaces, *Chasing Amy* locates its story in the figuratively queer – that is, alternative – world of comic book artists and aficionados, one presumably more familiar to Smith's core audience. Negotiating unfamiliar terrain (queer female subcultures) by way of a familiar route (a primarily heterosexual male subculture) allows for the metaphorical negotiation of bisexuality through an analogous – but safer – transgression of social norms. This narrative device, which I've named *bi-textuality* (to be discussed at greater length in my introduction), works through bisexuality by analogizing it to other "deviant" identity constructions that also resist the terms imposed by binary thinking. While *Chasing Amy*'s articulations of bisexuality are far less subtle than those of a number of films explored in this study (hence its serving as the sine qua non of screen bisexuality), the comics subculture it depicts clearly functions as more than a backdrop. *Chasing Amy*'s opening scene, set at an annual comics convention in lower Manhattan, establishes the similarities between it and the queer subculture it parallels, with the fanboys' (and some fangirls') elaborate getups and idiosyncratic factions mirroring the bondage gear and subdivisions based on self-presentation and preference within queer communities. During a panel discussion, Afrocentric comic artist Hooper (Dwight Ewell) delivers an enraged diatribe about racist subtext in the original *Star Wars* trilogy, only later to reveal privately that his militant image is designed to sell books. Actually, Hooper is a gay black man ("notoriously the swishiest of the bunch," he points out) who attempts at length to convince Banky that Archie and Jughead are lovers (more subtext, this time of the queer variety). Offering an immediate reminder that queerness is not always visible, this opening scene foreshadows Alyssa's own invisibility by depicting Hooper "passing" as black and proud – rather than gay and proud – for professional respect.

P.2. Alyssa (Joey Lauren Adams) demonstrating what lesbians do in bed.

Giving the straight male character and viewer a guided tour through "gay New York," *Chasing Amy* promotes empathy and tolerance for a subculture not so very different from that to which the film's comic artist heroes and their fans, as well as Smith's fans, belong.[1] In its metaphorical linking of different subcultures for the education of straight male viewers, *Chasing Amy* provides sensitivity training through the "lessons" Holden learns from Alyssa, who begins by disabusing Holden of his notion that lesbian sex is "not real sex," describing with suggestive hand gestures what it is that women actually do together in bed. To take measure of this overt demonstration of the mechanics of lesbian sex, it is useful to consider how comparatively uninterested in educating straight viewers was the roughly contemporaneous *Go Fish,* a film that touted itself as being by, for, and about lesbians. Analyzing that film's textual references to the lesbian community, Lisa Henderson recalls how a protracted scene in which two women prepare to consummate their romance by clipping each other's fingernails sent lesbian spectators falling into the aisles laughing, though this reference to sexual hand play, never clearly articulated within the dialogue, was likely lost on the rest of the audience.[2] *Chasing Amy* seems ethnographic by comparison, constructing its lesbian references not merely for the delectation of those in on the joke, as it were, but taking equivalent interest (and delight, given the priceless expression Alyssa prompts from the dumbfounded Holden) in informing those not in the know.

Alyssa will go on to justify her active sexual past alongside her queer identity by saying, "I was an experimental girl – I wasn't given a fucking map at birth." Concurrently, the homophobic perspective is voiced by the un-self-censoring Banky, who delivers an ongoing tirade against "faggots" and "man-hating lesbians" yet otherwise is presented not as a stereotypical gay-bashing ignoramus but rather as the voice of reason to Holden's love-struck sap, naive enough to fall in love with someone so clearly unavailable. In articulating the common-sense perspective, Banky sees through politically correct platitudes and offers homophobia-inclined male viewers a not-unsavory role model with whom to identify. Even so, persistent references are made to the homoerotic dynamic between this male duo who, like Batman and Robin (and perhaps Archie and Jughead), share a professional and domestic partnership as comic artists and roommates – until Alyssa threatens to come between them. The film repeatedly stages pairs of scenes to mirror one another in composition and content so as to illustrate Alyssa's physical infiltration into the "men's world." Moreover, Holden and Banky's suggestively close relationship is referenced in ways both comic (Smith regular Jason Mewes, playing his recurring stoner character Jay, addresses Holden with "Why the long face – Banky on the rag?") and serious (as Hooper tells Holden in regard to Banky, "Don't kid yourself – that boy loves you in a way that he ain't ready to deal with"). Banky himself refers to their being something more than buddies when he explains his resistance to Alyssa as intended "to ensure all this time we spent together building something wasn't wasted." "She's not going to ruin the comic," Holden protests. "I wasn't talking about the comic," Banky replies.

In these and other ways, *Chasing Amy* serves as a meta-commentary not just on gay identity but on gay identity *films*, in which the teleological resolution insists on a definitive acknowledgment of a questioning character's monosexual identity. The romantic-erotic triangle, a trusty cinematic trope (as we will see) for problematizing monosexuality and thus indirectly working through bisexuality, organizes *Chasing Amy*'s narrative infrastructure. From the opening credits' chronicle, via comic book narration, of Holden and Banky's superheroic success in the comics world, *Chasing Amy* follows the formula of the male buddy film in staging the homosocial bond under threat from a heterosexual love interest and vice versa, but through its triangulated structure also challenges the three leads' monosexual identities. The resulting hybridization of buddy film, romantic triangle film, and comedy of remarriage serves to make *Chasing Amy* an important antecedent of a more recent Hollywood phenomenon, the *bromance*, to which I will return in chapter 3.

Whereas in the first act it dawned on Holden that femme women could like women too, in the third act it occurs to him that, as he tells Banky, "you're in love with me" – a revelation that, in Holden's view, explains Banky's jealousy of Alyssa, his homophobia, and his sense of humor (lots of what Holden calls "dick jokes"). Ostensibly to prove his point, Holden kisses Banky on the lips in a provocative though not unreservedly progressive display of filmic homoeroticism. When Holden then proposes his "perfect solution" for defusing the tension – a three-way with Alyssa – Banky agrees, though seemingly reluctantly. He acts visibly relieved a moment later when Alyssa refuses, telling Holden "I'm not your whore," and that, for her, being in love means "I would never want to share you." Again bypassing a titillating scene for one that openly mocks Holden's fantasy of its being, as he says, "the perfect solution," *Chasing Amy* also departs from the utopian resolution typically imposed by the gay coming-out relationship drama *and* the heterosexual Hollywood romance, in not allowing its newly created (straight) couple to live happily ever after.

Instead, at film's close, all three of the principal characters are separated. Alyssa is again dating a woman, but because in her short time onscreen it becomes clear that her new girlfriend is every bit the "rag" Alyssa accuses her of being, her choice is hardly endorsed and may even signal that Alyssa again is choosing on the basis of gender over heartfelt attraction. That the failure of the romance between "soul mates" Holden and Alyssa does not work out is ascribed to Holden's paranoia – about Alyssa's so-called promiscuous past *and* about her past lesbianism. As Banky reminds him, Holden would always be wondering "when the other shoe was going to drop." But because Banky does not clarify his meaning, promiscuity and bisexuality are collapsed together as mutually re-inforcing traits – either way, Alyssa is bound to betray him. Finally, even Holden and Banky have gone their separate ways, professionally and personally, though their parting seems to have been fairly amicable. In *Y Tu Mamá También* (Alfonso Cuarón, 2001) and the unimaginatively named *Threesome* (Andrew Fleming, 1994), consummated encounters between male friends lead to awkward mornings after, best pals parting, and (at least in the former case) the woman who encouraged their sexual exploration having to die. Even without the threesome's actually hav-ing taken place in *Chasing Amy,* the fact of two straight-identified men overtly acknowledging their attraction to one another precludes their remaining buddies. Banky fails to reform completely by film's end – he's still telling dick jokes – but he and (if the film's aim is successful) the straight male viewer have gained some sensitivity and at least a minimal recognition of their own potential desires.

For a more or less "mainstream" film, *Chasing Amy* is unusual in its willingness to voice in any sustained way the struggle to move be-yond what I call *compulsory monosexuality.* This neologism along with the attendant *compulsory monogamy* (description also to follow) are of course drawn from Adrienne Rich's seminal concept "compulsory het-erosexuality," by which she indicated one facet of the ideological and in-stitutionalized means of suppressing lesbianism so as to control women. Writing in 1980, Rich was arguing unabashedly for a desexualized no-tion of *lesbian,* redefined as woman-identified women, so to encourage same-sex loyalties and with them feminist political affiliation across the then-widening lesbian/heterosexual divide.[3] I have adjusted Rich's for-mulation to account for contemporary society's accommodation of gay identity, albeit within certain boundaries of mainstream acceptability. In the contemporary United States, these boundaries get largely defined as assimilated and domesticated but not (to use the sacrosanct term) married. Monosexuality, signaling desire enacted with partners of only one gender, is systemically reproduced by pressing social-sexual subjects to conform to *either* heterosexuality *or* homosexuality, and by keeping bisexuality (in)visible. By emphasizing the importance of physical, emo-tional, and material determinants (as much if not more than the gender of one's object choice) in informing sexual desire, behavior, and identity,

Chasing Amy delivers on the promise of its secondary tagline: "Finally, a comedy that tells it like it feels."

Yet what *Chasing Amy* noticeably does not do, despite a dialogue-heavy script that consistently circles around sexual-identity issues and a female lead who *behaves* bisexually, is ever use the term *bisexual*. To be fair, the term *queer* is also omitted, likely in deference to the film's primarily straight audience and more centrist leanings, as well as for purposes of verisimilitude – *queer* remaining a term still little-used, except as a slur, outside of the BGLQT (bisexual, gay, lesbian, queer, and transgender) community and academe. *Bisexual,* I would argue, has more valence than *queer* among the population at large, and continues in usage as an identity formation especially among younger individuals.[4] Or perhaps it was Smith's intention to do away with identity labels in the wake of Alyssa's rethinking of her lesbian identity. Whatever the case, is it important that the film actually use the B word? Not necessarily; as we will see, the degree to which screen texts contribute insight to the discourse on bisexuality bears little relation to the number of times they dare speak its name. Consider, for example, the discrepancy in this regard between the pre-sound-era film *Pandora's Box* (G. W. Pabst, 1929), in which Louise Brooks's libertine Lulu is made to suffer silently the sexual intolerance of those around her, and the cacophony of MTV reality-style show *A Shot at Love* (Riley McCormick, 2007–2009), which I discuss in chapter 4. But in so meticulously avoiding its explicit articulation, *Chasing Amy* emerges as a consummate case of bisexual (in)visibility – the unnamed, elusive quality of bisexual representation that I find symptomatic of our cultural fascination-anxiety about bisexual desire and subjectivity.

Far more troubling than *Chasing Amy*'s avoidance of the B word itself is the film's ultimate resistance to what the B word signifies. As expressed by Robin Wood,

> Bisexuality represents the most obvious and direct affront to the principle of monogamy and its supportive romantic myth of "the one right person"; the homosexual impulse in both men and women represents the most obvious threat to the norm of sexuality as reproductive and restricted by the ideal of family.[5]

Modern Western discourse constructs sexuality to seem the inevitable corollary of one's gender (itself deemed an innate marker of biological sex) so as to perpetuate a seemingly natural progression toward sexual partnership with opposite-gendered individuals for the purpose of heterosexual procreation and propagation of heteronormativity. Given the degree to which same-sex parenting has proliferated within Western society, Wood's sentiments require a slight readjustment: it is now overwhelmingly the *bisexual* rather than the homosexual impulse that threatens heteronormativity's armature – and that of *homonormativity,* the term popularized by Lisa Duggan to refer to the sexual (non) politics of gay neoliberalism, which "does not contest dominant heteronormative assumptions and institutions but upholds and sustains them while promising the possibility of a demobilized gay constituency and a privatized, depoliticized gay culture anchored in domesticity and consumption."[6] Homonormativity is thus complicit in compulsory monosexuality – the ideological and institutionalized privileging of *either* heterosexuality *or* homosexuality as the two options for mature sexuality that are socially recognized and perceived as personally sustainable. The social drive toward compulsory monosexuality remains pervasive and relentless on both sides of the aisle, with compulsory monogamy – the enticement toward marching down another aisle, the one ending in marriage vows – providing the engine toward, and enforcement of, monosexuality.

Even as *Chasing Amy* departs from the conventional Hollywood conclusion in which, Judith Mayne observes, "heterosexual symmetry is usually restored with a vengeance," the naturalness of (opposite-sex or same-sex) coupling itself goes unquestioned.[7] The line of dialogue quoted at the start of this prologue suggests how *Chasing Amy* subscribes to a romanticized ideal of "true love" between "soul mates," with an accompanying conviction that monogamy with "that one person who just gets you" is the ultimate goal of a fulfilling life. In its reluctance to move beyond this heteronormative way of thinking, *Chasing Amy* ends up re-inscribing the same cultural assumptions and restrictions around sexuality that it purports to dismantle, and so finally demonstrates just how naturalized the twin tenets of monosexuality and monogamy continue to be. When Holden tells Alyssa, "I want us to be something we can't be – a normal couple," we have seen enough to know that Holden's notion of what constitutes "normal" needs troubling – and by film's end

Holden has learned his lesson on that count. But he has also learned that love means never having to share. Just as his relationship with Alyssa has concluded, so too is his personal and professional partnership with Banky over – as Holden learns, "some doors just shouldn't be opened." It is this book's aim to open those doors.

A text is queer, regardless of the queerness of its authorial persona, if it carries the inscription of sexuality as something more than sex.

TERESA DE LAURETIS,
"Queer Texts, Bad Habits, and the Issue of a Future"

Binary Trouble and Compulsory
Monosexuality

WHY IS IT THAT *CHASING AMY,* RELEASED IN 1997, COMES NO closer to "speaking" bisexuality than Stanley Kubrick's 1960 film *Spartacus*? In a now-legendary scene, cut from the original release, Crassus (Laurence Olivier) suggestively tells Antoninus (Tony Curtis) that his "taste includes both snails *and* oysters." Or, in the considerable critical literature on David Lynch's 2001 film *Mulholland Drive* that I discuss in chapter 1, why is the female lead's (or leads') bisexuality only faintly acknowledged, an elision with significant consequences for that film's interpretation? I call these textual and critical elisions *missed moments,* and devote portions of each chapter to addressing the questions and meanings left unexplored when a monosexual perspective is imposed upon a text rich with bisexual potential. Drolly noting the (at best) marginalization to which bisexuality is relegated within the realm of queer studies, Christopher James terms this tendency to claim bisexually suggestive characters and narratives as queer, gay, or lesbian "appropriation without representation."[1] Another missed moment permeates the sexploitation cinema cycle devoted to so-called "lesbian" vampires, figures whom I find more meaningful to discuss in terms of their compelling bisexual resonance. A phallic femme, deceptive in appearance, who straddles the line between alive and dead, richly evokes the characteristic tropes of bisexuality – for as we will see in chapter 2, the fascination and anxiety the vampire provokes stems expressly from her liminality and (in)visibility. Yet another potent site of missed bisexual meaning lies in wait within *Wedding Crashers* (David Dobkin, 2005) and the contemporary Hollywood bromance cycle it helped to initiate. Chapter 3 parses how these popular, often enormously lucrative films foreground homosocial love, and so provoke a reevaluation of binary logics of desire within the cultural mainstream. Turning finally to contemplate how medium specificity affects bisexual (in)visibility, chapter 4 addresses the rich (though rarely realized) potential of television narrative to enable bisexuality's emergence through a consideration of missed moments in two provocative shows: MTV reality-style series *A Shot at Love* hosted by self-proclaimed "bisexual bachelorette" Tila Tequila, and FX dramedy *Rescue Me* (Denis Leary and Peter Tolan, 2004–2011).

BISEXUALITY AND ITS VICISSITUDES

I didn't say I was gay, I said I was in love.

EVIE (Nicole Parker), *The Incredibly True Adventures*
of Two Girls in Love (Maria Maggenti, 1995)

In the great majority of screen representations and the critical readings they inspire, the perspective on sexuality expressed remains monosexist and fixated on gender above all other determinants of object choice, be they sensory response, emotional alliance, time, space, or need. As a culture we remain mired in binary trouble, even if we can rationally recognize that human sexuality and desire are irreducible to and always already in excess of binary ways of thinking. Bisexuality as a concept is produced through this crisis of signification – the contradictions and omissions that binary constructions of gender and sexuality have constructed. But whereas monosexuality is institutionally and ideologically naturalized to *seem* innate and ubiquitous – as Judith Butler notes, "The illusion of a sexuality before the law is itself the creation of that law" – bisexuality is rendered (in)visible, to conceal the challenge it poses to monosexist assumptions.[2]

While I aim both to parse further the reasons for bisexual (in)visibility and to illuminate cinematic texts through a bisexual perspective, my goal nonetheless is not to disambiguate bisexuality altogether. It is precisely bisexuality's epistemological and textual polysemy that generates its subversive potential to lay bare the mutability, contingency, and inherent transgressiveness of desire. This complex, queer understanding of bisexuality I use to analyze it and its representations construes "the B word" as a pluralistic construct rather than as a totalizing essence, but one which nonetheless possesses a distinct ontology, in emphasizing the importance of physical, emotional, and material determinants (as much if not more than the gender of one's object choice) in informing sexual desire, behavior, and identity. In this conceptualization, bisexuality's ongoing necessity as a term stems from an insistence on bisexuality's historical and idiomatic specificity, both as subjectivity and as epistemology (taking these to be different if not necessarily conflicting), coupled with a willingness to explore and to question the contours of and rationale for that specificity. To that end, I posit no ontological conclusion as to *who* is bisexual or what bisexuality *is* – at least, not in the sense of formulating a set of variables constituting a litmus test for identifying bisexual characters or textual instances of bisexuality. My approach makes no claims for an essential or universal bisexuality, but neither does it deny or render wholly abstract the internal alterity of particular individuals' experience of bisexuality. As the Scarecrow remarks along the yellow brick road in *The Wizard of Oz* (Victor Fleming, 1939), "Of course, people do go both ways."

Nor am I interested simply in illuminating instances in which bisexuality is euphemistically or "subtextually" concealed. I wish rather to demonstrate ways in which bisexuality is already present, if obscured – hidden in plain sight – by modes of representation and reading confined within monosexual logic. If bisexual readings of texts in which there is no explicit display of queer sexuality rely on evidence that seems at times tenuous or opaque, it is not only because those texts were crafted in deference to an audience presumed to be predominantly straight, but also because, as Alexander Doty observes, "heterocentrism makes the queer erotics of mainstream films invisible or 'subtextual' for most people in the first place."[3] In her survey of the cultural geography of what she terms *bisexual spaces*, Clare Hemmings takes as her subject those "contemporary sexual and gendered spaces where bisexuality informs the development or specific manifestation of sexual subjectivity, identity, or community, whether or not bisexuality is visible or named as such."[4] What we can single out as screen media's bisexual spaces are those that represent and appeal to interstitial, fluid spectatorial identifications and desires, and thus have the potential to subvert, or "unthink," monosexuality.

As viewers of screen media, we inhabit positions and accommodate pleasures more broadly than one's publicly performed identifications and behaviors might indicate. Cinematic eros, structured by the process of fantasy that Jean Laplanche and J.-B. Pontalis describe as a staging (*mise en scène*) of desire, involves multiple eroticized modes of identification and visual pleasure that suggest and indeed encourage a bisexual desiring gaze as well as a gender-fluid subject position.[5] Viewer predilection for experiencing films bisexually – what we might call *bi-spectatorship* – was acknowledged by early cine-feminism's responses to arguments that placed spectatorship within a monolithically heteropatriarchal framework. Post-Mulvey accounts (including those by Mulvey herself) conceived women's experience of and pleasure in classical Hollywood cinema as both passive and active, heterosexual and homosexual – with evidence ranging from feminist and lesbian histories (such as those by Miriam Hansen, Jackie Stacey, Shelley Stamp, and Andrea Weiss) of female movie fandom in the silent and classical eras, to Carol Clover's discussion of how viewer identification traverses gender binaries in slasher films, to the ardor with which heterosexually identified women across America weepingly embraced *Brokeback Mountain*'s (Ang Lee, 2005) leading men, helping that film to bring in over $100 million at the box office.[6]

To twist Richard Dyer's remark that "we're all in the closet when we're watching films," one might suggest that in fact we are welcomed *out* of the closet by the cinematic experience.[7] While screen media offer a liberating space for the accommodation of subjectivities and desires beyond monosexuality, we must consider to what degree, and at what cost, such spaces remain utopian and escapist. Just as we are hardly inclined to name ourselves bisexual (or even to shape our sexual behavior) on the basis of our identifications and interactions in media space, virtually no screen characters so identify. To limit the focus to characters who proclaim their own bisexuality would overlook the ambiguous and liminal spaces that alternatives to monosexuality actually inhabit, and moreover would make for a diminutive sample, given how prone explicitly bisexual characters are to expiring prematurely within the diegesis (as we will see). The dearth – and death – of confirmable bisexual characters has to do both with compulsory monosexuality and with the correlated issue of bisexual *representability.*

I parse a diverse sample of texts – diverse both in their position within the system of media production and consumption, and in their openness to disruptions of monosexuality – for their narratives of bisexuality as well as their construction of bisexual subjectivity. My focus on films produced since the 1960s stems from my interest in considering how bisexuality remained (in)visible even after it became a publicly, politically articulated identity, and after its explicit cinematic referencing became acceptable practice, at least in theory. This study is organized around four occasionally overlapping but aesthetically and industrially distinct modes of screen media: international art cinema, "sexploitation" cinema, contemporary Hollywood cinema, and English-language television. I examine a range of cinematic and televisual types to illustrate how bisexuality is constructed in ways specific to the material, formal, and ideological context in which media texts are produced, yet exhibits similarities and consistencies over time and across heterogeneous works. The element that characterizes and unites these texts – and determines their inclusion herein – is their shared interest in thinking through bisexuality, and in thinking bisexually. This is not to say that I have selected only texts which explicitly or even knowingly engage in bisexual discourse, or are uniformly affirmative of bisexuality; several instances of bisexual representation considered here ultimately work to contain notions of fluid sexuality.

As Doty points out, "it makes sense that mainstream films produced within a capitalist system keep the range of erotic responses available for audiences as open as possible."[8] Strategic ambiguity is part and parcel of the way screen narratives have historically catered to a crossover viewership beyond their designated target demographic market. *Chasing Amy* provides one such instance, with heterosexual males and queer females being offered different reasons to embrace the film. Appealing to variable spectatorial identifications, desires, and readings enhances commercial prospects, so long as representations of sexuality do not stray too radically from contemporaneous standards of mainstream acceptability (hence the preponderance of celibate gay male characters in Hollywood films long after the Production Code's extinction).[9]

Film stars who project erotic malleability possess the power to embody the fantasies of a diverse fan base. Consider the star texts circulating around James Dean, Marlene Dietrich, Greta Garbo, and Rudolph Valentino, whose bisexual personae extended the breadth of their appeal – they could be anything their fans wanted them to be; their desirability cut across genders and sexualities. Furthermore, the studio publicity machine of the classical Hollywood era was not loath to keep rumors afloat about certain (read: female) stars' sexual transgressions when such rumors served to intensify these women's intrigue. Even then, the aura of European decadence that added to Dietrich's and Garbo's allure proved devastating to homegrown stars such as Lizabeth Scott, whose rising career reputedly was torpedoed by tabloid allegations of her lesbianism. Certainly there were multiple cases in which contract players were pressured into sham public appearances and even relationships (including marriage) designed to keep their images heteronormative, and closeted actors such as Rock Hudson and Tab Hunter were subject to especially strict management lest any word of their homosexuality leak out. Nevertheless, as Andrea Weiss remarks, "Hollywood studios went to great lengths to keep the star's image open to erotic contemplation by both men and women."[10] It made good business sense to do so, and still does.

In *Gay Fandom and Crossover Stardom,* Michael DeAngelis argues that the unmistakable yet largely unarticulated – (in)visible – bisexuality attributed to certain classical stars mirrors that operating today as a means of endowing star images with a transgressive glamour – essential, I would add, in an industrial marketplace that necessitates crossing over to audiences of different sexual preferences and proclivities.[11] DeAngelis astutely points out the importance of the under-thirty demographic in this equation, as they are the prime consumers in today's moviegoing market. Focusing specifically on the bi-suggestive star persona of Keanu Reeves, DeAngelis demonstrates how discourses of liminality and ambiguity are circulated throughout Reeves's collective star text (including films, music videos, interviews, biographies, promotional materials, chat rooms, and fanzines). Though Reeves and Angelina Jolie, whom I discuss in chapter 2, are clearly exceptional in the extent to which they embody this erotic flexibility (as Dean, Dietrich, Garbo, and Valentino were in their time), contemporary stars, as Barry King argues, "epitomize the postmodern self, a de-centered subject, deeply reflexive and disdainful of the claims of identity ... prepared to be anything as the occasion demands."[12]

The sexual ambiguity of not just stars but the characters and narratives they inhabit is also worked into promotional discourse – the meticulously researched, increasingly expensive marketing campaigns that herald high-profile projects – as a means to distinguish and broadly disperse product across demographic boundaries. Indeed, bisexuality's universality is precisely the reason for its commercial and ideological import, as Katie King underscores:

> Bisexuality, rather than the identity the bisexual, may be the formation in greatest global circulation today. As one global gay formation, bisexuality has currency in a globalized economy of niche markets where the most circulated objects are those that can be viewed within the greatest range of divergent local markets as "like-us." This doesn't mean that bisexuality is actually "all things to all people," but rather that a highly commodified version of bisexuality can be exploited ... by a wide range of markets, especially media markets.[13]

Openness to queer erotics both establishes one's hipness *and* serves as a marketing strategy; contemporary queer visibility and queer consumer dollars create incentives for even – or especially – purely commercial media to encourage alternative readings. Opportunities for "pleasurable negotiations," to use Christine Gledhill's term for revisionist reading practices, multiply as queer chic pervades visual culture.[14] Cinematic displays of femme "lesbian" eroticism (or, in the aforementioned terminology of the adult movie industry, "girl-on-girl action") titillate straight male viewers, yet serve simultaneously to enable self-recognition and gratification for queer women – especially back in the pre–*L Word* era when, as Susie Bright once put it, "we'll sit through anything if there's the smallest chance that two women might get it on."[15]

So perhaps this predilection for "having it both ways" deserves not to be viewed in wholly cynical terms. Here I appropriate a charge made against bisexuals, that they exploit a convenient middle ground of so-called "bisexual privilege" that enables them to access a greater number of potential sexual partners and enjoy the thrill of sexual transgression while maintaining the option of a recourse to heterosexual privilege.

Bisexuals thus are said to reap the fruits of gay liberation without the political and personal challenges of gay identification and alliance. Or, as Woody Allen once joked, "Bisexuality immediately doubles your chances for a date on Saturday night."[16] In diverting this allegation of sexual profiteering lobbed at bisexuals back toward the media industry, I identify a mode of queer commodification that mobilizes bisexuality to appeal to a queer audience without threatening straight spectators. In this way, screen media deploy the "commodity lesbianism" tactics that Danae Clark identified in women's fashion advertisements of the 1980s and early 1990s: a "dual market approach thus allows a space for lesbian identification, but must necessarily deny the representation of lesbian identity politics."[17] Whether originating from Madison Avenue or Hollywood, this compromise (and compromised) version of bisexuality always risks becoming either sensationalized, as in *Basic Instinct* or *Wild Things* (John McNaughton, 1998), or diluted and assimilatory, as in *Kissing Jessica Stein* (Charles Herman-Wurmfeld, 2001), in either case imagining bisexual space as apolitical, superficial, and transient. Chapter 3 examines two recent cases of bisexuality mainstreamed to triumphant commercial effect: the crossover "art film" *Brokeback Mountain* and the blockbuster bromance *Wedding Crashers*, respectively responsible for making it safe (and profitable) to screen homosexuality in the heartland and in R-rated comedies in the teen-dominated multiplex. On what terms, and at what cost, these narratives of male same-sex desire are formulated for mainstream audiences are questions I take up therein.

The task I undertake in this study, then, is both historical and theoretical: asking how, over time and space, bisexuality has been constructed onscreen, and questioning why bisexuality is so frequently elided – made (in)visible – there and in screen studies discourse, despite its perceptibility and, indeed, ubiquity throughout visual culture. I focus most keenly on identifying sites (textual and extratextual locations) and sights (ways of seeing) that resist monosexuality and that attribute desire to physical, emotional, and material determinants beyond gendered object choice. Texts, in other words, which seem to grapple with bisexuality's elusive representational and cultural history, drawing bisexuality onto the stage (or screen) of contemporary discourse so as to effect a reconceptualizing of our cultural logic of desire. But while my admitted aim is to unthink monosexuality, my approach is more exploratory than recuperative, more contemplative than prescriptive. Because I view bisexuality's ontology in socially relative rather than essentialist terms, I find its manifestation onscreen often to be in the eye of the beholder, dependent on the differences of our individual desires and corresponding sightlines. To some degree, we see what we want to see. In their ontological uncertainty, screen constructions of bisexuality resemble the similarly shifting (not to say shifty) conceptualizations of "real life" bisexuality over the past century, to which I now turn.

> Matt (Ivan Sergei): For your information, I'm bisexual.
>
> Lucia (Lisa Kudrow): Please. I went to a bar mitzvah once.
> That doesn't make me Jewish.
>
> *The Opposite of Sex* (Don Roos, 1998)

The genealogy of bisexuality dates from the late nineteenth century, and emanates largely from the fields of psychology (Wilhelm Fliess, Sigmund Freud, Fritz Klein, Juliet Mitchell, Jacqueline Rose), sexology (Havelock Ellis, Alfred C. Kinsey, Richard von Krafft-Ebing, Wilhelm Stekel), and sociology (Margaret Mead, Paula C. Rust, Charlotte Wolff), and from the perspective of sexual identity politics (Amber Ault, Jo Eadie, Amanda Udis-Kessler). Within psychiatry, the treatment of bisexuality both theoretical and therapeutic can be traced to Fliess's supposition circa 1890, soon taken up by Freud, that all humans are endowed constitutionally with both masculine and feminine sexual dispositions.[18] In his *Three Essays on the Theory of Sexuality* (1905), Freud proclaims definitively that

> since I have become acquainted with the notion of bisexuality I have regarded it as the decisive factor, and without taking bisexuality into account I think it would scarcely be possible to arrive at an understanding of the sexual manifestations that are actually to be observed in men and women.[19]

Although in contemporary usage *bisexuality* refers generally to an erotic disposition toward both men and women, Fliess and Freud used the term more precisely to designate the idea of a duality of gender – that is, a body or self-image that resists categorization as *either* masculine *or* feminine.

This concept of bisexuality, closer to what we would today term transgender, gestures at a connection between bisexual and *trans* identities and perspectives that paradoxically stems from the Victorian-era conflation of sex and sexuality, wherein same-sex object choice was considered a symptom of pathological "gender inversion."[20] Much as trans discourse works to dispel the presumption that a trans identity entails a homosexual orientation, unthinking the naturalized link between gender and sexuality is a central project of critical bisexuality theory.

Although Freud proclaimed bisexuality "the decisive factor," he initially perceived it as a primary instinct requiring repression in order for healthy sexual maturation to be achieved. Those who persisted in exhibiting a bisexual disposition past what Freud believed to be an appropriate age he labeled "psychosexual hermaphrodites," those "[whose] sexual objects may equally well be of their own or of the opposite sex," noting also in his 1931 paper "Female Sexuality" that bisexuality "comes to the fore much more clearly in women than in men."[21] Yet Freud conceded the prevalence of so-called "sexual perversions" (any deviations from the sexual aim of genital-to-genital copulation), cautioning that psychoanalysis should not overvalue the sexual object. "We are thus warned to loosen the bond that exists in our thoughts between instinct and object," he writes in *Three Essays on the Theory of Sexuality*. "Under a great number of conditions and in surprisingly numerous individuals, the nature and importance of the sexual object recedes into the background."[22] Freud's findings, often too hastily discredited for their tendency toward essentializing, universalizing, and pathologizing, in this instance point clearly toward contemporary conceptualizations of bisexuality and queer alike as constituting a move beyond gendered object choice and other sexual orthodoxies. Informed by Jacques Lacan's rereading of Freud, contemporary conceptualizations of bisexuality opt for a constructivist account of bisexuality rather than viewing it as biologically innate.[23] Even as it aims to expand understandings of desire, critical bisexuality theory actively resists associations of bisexuality with nostalgic retrospection to a "pure state" of desire or utopian aspiration to a pansexual ideal. Chapter 1 will examine several texts that grapple with these associations of bisexuality with nostalgia and utopianism, embodied by the recurring *bisexual-bohemian* figure of art cinema.

Only 50 per cent of the [male] population is exclusively heterosexual throughout its adult life, and . . . only 4 percent of the
population is exclusively homosexual throughout its life.

ALFRED C. KINSEY, *Sexual Behavior in the Human Male*

These revelations about mid-twentieth century Americans' sexual
behavior from *Sexual Behavior in the Human Male* (1948), as well as those
in Kinsey's subsequent study *Sexual Behavior in the Human Female* (1953),
were considered shocking at the time. The culturally equalizing effect
that Kinsey anticipated failed to materialize within America's McCar-
thyite Cold War climate; indeed, Kinsey's findings provoked the opposite result, as Chris Cagle documents: "Kinsey's insistence that sexual
identities were fluid and that same-sex desire was an innate physiological
capability fed fears that gays could seduce and corrupt even the best of
men and governments."[24] While Kinsey's aspirations may have fallen
short of liberating public sentiment about sexuality, his insistence that
the truth of sexuality was far from the socially sanctioned norms made
him an enduringly divisive figure – as indicated by the controversy that
greeted Bill Condon's 2004 biopic *Kinsey*.[25] Kinsey's attempt at reforming
American sexual politics proved largely ineffectual, and only with cultural anthropologist Margaret Mead's widely read 1975 article "Bisexuality: What's It All About?" did bisexuality reenter the American popular
lexicon in a significant way.

The time has come, I think, when we must recognize bisexuality as a normal
form of human behavior. . . . We shall not really succeed in discarding the
straitjacket of our cultural beliefs about sexual choice if we fail to come to terms
with the well-documented, normal human capacity to love members of both
sexes. Even a superficial look at other societies and some groups in our own
society should be enough to convince us that a very large number of human
beings, probably a majority, are bisexual in their potential capacity for love.

MARGARET MEAD

When Patti (Lisa Lucas), the precocious teenager of Paul Mazursky's
1978 film *An Unmarried Woman*, declares, "I think we're getting to an age
where the dominant cult figure is bisexual," she registers the powerful
influence of such figures as David Bowie and Mick Jagger, but like Kin-

sey she underestimates the force required to reshape American sexual norms. While bisexual chic spiked in the 1970s, a bisexual movement and community has never emerged on the same scale as the others gathered under the BGLQT banner. The movement's curtailed momentum is most succinctly symbolized by the Bisexual Center of San Francisco (1976–1985), an early nexus, which closed prematurely amid the cultural backlash of AIDS paranoia and Reaganite politics.

As Eve Kosofsky Sedgwick once commented, "I'm not sure that because there are people who identify as bisexual there is a bisexual identity."[26] To identify as bisexual is to be obliged to defend, paradoxically, both bisexuality's essence and existence – "everyone is bisexual" and "there is no such thing as bisexuality" persist side by side in common wisdom. As recently as 2005, Dr. J. Michael Bailey of Northwestern University authored a study that claimed to prove the nonexistence of bisexuality by crudely monitoring subjects' genital response to viewing pornographic material; the study's findings, that arousal patterns of bisexually identified subjects were indistinguishable from those identifying as gay, have been widely disseminated albeit disputed.[27] Within accounts by those self-identifying as bisexual, there is considerable variation with regard to the importance (or lack thereof) that gendered object choice holds for determining desire and sexual subjectivity. As Kathleen Bennett describes:

> Some bisexuals say they are blind to the gender of their potential lovers and that they love people as people; others are aware of differences between their male and female partners but are able to be attracted to each in different (but overlapping) ways. For the first group, a dichotomy of genders between which to choose doesn't seem to exist; the second group simply disregards the social obligation to choose.[28]

What unites these positions is a leveling of gendered object choice to on par with (or below) other determinants of desire, coupled with a sense of unpredictability concerning the gender of future object choices. Though one can speculate only so far about any universal consistency to bisexual alterity, this sense of gender impartiality positions bisexual subjectivities as different from monosexual subjectivities, and as distinct (though not disassociated) from other queer subjectivities. The specificity of bisexual subjectivity, then, involves a perception of the strangeness of monosexuality's prioritization of gendered object choice, about which Jane Litwoman ventures this self-appraisal:

> The clearest way for me to understand lesbians and straight women is to understand them as fetishists. From my viewpoint straight women are malegenderfetishists and lesbians are femalegender-fetishists who are so culturally supported in their sexual attractions that most of the time they hardly understand my different reality.[29]

Of course Litwoman's assessment is meant somewhat facetiously; if asked to name those qualities found to be romantically or erotically appealing, few people will produce a list of exclusively gender-specific traits. Why then do the majority of people foreclose any real consideration of intimate involvement with same-gendered individuals, in defiance of *Chasing Amy*'s admonition not to "immediately halve your options"?

BISEXUALITY AND ITS DISCONTENTS

> Shane (Katherine Moennig): Dana, I'm impressed. You're into someone and you want to know if she's down . . .
>
> Dana (Erin Daniels): *Down?*
>
> Alice (Leisha Hailey): Whether she plays for our team – the gay team.
>
> Dana: Don't bisexuals have their own team?
>
> *The L Word* ("Let's Do It," 1/25/2004)

If the knowing smiles and laughter that greeted Dana's sarcastic question are any indication, not only don't bisexuals have their own team, the very notion is naive. While the 1970s were the "golden age" for celebrity bisexuality (though several recent calendar women, including Anna Paquin, Evan Rachel Wood, and Lady Gaga, have emerged), the academic study of bisexuality experienced its most vigorous period in the 1990s, expanding into the humanities with rich work by Alexander Doty, Marjorie Garber, and Donald Hall and Maria Pramaggiore.[30] Yet bisexuality theory would shortly thereafter be absorbed and summarily outsourced by queer theory, which tended to consign bisexuality to habitual secondguessing, footnoted afterthought, or outright omission – in part because of the epistemological challenges of navigating what Clare Hemmings calls the "minefields of meaning" that bisexuality erects.[31]

Binary systems begin to look unstable and inadequate when the complexity and range of our differences *and* sameness are acknowledged. For this reason, Garber proposes, the only apparently more radical term *lesbian* enjoys greater visibility in cultural discourse:

> [Is] it because lesbianism is so clearly the "other," the not-self, and therefore readily demonized ... [whereas] bisexuality – since it [is] not so easily regarded in the mainstream press as "them" not "us" – pose[s] an even more palpable threat? Conversion, sexual fluidity, the capacity to attract and to be attracted by members of both sexes – these are genuinely dangerous attributes.[32]

Given that bisexuality undoes the perceived stability of the poles on which compulsory monosexuality rests and (in some measure) on which the political rights and social recognition awarded gays and lesbians are founded, it is little wonder that bisexuality-as-identity is viewed with suspicion and hostility by straight *and* gay and lesbian communities. In an extensive 1990s study of the opinions on female bisexuality held by heterosexual women and lesbians, sociologist Paula C. Rust found these two groups surprisingly similar in their attitudes. Rust's findings revealed a widespread conception that bisexuals are by nature licentious and incapable of monogamy, and that they use their bisexuality as an excuse not to commit to relationships. Rust detected a pervasive skepticism of bisexuality on the part of lesbians in particular, many of whom held the perception that "claims of bisexuality are the result of confusion, youthful immaturity, lack of self-knowledge, indecisiveness, conformism, mental illness, or attempts to gain the acceptance of both the lesbian and heterosexual communities, to get the best of both worlds, to avoid stigma, or to avoid taking a political stand."[33] Chapter 3 will examine the political expediency of compulsory monosexuality to gay rights activists, specifically in relation to marriage equality legislation, and the result whereby bisexuality is subject to a persistent "politics of delegitimization."[34]

Whereas the cultural presumption of heterosexuality gives way in certain spaces (a gay bar, for instance) to a presumption of homosexuality, in virtually no situations or contexts are people presumed bisexual. Bisexuality as a critical category endures a similar nowhere-ness. Those queer theorists skeptical of the continuing use of bisexuality as a discursive concept protest that it simply substitutes a trichotomy (hetero/ homo/bi) for the entrenched dichotomy, and thereby re-inscribes dominant notions of sexuality as innate and fixed – even as bisexuality itself is regarded as contrived and fleeting. As Elizabeth Däumer notes, "tropes of bisexuality as either neatly divided between or integrating heterosexuality and homosexuality threaten to simplify bisexuality [by retaining] a notion of sexuality – and sexual identity – based exclusively on the gender of object choice."[35] The unfortunate prefix *bi* (from the Latin, meaning "two"), is partly to blame for the situation, as it reinforces the notion of two "true" sexual orientations as well as two "natural" genders (masculine, feminine) and sexes (male, female). Such a literal, and facile, definition obscures the complex meanings encompassed within bisexuality, which nonetheless must defend its ontological status – and even its radical potential – whereas heterosexuality and homosexuality are presumed ontologically self-evident. Likewise, gay and lesbian studies have won widespread acceptance as legitimate frameworks of intellectual inquiry while bisexual studies must continually defend its epistemological grounding. Within the academy, skepticism around bisexuality often comes couched in a curiously insistent promotion of *queer* as superior nomenclature for any form of alternative sexuality, on the grounds of its ever-widening embrace of non-normative subjectivities and desires, and as a more highly evolved concept given bisexuality's taint of having been handed down by heteropatriarchal culture.

Apart from these tensions, bisexuality studies generally harmonize with queer studies' concepts and aims to advance its goals; by no means does queer studies render bisexuality studies redundant or outmoded. Possessing a distinct discursive history and idiom, bisexuality studies is as much an indispensable and unique subset of queer studies as discourses of trans, intersex, and BDSM, all of which share bisexuality's emphasis on determinants beyond gender-differentiated bodies, but none of which are rendered redundant by or entirely subsumed within the concept "queer."[36] Like those terms, *bisexual* can remain a viable signifier so long as its meaning remains unfixed, much as Judith Butler defends her use of *lesbian* by making it "permanently unclear what precisely that sign signifies," while Valerie Traub encourages viewing that term as

less a person than an activity, less an activity than a modality of pleasure, a position taken in relation to desire. Its problematic ontological status suggests that
it is better used as an adjective (e.g. "lesbian" desire) than as a noun signifying a
discrete order of being.[37]

As Maria Prammaggiore defines it, "Bisexual epistemologies [are] ways
of apprehending, organizing, and intervening in the world that refuse
one-to-one correspondences between sex acts and identity, between
erotic objects and sexualities, [and] between identification and desire,
[so as to] acknowledge fluid desires and their continual construction and
deconstruction of the desiring subject."[38] Or, as Hemmings states, to say
"'I am bisexual' is to say 'I am not "I."'"[39] In this formulation, bisexuality
transcends its relegation to temporary place marker between (and, it is
implied, complicit with) the monosexual binary, serving instead to de-
stabilize heterosexual and homosexual poles by revealing their affinities,
interdependency, and ultimate pliability. Because bisexuality is already
"positioned both 'between' and outside gender and sexuality binaries,"
as Doty notes, it serves as a productive route for exploring texts, spectator positions, pleasures, and readings that operate both through and in
excess of gender and sexuality orthodoxies.[40]

BISEXUAL REPRESENTABILITY

For it is upon the repression of bisexuality that the organization of sexual
difference, as enacted within our culture and as represented upon our
cinema screens, is constructed.

ROBIN WOOD, *Hollywood from Vietnam to Reagan . . . and Beyond*

Outside of the erotically transgressive realms of art cinema and pornography, screen as well as "real life" bisexuality is effaced not only by
compulsory monosexuality but also by compulsory monogamy. For
bisexuality, unlike heterosexuality and homosexuality, seems to rely on
a temporal component for its (practical or conceptual) actualization.
That is, at any given moment a bisexual person or film character might
appear heterosexual or homosexual depending on his or her present
object choice, a situation that significantly contributes to bisexual (in)
visibility in society – even uncloseted bisexuals may feel as if they are
leading a double life – and that challenges bisexual representation in

film. Writing in 1996, Biddy Martin notes the way in which butch-femme coupling contributes to lesbian mainstream visibility: "as a femme alone, her lesbianism would be invisible."[41] Fifteen years later, we as a culture have grown increasingly accustomed to images of femme lesbians (indeed the butch is a far rarer species within screen media), but the assumption remains that the gender of one's current object choice indicates one's sexuality. The onus is thus regularly on bisexuality to "prove" itself – which seems to demand, for the individual bisexual, a roster of previous and current partners. Given that bisexuality is also thought to be a way station on the path to monosexual maturity, providing credentials for an identity deemed impermanent or nonexistent seems specious. Why, as Ed Cohen bluntly puts it, do we "make an identity out of whom we fuck?"[42] Or, because many people's sexual behaviors diverge from their identities, and because many others have sexual desires that remain unacted on, why do we make an identity out of the gender of (only) those with whom we pair publicly?

Admittedly, the act of reading bisexually is often prompted by the undecidability of an image or instance in question – that is, textual resistance to pinning characters or narrative elements down as *either* straight *or* gay/lesbian in persuasion or perspective. This would seem to certify a given film's bisexual/ity by who, or what, it is *not,* a strategy of definition through negation that might threaten to negate bisexuality itself. Yet, as Michael du Plessis urges, "we may well insist on our visibility by working through the conditions of our invisibility. . . . We can begin naming ourselves and our various bisexual identities by, paradoxically, negation."[43] Without subscribing to the simplistic premise that more affirmative representations of bisexuality will cure bi-phobia, it is hardly naive to imagine, as critical bisexuality theory does, that "film's images might have the power to break or smash 'sacred' images of sexuality, offering us other possibilities of intimacy – even if unnamed as such."[44]

In *UnInvited: Classical Hollywood Cinema and Lesbian Representability,* Patricia White argues that the PCA mandate against implications of what it deemed "sex perversion" resulted in lesbianism's manifestation on screen as a spectral presence, perceivable by spectators in the know but sufficiently opaque so as not to offend the mass audience that the PCA claimed to be protecting. Echoing Terry Castle's apparitional trope for lesbian representation, White links the PCA's conscious censorship to that of psychological censorship: the processes of disavowal summoned by the unconscious. Owing to its particular problems of legibility, bisexuality retains its slipperiness of signification even with newfound freedoms for sexual explicitness, maintaining its "legacy of absence" through spectral narrative connotation and spectatorial inference.[45] But the continuing (in)visibility of screen bisexuality is also attributable to a cultural disavowal of bisexual desire, reinforced by the questions and meanings left unexplored by the specifically lesbian framework of studies such as White's. Adopting White's neologism *representability* signals my shift away from conceiving the textual images and instances under discussion here as (in)visible, toward an acknowledgment of their readability as bisexual.

Open-ended conclusions, particularly those that leave unresolved the question of a character's future object choice(s), compel us to regard individuals' orientations and attractions as continually in flux. Much as we could not necessarily determine one's sexual identity on the basis of one's most recent partner, Marcy Jane Knopf suggests that to read bisexually necessitates moving beyond the typical inclination to read characters' sexual orientations "based upon the desires or relationships at the end of a text – rather than looking at the fluctuations and variations of desire throughout the novel [or film]."[46] Chapter 1 describes the ways in which art cinema's characteristic ambiguity opens a space for bisexual representability. But paradoxically, textual resistance to or incapacity for monosexuality also are suggested by characters and texts that resolve the "conflict" of bisexual desire so tidily that they seem to protest too much. Postclassical Hollywood films such as *The Deer Hunter* (Michael Cimino, 1978) and *Top Gun* (Tony Scott, 1986) that make such excessive spectacle out of homoeroticism – in poignant scenes of wartime mourning in the former, and in the glisteningly virile displays of locker room and beach volleyball preening in the latter – so anxiously cast off the bisexual desire they have constructed in the course of the narrative that the "happily monosexual after all" conclusions often ring false or seem bewildering. This mode of resolution whereby monosexuality is reestablished attempts, though not terribly convincingly, to posit that bisexuality (as identity or practice) is unworkable as a long-term option – a sentiment that can be found alongside affirmations of homosexuality, as we saw in *Chasing Amy*. In the steady spate of lesbian romantic comedies released in the last two decades – including *Imagine Me & You* (Ol Parker, 2005) and *When Night is Falling* (Patricia Rozema, 1995) – an initially heterosexual-identified woman falls for a self-assured lesbian and henceforth lays claim to a newfangled lesbian identity herself. Whether these stories of new love assert or challenge the idea of a universal monosexual destiny remains a vexed question.

Hinging especially closely on the formation and sustenance of same-sex bonds, the male buddy film and its counterpart the female friendship film offer up particularly potent sites of bisexual representability. Same-sex couples such as Frodo (Elijah Wood) and Sam (Sean Astin) in Peter Jackson's *Lord of the Rings* trilogy (2001–2003) and Joe Buck (Jon Voight) and Ratso Rizzo (Dustin Hoffman) in *Midnight Cowboy* (John Schlesinger, 1969) are bi-suggestive in giving, just as Doty notices about *Gentlemen Prefer Blondes* (Howard Hawks, 1953), "roughly equal emphasis to both same-sex and opposite-sex relationships, perhaps focusing somewhat more upon the importance of same-sex intensities, which has the effect of challenging straight-favoring cultural biases."[47] Depicting the largely unspoken, unacted-upon desire between these screen couples encourages viewers to consider how these relationships would work differently if not governed by a monosexual logic of desire. Though the heterosexualization of female relationships in films such as that between Celie (Whoopi Goldberg) and Shug (Margaret Avery) in *The Color Purple* (Steven Spielberg, 1985) and between Idgie (Mary Stuart Masterson) and Ruth (Mary-Louise Parker) in *Fried Green Tomatoes* (Jon Avnet, 1991) may seem similarly monosexist, these films often make oblique reference to consummation (in whatever form) having taken place, in so doing complicating our reading of specific characters' sexualities.

Even when (as in the cases of these novel-to-film adaptations) such implications are erased or obscured for narrative purposes or straight viewers' comfort, we should not be too hasty to rule out the potential for a bisexual reading. To do so would be to fall prey to the heterosexist fallacy of "straight until proven otherwise," which stems from a systemic logic of desire in which the (homo)erotic and the "merely" (homo)social are sharply divided. Even in the relatively permissive post–Production Code cinema that is my focus, "proof" of bisexuality depends on behaviors that a character is hard-pressed to demonstrate within the confines of a feature-length film, in which not just running time but narrative circumstances can foreclose the development of a character's bisexual potential. The heroines of *Thelma & Louise* (Ridley Scott, 1991), to take another instance from the female "friendship" canon, would presumably have found occasion to explore their burgeoning attraction had they not been on the run from the law; as it is, they have only enough time for a quick kiss before speeding over the Grand Canyon's rim. The serial format of television drama makes it the medium with the most *bi-potential* in this regard, as its (multi-)seasonal arcs allow time for bisexuality to develop. The extent to which that potential is realized is the focus of my final chapter.

Given these accumulated roadblocks to defining and representing bisexuality, alongside the eclipsing of bisexual activism and political visibility, it makes sense that bisexual readings of cultural texts have benefited little from the considerable energies devoted in recent times to queer appropriation and canonization. Attempting to compensate for the dearth of explicitly BGLQT images, queer film criticism focused for a time on revealing subtextual or subcultural meanings in ostensibly "straight" narratives. "The pleasures of such readings are simple," writes Paul Burston. "What better revenge on a culture that seeks to exclude you than to demonstrate how you were there all along?"[48] This reading "against the grain" risks re-inscribing queerness within the shadowy realm of connotation – the textual closet, so to speak – without dispelling the presumption of the text's inherent straightness. "It implies taking a thing that is straight and doing something to it," Doty observes, proposing instead that we view "queer discourses and practices as being less about co-opting and "making" things queer . . . and more about discussing how things are, or might be understood as, queer.[49] Following Doty, I am most interested in defamiliarizing images and expressions of desire assumed to be monosexual, and in examining the processes of signification and subjectification whereby representations of bisexuality are constructed yet made (in)visible. Ultimately I aim to gauge how screen bisexuality "looks" over time, bisexuality's relation to other identity constructions, and the meanings these hold for understanding our logic of desire. These spaces of queerness, fluidity, and liminality indicate the extent to which screen media serve as a singular cultural forum for imagining and negotiating desire of many stripes.

READING BISEXUALITY, READING BISEXUALLY

"Il n'y a pas d'amour, il n'y a que des preuves d'amour."
("There is no love, there is only proof of love.")

Les dames du Bois de Boulogne (Robert Bresson, 1945),
dialogue by Jean Cocteau

"A bisexual perspective," writes Clare Hemmings, "is a way of looking, rather than a thing to be looked for."[50] Bisexual desire need not be explicitly visualized or voiced; to expect such would be to think rather unimaginatively about what might constitute the erotic. To read a film *bisexually*, then, is to resist the monosexist assumptions of dominant cultural discourses by recognizing ways in which dialogue, framing, performance, and other channels for expression create and sustain the impression of an individual character's potential bisexuality, or to suggest a bond between same-sex characters that bears an erotic charge – such as that Doty notices between Lorelei (Marilyn Monroe) and Dorothy (Jane Russell) in *Gentlemen Prefer Blondes,* discussed in chapter 3.[51] To argue from a bisexual subject position that certain characters or plots arouse desire and/or encourage identification may not itself "prove" bisexuality, but it is proof of bisexuality.

Throughout this study I frequently take as instances of bisexual representation those characters and texts which resist monosexuality through their actions, depictions, or significations, even if the majority of my examples are conspicuously bi-suggestive in depicting characters acting on or fantasizing about desires for both men and women. Orienting my bisexual corpus by these coordinates, however, should not be understood as re-inscribing sexual difference or re-prioritizing gendered object choice. Representations of desire for both men and women indicates potential bisexuality, but it is the reverse formulation that I wish to emphasize: bisexuality, in looking beyond gendered object choice to other physical, emotional, and material determinants, suggests the *prob-ability* that desired object choice will not be limited by gender exclusiv-ity. Admittedly, many elements of the screen characters and imagery I will argue are bi-suggestive could also be – and often are – perceived as homoerotic, or alternatively as "girl-on-girl." In the readings to come, I will term certain subjects bisexual because (to twist a phrase of Terry Castle's) I think it meaningful to do so.[52]

Occasionally I consider a character who complicates conventional assumptions that behavior and identity should correspond; Violet (Jen-nifer Tilly) in the cult queer film *Bound* (Andy and Larry Wachowski, 1996) offers a significant case in point. Violet is behaviorally bisexual in that she is both the longtime moll of gangster Caesar (Joe Pantoliano) and eager to seduce the butch ex-con Corky (Gina Gershon) who moves in next door. But in a speech she gives the skeptical, bi-shy Corky, Vio-let explains that she considers her heterosexual activities to be merely "work," saying confidently "I know what I am." Her meaning is clear – Vio-let considers herself a lesbian – and not a whisper of the B word is to be heard throughout *Bound*. Yet while Violet may be more meaningfully discussed as lesbian, *Bound* by all means calls to be read bisexually for its overturning of heteronormative assumptions made toward those engag-ing in relations with the opposite sex, and for directly articulating factors beyond gendered object choice (for Violet, financial incentive and, given Caesar's mob ties, self-preservation) in determining sexual relations. In this way, *Bound* presents a clear instance of *bisexual space* even if it does not produce an unproblematically bisexual character.

Perhaps the real genius of the PCA–ruled classical Hollywood stu-dio system was its mandating a level of discretion that kept films open to multiple readings, pleasing (and flattering) sophisticated spectators without offending more conservative, oblivious sensibilities.[53] Even with the Code now defunct, Hollywood's aim to "appeal to everyone, offend no one" remains very much a part of its contemporary family-friendly agenda – though one not so airtight as to snuff out the R-rated comedy's recent revitalization (wholesomeness being expendable when there's a buck to be made). But unlike Code-era films and recent animated films' use of adult humor that goes over the heads of the children in the audi-ence, the newly popular sex comedies are hardly subtle. Whether their explicit homoeroticism is a sign of sexual liberation is a question I take up in chapter 3, but what seems inarguable is that the decade-long box office success of films representing male desire that evades or exceeds heteronormativity makes reading bisexually ever more vital, as Maria Pramaggiore avows.

> If... the contemporary film industry, need[s] to "cheat" their representations of homosexualities for mass audience appeal – making them legible to those on both sides of the fence – it may be the case that the ambiguities, doubleness, and "both/and" of bisexual desire are encoded in contemporary films and may, in part, make bisexual reading practices possible and necessary.[54]

BISEXUALITY AS TRIANGULARITY

Mr. Roper (Norman Fell): I wonder what's going on up there.

Mrs. Roper (Audra Lindley): Oh, probably something kinky that only three can play.

Three's Company ("A Man About the House," 3/15/1977)

The romantic-erotic triangle or "threesome" can efficiently suggest bisexuality or even act as an indirect mode of conveyance within narratives featuring same-sex desire that goes unacknowledged or unconsummated. In other words, triangles are time-saving structures that overcome the problem of temporality by allowing for a character's simultaneous exploration of same-sex and opposite-sex desire. But because such narratives are often structured around the question of a bisexual character's "true" (read: monosexual) identity, the triangle tends to turn on stereotypical notions of bisexuality as indecisiveness, as wanting to have it all, and as a phase to be outgrown. Since not only compulsory monosexuality but compulsory monogamy as well are enforced as cultural norms, the narrative resolution of the triangular structure almost always involves a questioning (or questionable) character's ultimate self-discovery as *either* heterosexual *or* homosexual, a revelation reinforced by the notion of a fated "one true love." And yet the romantic-erotic triangle, by virtue of its ubiquity in so much of art and literature, could be said to denaturalize by delaying (and, as in the case with *Chasing Amy,* occasionally denying) the reproduction of the straight *or* gay couple,

thereby unsettling cultural beliefs in the natural(ized) progression toward monosexual coupling. In films such as *Les Biches* (Claude Chabrol,
1968) and *Personal Best* (Robert Towne, 1982), the triangle plot acts as
another fruitful site of bisexual representability with its emphasis on the
space between monosexuality and monogamy.

Even when no character behaves bisexually – as in *The Children's Hour*
(William Wyler, 1961) and *Jules et Jim* (François Truffaut, 1962) – triangularity accommodates bisexual representability in a way that circumvents the temporal problem of "proving" bisexuality. Take, for example,
the two unusually intelligent teen films that writer John Hughes and
director Howard Deutch collaborated on in the 1980s. The high school
love triangles of *Pretty in Pink* (1986) and *Some Kind of Wonderful* (1987)
encourage queer reading in that the "third term" is represented by a
socially ostracized and gender-nonconforming character (the flamboy-
ant Duckie [Jon Cryer] of *Pretty in Pink* and the soft butch Watts [Mary
Stuart Masterson] of *Some Kind of Wonderful*) who, though he or she
harbors an unrequited love for a member of the opposite sex, is easily
readable as a stand-in for queer identity and desire. Yet these films ultimately resolve themselves conventionally (if not particularly persuasively or gratifyingly), with the gender-conforming straight boy and girl
ending up together.[55] *Ferris Bueller's Day Off* (1986), written and directed
by Hughes, rounds out its love triangle with another queer-coded teen,
the fastidious Cameron Frye (Alan Ruck), who is clearly if covertly en-
amored of the eponymous charismatic rebel played by Matthew Broder-
ick. Here too we are served the conventional ending when Cameron and
Ferris surrender to going their separate ways, with Ferris subsequently
proposing marriage to his girlfriend. But perhaps the more noteworthy
and subversive aspect of these films' subtle referencing of bisexual desire
is its affirmation; though the queer couplings go unconsummated, in the
three cases mentioned here they are presented as the most emotionally
and narratively significant relationships within the film.

Bisexuality in screen narrative also frequently materializes in a way
that suggests what René Girard calls the mimetic character of desire.[56]
Just as spectators experience eroticized identification with characters
onscreen, for those characters the desire *to have* is often conflated with
the desire *to be*. Still other films portray a female pair as "unnaturally"

close, with one woman obsessively fixated on the other's identity and lifestyle; in *My Summer of Love* (Pawel Pawlikowski, 2004), for example, the adoration that working-class teen Mona (Natalie Press) displays in thrall to her posh friend Tamsin (Emily Blunt) is inextricably inspired by adolescent longing, class envy, and same-sex desire. As in ads that exude homoerotic suggestiveness, screen bisexuality emerges out of the impulse to connote yet disguise same-sex desire behind the smokescreen of one woman's fantasy of identification with the other. Fleshed out in narrative, this bisexual-suggestive representation accrues meaning through visual and thematic motifs that emphasize mother-daughter surrogacy, doubling, and even split personality, wherein bisexuality operates as a spoil of affluence or as a leveraging device for socioeconomic empowerment, laying bare the unavoidable if underacknowledged relationship between profit, power, and pleasure that I will take up in chapter 2.

The majority of triangle films still represent bisexuality as a temporary condition requiring a monosexual resolution – as in *Chasing Amy* and *The Fox* (Mark Rydell, 1967) – even as they create narrative suspense through maintaining the possibility that she (for it is nearly always a woman) could "go both ways." With the plot hinging on the question of the character's "true" sexual identity, here again bisexuality is imagined as something furtively and only temporarily concealing one's essential nature. The triangle plot allows for the inclusion of homosexuality as a valid and stable identity, but stops short of conceding the same of bisexuality. Contemporary triangle films regularly culminate in same-sex partnership, albeit typically involving a sexually "confused" character who ultimately discovers his or her "true" nature to be monosexual: lesbian, in films geared toward queer audiences, such as the coming-out dramas referenced earlier, *Imagine Me & You* and *When Night is Falling*; straight, in films emerging from and targeting a mainstream audience, as does the Jennifer Westfeldt–penned *Kissing Jessica Stein*. In a more radical vein, those films that avoid any implication that gendered object choice was the determining factor in couple formation exhibit a bisexual perspective even without uttering "the B word"; that the lovers-on-the-lam played by Joan Chen and Anne Heche in *Wild Side* (Donald Cammell, 1995), last seen successfully traversing the Mexican border, are ideal partners in crime *and* love does not undermine the intensity of both women's attachment to Christopher Walken's charismatic kingpin Bruno. Still more radical, and thus rare, is the choice to leave characters happily *un*coupled, which departs from mainstream conventions that regard remaining single, whether by choice or circumstance, as at best suspect, at worst tragic.[57]

In the triangle plot, bisexuality can be conjured out of the disavowed desire enfolded within a straight/straight/gay triad, as arises among the domestic threesome played by Meryl Streep, Kurt Russell, and Cher in *Silkwood* (Mike Nichols, 1983). The intimate emotional relationships shared by same-sex characters within this version of triangular desire are de facto platonic, based not on an unsatisfying attempt at erotic intimacy but rather on a rigid distinction between heterosexuality and homosexuality and between erotic and non-erotic feelings. This binary thinking by characters and texts is rarely self-aware or explicit; it need not be, for it takes for granted the impossibility of "overcoming" monosexual identity, as the following exchange between *Silkwood*'s female leads makes clear:

Dolly (Cher): I love you.

Karen (Meryl Streep): I love you too.

Dolly [*sarcastic*]: I don't mean "I love you too."

Karen: I know that's not what you mean. That's what I mean.

With this brief and veiled exchange, occurring fairly early in the film, the narrative closes down any possibility that Karen might be anything other than heterosexual, and simultaneously consigns Dolly to the "tragic lesbian" status she will occupy throughout. *Silkwood*'s resistance to considering the possibility of eroticism between these women typifies the disinclination on the part of both filmmakers and audiences that arises from Western modernity's clear division between the heterosexual and the homosexual, and between the homosexual and the homosocial.[58]

BI-TEXTUALITY

Queer connections can be insinuated powerfully and unobtrusively, especially if they fit in with ideas the audience already has at the back of its mind.

William Empson, *Some Versions of Pastoral*

Of course Empson (who was himself reportedly bisexual), writing around 1935, meant *queer* in the sense of curious and unexpected. But much like the double plot Empson observed in Elizabethan drama, a pervasive structural motif evident throughout the corpus of screen bisexuality gives rise to certain queer connections. As Empson indicates above, the double plot can create and sustain a metaphorical structure "so strong that it brings out other ideas which were at the back of the metaphor," through which "the interaction of the two plots gives a particularly clear setting for, or machine for imposing, the social and metaphysical ideas" being theorized therein.[59] As Empson notes of Shakespeare's metaphorical comparison of sexual and political standards in *Troilus and Cressida,* "the double plot was an excellent vehicle for [relating] them, if only because it could suggest so powerfully without stating anything open to objection."[60] In a substantial number of the films to which I will turn next, the double plot structure I name bi-textuality operates to formulate and convey just such a metaphor between bisexuality and an analogous identity construct that also resists containment within a binary taxonomy.[61] This, the text's two-pronged "identity crisis," attempts to work through bisexuality – which is occasionally rendered more connotatively than denotatively – by reading it through another discourse pertaining to economic class, cultural heritage, ethnicity, gender roles, mental health, or psychological states. Bi-textuality thereby operates dialectically to challenge monosexuality, revealing the disavowed spaces beyond dominant identity constructs governing socioeconomic strata, culturally identified groups, racial and gendered categories, and psychological classifications. Bi-textuality ultimately works, therefore, to expose the fallacy of ordering sexuality (or any identity construct) so simplistically and constrictively as binary systems do. Not every film under examination here is intentionally bi-textual, nor does a bi-textual structure ensure a "progressive" reading – that is, one which undermines monosexist assumptions. Bi-textual significations may even reproduce stereotypes, though to do so is not necessarily regressive but rather can serve to defamiliarize and question. These queer connections between bisexuality and other identity constructions provoke a reconceptualization of sexual desire and subjectivity suggested by our understanding of these other boundary-pushers.

As chapter 1 demonstrates, art cinema has proven the richest site for bisexual representability, primarily because of that cinematic form's propensity for candidly addressing alternative sexualities and eroticism more generally. Art cinema's characteristic narrative ambiguity and character opacity paradoxically allow for bisexuality's clearer enunciation. Given that explicit articulations of bisexuality are permissible in art cinema, the bi-textual system works less as a means to covertly connote bisexuality and more as a route to explore the associations between bisexuality and another related counterculture: bohemianism. This bi-textual analogy gives rise to a bisexual-bohemian figure, whom I trace through art or "specialty" films such as *Sunday Bloody Sunday* (John Schlesinger, 1971), *Sans toi ni loi/Vagabond* (Agnès Varda, 1985), and *Laurel Canyon* (Lisa Cholodenko, 2002), concluding with a sustained consideration of one markedly missed moment for a bisexual reading, Jane Campion's 1999 film *Holy Smoke*.

From there I turn to look at a group of films in which art cinema's characteristic ambiguity is intensified to the point where narrative distinctions between fantasy and reality are obscured. In conjuring uncanny worlds that call for new ways of seeing, these *dream films*, as I call them, engender their own recurring figure whom I name the *dreamgirl* (there are but rare instances of *dreamboys*, though Terence Stamp's character in Pier Paolo Pasolini's 1968 film *Teorema* is a memorable case). Through an intricate bi-textual structure that considers bisexuality in relation to gendered and ethnoracial performance (that is, "passing"), the dreamgirl defamiliarizes the social-sexual subject's constructed self and the binaries that work to maintain it. I focus on a trio of art films whose bi-textual dream discourse is intriguingly interconnected: *Persona* (Ingmar Bergman, 1966), *3 Women* (Robert Altman, 1977), and in another missed moment that yields intriguing bisexual meaning when unlocked, *Mulholland Drive*. Considered together, these related but independent strains of art cinema operate in concert to "unthink" monosexuality.

Chapter 2 appraises a mode of cinema that shares with art films a willingness to engage explicitly with bisexual discourse, but one with its own distinct aesthetic and industrial watermark: the soft-core form of erotica known as sexploitation. In assessing sexploitation in both its typically raw, low-budget version and in its more polished Hollywood incarnation, two additional bi-textual systems emerge. In the first, an analogue between bisexuality and socioeconomic privilege broaches an understudied topic – the cinematic representation of class – in probing sexuality's relation to power and need within Western late capitalism. By employing motifs of mimicry and the double, films such as *Black Swan* (Darren Aronofsky, 2010) and *Single White Female* (Barbet Schroeder, 1992) explore bisexuality's relation to mimetic desire and the eroticization of (cinematic) identification. Again recurring character types are constructed to embody this bi-textual negotiation; I name the resulting dyad the *rich bitch* and her *dependent double*, tracking their power play/s across sexploitation cinema to the culminating missed moment of the only apparently "lesbian" vampire film cycle.

Another, concentric bi-textuality structures the women's institution films of sexploitation, in which bisexuality's associations with promiscuity and pathology are scrutinized for their roots in medical and penal discourse. Sexploitation films that deconstruct this discourse do so in the context of the all-female institution (school, prison, mental hospital, coven), in which the emphasis is on same-sex relationships and their inherent resistance to heteronormativity. Such a liberating departure from compulsory heterosexuality combines with resistance to patriarchal (and occasionally matriarchal) authority to result in an escape from the ritualized reproduction of gender roles and monosexuality, as evident in such missed moments as *Foxfire* (Annette Haywood-Carter, 1996) and *Girl, Interrupted* (James Mangold, 1999). Whether low-budget or simply lowbrow, sexploitation readily engages camp aesthetics and appreciation that, in emphasizing the constructedness of performance and identity, open another space for the critique of normative sexualities.

One might initially assume filmmaking aimed at the mass market would steer well clear of suggestions of bisexuality, but as chapter 3 explores, contemporary Hollywood comedy is in fact actively invested in representing sexual fluidity. Charting the course of homoeroticism and homosociality in contemporary Hollywood comedies aimed at a broad audience, from the "buddy films" of the late 1960s and 1970s to the post-millennial bromance phenomenon, I uncover within these films' affirmation of male relationships anxieties stemming from (post-)feminism, queer culture, and recent public debates around marriage equality. Focusing on two runaway hits (and their promotional campaigns) released in 2005 – Ang Lee's *Brokeback Mountain* and the Vince Vaughn–Owen Wilson vehicle *Wedding Crashers* – I demonstrate how these missed moments of "mainstream" bisexual visibility are troubled by heteromasculinist values and tactics of assimilation and disavowal with regard to their transgressive content.

Finally, chapter 4 asks how medium specificity influences bisexual (in)visibility and representability, gauging the degree of candor and inclination allowed by network versus cable content standards and by serial television's extended narrative format. After surveying the as-yet-undocumented televisual history of bisexual representation, I hone in on two exceptional case studies: FX dramedy *Rescue Me*, unique both for centering its bisexual storyline on a lead male character and for maintaining it over an entire season; and MTV's *A Shot at Love*, a reality-style series that voices the B word more vociferously than any aforementioned text, but that nonetheless leaves compulsory monosexuality substantially unchallenged.

American movies are based on the assumption that life presents you with problems, while European films are based on the conviction that life confronts you with dilemmas – and while problems are something you solve, dilemmas cannot be solved, they're merely probed.

PAUL SCHRADER

ONE

Unthinking Monosexuality: Bisexual Representability in Art Cinema

THOUGH SCHRADER'S REMARK, CLEARLY INTENDED TO PROVOKE, may go too far in consigning popular commercial cinema and art cinema to opposing sides of the Atlantic, it offers a useful starting point for thinking about the expectations that filmmakers and audiences bring to different forms of filmmaking. For the majority of popular films classifiable as "mainstream" or "Hollywood" productions (both terms require troubling), it remains anathema to offer downbeat or ambiguous resolutions, longtime staples of art cinema. Conventional Hollywood narrative closure endorses compulsory monosexuality by reestablishing heterosexuality as the natural order and opposite-sex coupling as the ultimate goal. Characters who fail to conform to Hollywood's boy-gets-girl dictate are typically homosocialized (female friends, male buddies) or fetishized into spectacles either hypersexualized (lesbian vampires) or romanticized (gay cowboys). Since the 1980s, homonormative same-sex coupling is increasingly tolerated in across-the-aisle crowd-pleasers such as 1993's *The Wedding Banquet,* the low-budget romantic comedy that launched the career of its then-unknown director Ang Lee. Such films are made palatable for straight consumption through their downplaying of eroticism, and of the threat to social order represented by same-sex desire. Their feel-good tastefulness is a far cry from the 1990s New Queer Cinema, which featured films so defiantly nonassimilatory that they did not uniformly find favor even with the gay audience they targeted. In the sea of "positive images" and "gay role models" that has come to dominate the BGLQT film marketplace and media rhetoric since that brief moment of edgy irreverence, art cinema can still be counted on for a degree of narrative *and* erotic realism, daring, or complexity with regard to queer sexuality.

Whereas commercial cinema generally relies on clearly motivated, rational characters and Manichaean divisions between protagonists and antagonists to secure spectatorial identification, art cinema embraces ambiguity and illogicality as truthful rather than obfuscating. According to Robert Self, art cinema

> perceives the social subject as a site of contestation and contradiction that is constantly in the process of construction and crisis under pressure from forces in the cultural formation. The subject is a process not yet fixed but open to difference and transformation. . . . The art cinema demands a reading strategy that looks not for resolution but for multiplicity, not for linear causality but for indeterminacy. The art cinema asks to be read in its ambiguity.[1]

By preventing any complete, coherent understanding of narrative meaning and character psychology, art cinema undermines and frustrates the Cartesian ideal of rational self-knowledge. Notwithstanding the commercial incentive of "having it both ways," in its reluctance to resolve character identity or to desire monosexually, art cinema looks beyond Western modernity's division between heterosexual and homosexual, and between homosexual and homosocial. Art cinema's audiences respond in kind, adapting their modes of identification and perception to engage with enigmatic characters and to eroticize more freely. Previously I suggested that a primary way of gauging bisexual representability is to assess whether a film keeps open the possibility of bisexuality or relegates potentially bisexual characters and desires to fixed monosexual positions. In contrast to most popular cinema as well as "indie" films (a description more of a film's sensibility than of its actual financing model), art cinema historically and cumulatively has mounted a substantial critique of compulsory monosexuality with its willingness to probe the dilemmas of desire.

Clearly the financial stakes are lower for art films – smaller budgets, less risk – than for studio-produced films, a factor that encourages experimentation, bisexual and otherwise. And, of course, featuring sexual titillation is a proven strategy for art films seeking American distribution. Overall, however, there seems to be a saturation point in terms of fiscal risk on an explicitly bi-suggestive film. Consider Hollywood's experiments with relatively big-budget bisexuality: *Gigli* (Martin Brest, 2003), a film that despite going to great pains to disavow the sexual transgressions of its female lead (played by Jennifer Lopez) by having her fall for Ben Affleck's character, performed abysmally at the box office. As did *Domino* (Tony Scott, 2005), a high-octane adaptation of the life of Domino Harvey, Hollywood royalty turned bisexual bounty hunter, starring Keira Knightley. Other studio-produced and/or -distributed films that ventured into explicit representations of queer identity and succeeded have either, as in the much-awarded *Philadelphia* (Jonathan Demme, 1993), played their sensitivity and sentimentality to the hilt, or, as in the cases of *Boys Don't Cry* (Kimberly Peirce, 1999) and *Brokeback Mountain*, have hedged their bets with high publicity-to-production budget ratios and by avoiding significant formal disruptions. Despite the MPAA flap over *Boys Don't Cry*'s depiction of oral sex, all three of these films kept the display of sexual activity muted.[2] More recently, the bisexual female rebel-heroine Lisbeth Salander of Stieg Larsson's Millennium Trilogy survived her Hollywood importation with bisexuality intact, in David Fincher's 2011 adaptation; as I discuss in my conclusion, this recent remake could challenge industry thinking on big-budget bisexuality (if not the characteristic representation of it). I will explore this topic of Hollywood-financed queer representation more fully in chapter 3's discussion of the bromance, but the pertinent point here is that the relative affordability of art cinema production fosters bisexual representability, as does the embrace of narrative ambiguity and complex characterization that art cinema's specialized market niche allows. To represent sexualities and stories outside of the norm and in nonprescriptive, open-ended ways is a risky venture that violates studio productions' preference for the proven and the palatable. Art cinema's sexual frankness and associations with decadence (or deviance) enable it – perhaps more pervasively and pronouncedly than any other cinematic category – actively to open bisexual spaces. The question of what exactly constitutes art cinema is a fair one, especially amid contemporary industry phenomena such as the studio-produced "indie" film and the mainstream "art" film. Yet as David Bordwell put forth and more recent scholars continue to concur, there are distinctive if not necessarily disqualifying criteria for categorizing films as more or less attuned to the art film tradition.[3] As I discuss below, the most prominent of those criteria are qualities that yield marked bi-potential, as illustrated by this chapter's sampling of titles recognizably classifiable as art films.

Art cinema's flexible meanings and open-ended resolutions obviate the need for bisexuality to name itself through dialogue or prove itself through action, making art cinema texts available for bisexual readings, Maria Pramaggiore describes:

> Chronological narrative structures that assign more weight and import to the conclusion – typical of Hollywood film rather than, say, European art cinema – may be less compatible with bisexual reading strategies, which focus on the episodic quality of a nonteleological temporal continuum across which a number of sexual acts, desires, and identities might be expressed.[4]

Echoing Paul Schrader's epigraph at the start of this chapter, Pramaggiore also overdetermines art cinema's Europeanism, yet both their associations are predicated on the historical precedent whereby the European film industry receives substantial public support relative to that of the United States, thereby permitting greater artistic experimentalism. Although free of the intense focus on profits that characterizes major studio filmmaking, art cinema is hardly indifferent to the commercial advantage of polysemy to encourage multiple readings, both across diverse audiences and on the part of individual spectators. Art cinema facilitates, invites, and benefits from variable interpretations, making it widely dispersible and more likely profitable. A key component of this multivalence is bisexuality. Positioned industrially and aesthetically between popular Hollywood-style cinema and the more radical/experimental avant-garde, art cinema is formally accessible to a broader swath of spectators than the latter, regularly crossing over to a mainstream audience lured by star casts, genre markings, or titillating content.

Regarding the latter, despite the axiom "sex sells," commercial film-making – intent on ensuring that no significant audience segment is shut out – has been decidedly sex-averse since the late 1970s. To fill the residual demand for adult content, Steve Neale observes, "Art Cinema has stabilised itself around a new genre: the soft-core art film."[5] In its willingness (and that of its audience) to explore alternative sexualities at both representational and discursive levels, art cinema and the film festival/art house/digital streaming circuit central to its distribution is the primary remaining bastion (save the adult film industry) for depictions of graphic sexuality. Again, its willingness to forego blockbuster profits makes art cinema more willing than popular cinema to risk the R (let alone NC-17) rating, feared to be sufficiently risky that studio directors often are contractually obligated to bring films in with a rating short of R. The recent success of the R-rated bromance has mitigated somewhat Hollywood's reluctance in this regard, as chapter 3 will discuss, but R-rated studio fare remains largely bereft of queer eroticism. As Mark Betz demonstrates, art cinema advertising since at least the 1960s has taken its lead from exploitation cinema's sensationalist tactics, teasingly referencing queer desire that never fully materializes or that resolves itself heteronormatively, as does the road trip of erotic awakening chronicled in *Le Voyage en Douce* (Michel Deville, 1980), in which the same-sex intimacy and impromptu three-way explored by sisterly best friends Hélène (Dominique Sanda) and Lucie (Geraldine Chaplin) ends anticlimactically with each returning to the stultifying marriages they were initially intent on escaping.[6] While certainly not impervious to the pull of compulsory monosexuality that challenges bisexual readings, art cinema's comparative freedom to openly, unapologetically depict eroticism should in theory make bisexuality legible where it is elsewhere relegated to the connotative closet – that is, made (in)visible.

Despite Schrader's and Pramaggiore's demarcation of American versus European sensibilities, transnational art film coproductions have long troubled the conceptual and industrial borders of national cinemas similar to the way that bisexuality challenges monosexual boundaries. Art cinema is a cinema of exile insofar as its financing, postproduction, and exhibition are frequently dislocated from their local contexts. In certain cases, namely for Iranian and mainland Chinese filmmakers, this exile is politically determined; for filmmakers elsewhere it is economically driven, as figures such as Michael Haneke, Alejandro González Iñárritu, David Lynch, and Raoul Ruiz seek out more amenable funding sources and reception outlets for projects deemed noncommercial in their native markets.

These culturally and industrially hybridized aspects of art cinema mirror the blurring of borders and troubling of binaries that bisexuality accomplishes. Moreover, in its critique of compulsory monosexuality, bisexuality theory shares with postcolonial theory an aim to deconstruct, or "unthink," entrenched Western structures of knowledge and power. Bisexuality theory challenges the hierarchical binary heterosexual/homosexual in a way that recalls postcolonial theory's disruption of the colonizer/colonized dyad in favor of hybridity as a conceptual strategy for unthinking Eurocentrism. Like bisexuality, the term *hybridity* provokes anxieties with its unfixedness and evocation of miscegenation, as tourism theorist Anne-Marie d'Hautserre reflects:

> Hybridity brings with it ambiguity, and thereby threatens the orderliness of the schematized reality of tourists. Hybridity is redolent of miscegenation, which was one of the greatest fears of most self-respecting travelers.... Hybridized identities are sometimes said to have lost authenticity, and thus authority.... Relationships with visited "others" are difficult to enact because of a continued fear of pollution or contamination.[7]

Without suggesting that the ontology and experience of bisexuality is identical to that of other hybrid identities, this passage's description of dominant cultural perceptions about hybridity evokes analogous anxieties and stigmas around bisexuality, which itself is often alleged to constitute a sort of sexual tourism (that is, heteroflexible experimentation free of the responsibilities of gay identity). Much as contemporary tourist theory appropriates hybridity to critique the tourist/other binary, bisexuality theory appropriates bisexuality to critique monosexuality.

Furthermore, bisexuality is subject to figurative colonization by heteropatriarchal capitalism, which operates in a way that is *conceptually* analogous to the literal colonization of subaltern peoples and territories insofar as, tourism theory notes, "exotic places are controlled by being familiarized and domesticated through a language that locates them in a universal (meaning Western) system of reference that visitors recognize and can communicate about."[8] Bisexual chic is enabled and fed by a safe exoticizing or assimilation of bisexual images and spaces, much as "third world" tourism under Western capitalist (models of) control makes it safe for Western travelers to venture into unfamiliar territory so as to pleasurably consume images of otherness and the labor of impoverished others. Rhetoric of "universalizing" sexual or cultural difference defuses the threat of otherness even as dominant ideology redoubles efforts to contain the colonizer/colonized duality by subsuming difference within a binary division that sees otherness only in relation to the dominant/ normative. What follows is a consideration of this bi-textual analogy "bisexuality as cultural hybridity" through its personification in a recurring figure in art cinema: the bisexual-bohemian.

MORE THAN A TOURIST: THE BISEXUAL-BOHEMIAN AND CULTURAL HYBRIDITY

"Bisexuality as the expression of fullness of an individual – and an honest rejection of the – yes – perversion which limits sexual experience . . . "

SUSAN SONTAG, *Reborn: Journals and Notebooks, 1947–1963*

Fittingly conjoining bisexuality and art cinema by embodying their shared signification of displacement from normative values, art cinema's bisexual-bohemian is typically a privileged white woman who straddles two worlds: her native Western culture, characterized as stifling and heteropatriarchal, and an alternative (usually non-Western) realm shown to be seductive and liberating yet potentially dangerous and perverse. In rejecting social convention in favor of a liminal existence and personal liberation, the bisexual-bohemian becomes susceptible to representation as a naively idealistic hedonist or (worse) deviant, destined for redemptive rescue or pessimistic ruin. Her troublingly in-between position invokes the possibility – at once fear and fantasy – of becoming Other, with the narrative drive working to reconcile or contain this enticing yet threatening alternative lifestyle. While what is most explicitly at stake is the Western woman's "purity" (both sexual and racial), behind the fear of miscegenation looms greater anxiety about insubordination by oppressed groups that portends radical social reorganization. The literary and cinematic tradition that gives rise to the bisexual-bohemian betrays its often conservative colonialist sensibility by subjecting her to a deprogramming of her social/sexual deviancy: decontaminating and domesticating her body, agency, and desire as safely gender-conforming and heteronormative, and re-Westernizing her adopted "third world" exoticism (or re-Americanizing her adopted "European-style" eroticism), maligned as perverse and promiscuous. Occupying a position both normative and Other, millennial art cinema's bisexual-bohemian literally inhabits a transcultural space and metaphorically inhabits a bisexual space. In Jane Campion's *Holy Smoke*, the missed moment discussed below, the bisexual-bohemian's struggle to shape and sustain a hybrid self-identity constitutes the film's chief narrative conflict.

Both art cinema and bisexuality are associated with privilege, decadence, and bohemianism, wherein artistic and bisexual tendencies are perceived as the products of affluence, self-indulgence, and jadedness. Both arouse suspicions of elitist transgressions from mainstream norms (popular cinema, monosexuality) while simultaneously being accused of half measures and apolitical frivolity from the "radical" margins (avant-garde cinema, queerness). Bohemian alternatives to social and sexual orthodoxies have often been mobilized by narratives both celebrating and condemning non-normative female sexualities. As Frann Michel observes, a recurring use of the conventionality-versus-bohemianism dyad in 1950s lesbian pulp novels serves to negotiate "the choice between the conformity of heterosexual marriage and the independence of lesbian subculture" in ways that ultimately "correlate lesbian subculture and relationships with personal freedom and with intellectual, artistic, financial, and spiritual self-fulfillment."[9] In contrast to these subcultural endorsements of Sapphic loves and lives, contemporaneous Hollywood films of the late classical studio era, still subject to PCA censorship, treat the (implicitly) bisexual-bohemian to the same fate as other queer-coded characters: with the redemption through marriage and domesticity granted Johnny (Glenn Ford) in *Gilda* (King Vidor, 1946); with the shaming castigation doled out to Amy North (Lauren Bacall) in *Young Man with a Horn* (Michael Curtiz, 1950); or, as in the fate of Hallie (Capucine) in *Walk on the Wild Side* (Edward Dmytryk, 1962), with even grander punishment: a dramatic death. Even postclassical American and European art cinema depict bisexuality as symptomatic of anomie among the complacent leisure class intelligentsia, as in *Il Conformista/The Conformist* (Bernardo Bertolucci, 1970) and *La Dolce Vita* (Federico Fellini, 1960), or of the hedonistic pursuits of preening artistes such as those in *Cabaret* (Bob Fosse, 1972), and *To Live and Die in L.A.* (William Friedkin, 1985). The bisexual-bohemian consistently served as scapegoat for what was viewed as a dangerously and destructively lax culture.

The problem here is not the dearth of positive images so much as the way that art cinema renders bisexuality hypervisible only to conflate it with an overdetermined bohemian lifestyle – which, it is implied, would make anyone and everyone bisexual. This becomes an especially reductive maneuver when claiming to represent a real-life bisexual such as Simone de Beauvoir, the media construction of whose public persona Miriam Fraser uses to demonstrate how

> bisexuality is not perceived to be constitutive of the self (as other sexualities, particularly heterosexuality, are); instead, de Beauvoir's sexual behavior is informed by her bohemian milieu. If it had been possible to "separate" this lifestyle from de Beauvoir, the press imply, her "capricious" sexual behavior might also (by her own preference even) have been circumvented.[10]

Bisexual legibility and viability is similarly suppressed through conflation with bohemianism within films that claim to represent historical bisexuals, who would presumably protest that their bohemian lifestyle did not determine but simply made it possible to act on their bisexual desire. Two such artists' biopics, leaning heavily on art film trappings, exoticize bisexuality as an element of decor in the glamorous depiction of bohemian life: recounting the adventures of Anaïs Nin (Maria de Medeiros) with her bohemian consorts Henry (Fred Ward) and June Miller (Uma Thurman) in 1930s Paris, the NC-17-rated *Henry and June* (Philip Kaufman, 1990) glossily and superficially aestheticizes Nin's journalistic introspections on fluid eroticism. Similarly, in playing the eponymous bisexual artist in Julie Taymor's *Frida* (2002), Salma Hayek joins Ashley Judd (as Tina Modotti) to recreate *Il Conformista*'s languorously lesboerotic tango, again for the delectation of onlookers both diegetic and nondiegetic. In the film overall, however, Kahlo's affairs with women are given little narrative weight, her bisexual desire subordinated to – and implied as largely an effect of – her ongoing struggle to endure the infidelities of husband Diego Rivera (Alfred Molina).

The peak for art cinema's bisexual-bohemian figure fittingly coincides with the late-1960s and early-1970s sexual liberation movements, when alternative sexualities received greater public visibility, and cinematic eroticism (led by a European soft-core art film boom) was allowed more graphic screen representation. However, representations of the bohemian "hippie" remained at their core little changed in either the popular or specialty cinemas of this "morning after the revolution" moment, when countercultural ideals are shown to have soured into naive utopianism at best or hedonistic narcissism at worst, both of which the bisexual-bohemian serves to personify. These "hippie hangover films," as I think of them, soberly survey the excesses and dashed hopes of living according to the hippie creed, in so doing cynically conflating bisexuality with social ills and personal afflictions.

One of the more harrowing celluloid depictions of the ravages of drug abuse, Barbet Schroeder's little known and fairly experimental debut feature *More* (1969) conjures a utopian social and sexual space only to resolutely dismantle it as wayfaring young couple Stefan (Klaus Grünberg) and Estelle (Mimsy Farmer), reveling in a carefree existence on a Mediterranean island, gradually succumb to erotic betrayal and chemical self-destruction. Estelle's introduction of another woman into their hallowed space is depicted as on par with her heroin peddling, wherein "free love," like narcotics, enticingly promises liberation but eventually destroys their coupled harmony. Similarly, the bohemian threesome of Nicolas Roeg and Donald Cammell's *Performance* (1970) – Turner (Mick Jagger), Pherber (Anita Pallenberg), and Lucy (Michèle Breton) – play house in a shabbily opulent Knightsbridge mansion that initially seems a welcome sanctuary for thug-on-the-run Chas (James Fox). But it is inside this ostensibly utopian space – insulated from the capitalist ills of the music industry and the vice trade that plague Turner and Chas respectively – that the latter goes mad, provoked by ceaseless psychosexual games orchestrated by temptress Pherber and narcissist Turner. As in *More,* the hippie ethos of "dropping out" is depicted as inevitably devolving into addiction and social irrelevancy, while the originally alluring wonderland of a nontraditional household dissolves into nightmare.

Written by former *New Yorker* film critic Penelope Gilliatt and directed by John Schlesinger (*Midnight Cowboy*), *Sunday Bloody Sunday* was much lauded for its maturely understated depiction, considered groundbreaking for the time, of a love affair between gay doctor Daniel (Peter Finch) and younger bisexual artist Bob (Murray Head). In art cinema style, the film's treatment of its various themes – religious conviction, personal loyalty and responsibility, and the difficulty of reconciling free love with emotional needs – are equally measured in tone. Yet here again

a parallel is drawn between the vagaries licensed by countercultural values and the emotional pain endured by Daniel and Alex (Glenda Jackson) in sharing Bob as a lover, in particular by two sequences curiously
incongruent with the film's realist tone and serving no explicit narrative
purpose: a surreal episode in a pharmacy littered with addicts provides a
solemn reminder of the needle and the damage done, and Alex's absurdist
discovery while babysitting for her bohemian friends' brood that even the
toddlers have parental consent to smoke marijuana. Though Schlesinger's moralizing remains subtle, incorporating such scenes alongside the
central tale of a doomed love triangle trains a spotlight on bohemia's
dark side. The attribution of blame, albeit also restrained, falls squarely
on bisexual Bob – whose stereotypically flighty narcissism is underlined
when he leaves Daniel and Alex for greener pastures in America. Like Bill
Condon's art film/biopic *Kinsey*, *Sunday Bloody Sunday* intently depicts
the emotional suffering that can accompany attempts to break out of the
monogamous paradigm, without wholly withdrawing endorsement of
nonmonogamous behaviors.

Though almost invariably gendered female (unsurprising given our
culture's greater comfort with imagining women's same-sex desire), the
1960s-1970s bisexual-bohemian might be regarded as counterpart to the
American New Wave cinema's contemporaneous *ramblin' man* archetype, that modern-day cowboy whose unwillingness to be tied down by
civilization or women was valorized throughout this era in films such
as *Easy Rider* (Dennis Hopper, 1969), *Five Easy Pieces* (Bob Rafelson,
1970), and the myriad male buddy films to be mentioned in chapter 3. Yet
whereas these male social dropouts are esteemed for "sticking to their
guns" (that is, maintaining a stoic resolve of anti-authoritarian self-sufficiency), their female equivalents are pathologized as loose women or, alternately, as women with a screw loose, in ways that portend the backlash
against women's liberation. In the bisexual-bohemian's infrequent male
incarnations – which include *Performance*'s Turner and *Sunday Bloody
Sunday*'s Bob as well as the angelic stud played by Terence Stamp who
seduces each member of a haut-bourgeois family in Pasolini's elliptical
art film *Teorema* – he is additionally transgressive in his gender-bending,
recalling how the hippie persona in some (but not all) ways allowed for a
non-normative standard of Western masculinity in promoting pacifism,

sensitivity, and even androgyny. But while the male bisexual-bohemian may share a social ethos with his contemporary, the ramblin' man, he is significantly more feminized a construction. *Easy Rider*'s Wyatt (Peter Fonda) and Billy (Dennis Hopper) may be mistaken for hippies by the rednecks who accost them in the deep South, but the distinction between hippies and the American New Wave's ramblin' men is actually more nuanced. As *Shampoo* (Hal Ashby, 1975)'s George Roundy (Warren Beatty), another ramblin' man mistaken for both a hippie and a homosexual, protests, "I'm not anti-Establishment!"

Agnès Varda's *Vagabond* investigates in quasi-documentary art film style the days leading up to the mysterious death of young drifter Mona (Sandrine Bonnaire), who attempts to claim the ramblin' man's prerogative for herself. In a departure from the tendency to confine the bisexual-bohemian to a supporting role and relatively opaque characterization, Mona dominates both frame and narrative, and though she too remains largely a cipher it is for reasons of purposeful ambiguity rather than two-dimensionality. Sharing the investigative narrative structure of *Citizen Kane* (Orson Welles, 1941), *Vagabond* gives it a feminist rewriting: instead of a privileged, powerful man whose fear of abandonment compels him to acquire massive material wealth, Mona is a disenfranchised woman attempting an unengaged existence on society's margins.[11] Tellingly, on the night before her death (simply enough from exposure, it is revealed), Mona is shown gazing longingly into a cozy scene of domestic bliss from which her independent lifestyle excludes her. The irony becomes that in chasing complete self-sufficiency, Mona makes herself entirely dependent on the kindness of strangers, including a professor named Madame Landier (Macha Méril) who offers Mona a day's worth of comforts: shelter, food, even (this being France) champagne. Although there is a perceptible erotic charge between these two unattached women that leads Mona to open up to Mme. Landier in a way that she does with no one else (and which the professor, while soaking in a bath, recounts to a friend via telephone in a way that underlines its eroticism), this dynamic remains unconsummated and simultaneously readable along mother-daughter lines. But in the way that all of Mona's relationships, sexual and otherwise, are based baldly on a system of exchange, she personifies bisexuality theory's pragmatic assessment of the way in which social circumstances often necessitate privileging material need over gendered object choice.

Chantal Akerman's *Je Tu Il Elle* (1976) presents a similarly unknowable (and unnamed) female character, played by the filmmaker herself, who appears to live in similarly self-imposed exile on society's fringes. In a protracted scene, Akerman's character, on her way to visit a former girlfriend, "repays" a truck driver who has given her a lift with sexual favors, though she appears to do so willingly and her general inscrutability makes it difficult, in any case, to ascribe motivation. *Vagabond*'s Mona refuses when a truck driver demands the same from her, although with other men along her route she does give in, both of free will and (in one instance) through coercion. Both *Vagabond* and *Je Tu Il Elle* depict bisexuality in some sense as a mode of survival for the bisexual-bohemian, but in each the relationship that is portrayed as the most convincingly erotic and emotional – though still founded on an "exchange" – is between women.

More recently, art films *Chloe* (Atom Egoyan, 2009), *Savage Grace* (Tom Kalin, 2007), and *Swimming Pool* (François Ozon, 2003) construct bisexual-bohemian ménages that are literally or quasi-incestuous, in which an older woman is fixated on both her literal child (or lack thereof, in the case of *Swimming Pool)* and another younger object of desire figured as a quintessential bisexual-bohemian. These films' repressed female protagonists are awakened to desires that seem predicated chiefly on possession of this younger bisexual-bohemian and the (biological or surrogate) child. In characteristic art cinema fashion, these family romances favor ambivalence over explicit judgment, even if in each case the unleashing of bisexual desire has murderous results. The quasi-incestuous (but nonmurderous) quadrangle of Lisa Cholodenko's *Laurel Canyon* reverses this structure to make the older woman the bisexual-bohemian, but one whose bisexuality does not overshadow other aspects of her personality, a refreshing change from queer characters in most American features. Jane (Frances McDormand) is an unconventional mother and successful record producer whose bisexuality is presented as a given, again implying that along with hanging out with rock stars and smoking dope, it comes with the bohemian territory. But in a rare turn of events, here it is the bisexual character who provides the moral compass in abstaining from acting on her attraction to her son's girlfriend. A similar structure informs Cholodenko's most recent film, *The Kids Are All Right* (2010), in which longtime partners Jules (Julianne Moore) and Nic (Annette Bening) find their domestic harmony threatened by the introduction into their family's lives of their sperm donor Paul (Mark Ruffalo). Though she embarks on an affair with Paul, Jules responds to Nic's demand "Are you straight now?" with a defiant "No! That has nothing to do with it." Despite an occasion for the B word going missing here (Nic does not think to question Jules about that), that Jules continues to affirm her lesbian identity despite behaving bisexually avoids ascribing her actions to a sexuality crisis and instead accentuates how she was steered by circumstance and emotional need. Together with her debut feature *High Art* (1998), Cholodenko's three films to date all refuse to resolve their (exclusively) female characters' sexualities as fixed or monosexual by film's end.

MISSED MOMENT: *HOLY SMOKE* (JANE CAMPION, 1999)

My final illustration of art cinema's bisexual-bohemian, like *Vagabond*'s Mona and *Laurel Canyon*'s Jane, is strongly feminist yet all too human, and is also the creation of a female filmmaker's vision.[12] In narrating the coming-to-consciousness of Ruth (Kate Winslet), a young Australian woman mesmerized by a local spiritual leader while traveling in India, *Holy Smoke* examines associations of both bisexuality and bohemianism with hedonism, idealism, exoticism, and exploitative mimicry. Set in the postcolonial milieus of Delhi (former capital of the British colony) and the Australian Outback (aboriginal lands colonized by white settlers of another British colony), *Holy Smoke* explores the bisexuality-as-tourism metaphor bi-textually to create a hybrid cultural and sexual identity for its protagonist – extending *Holy Smoke*'s gaze beyond that of the conventional travel film, and Ruth's gaze beyond that of cultural tourism and compulsory monosexuality.

As a bisexual-bohemian, Ruth provokes colonialist anxieties about cross-cultural contamination both social/sexual (miscegenation) and spiritual/psychological (brainwashing). While displaying explicit bisexual desire in key scenes, Ruth's sexual transgression chiefly involves desire that is interracial and intergenerational: a symbolic marriage to her guru Baba (Dhritiman Chatterjee) and a relationship deemed ethically and age inappropriate with PJ (Harvey Keitel), the cult deprogrammer enlisted by Ruth's family to "save" her from Baba's clutches. Moreover, the elaborate game of dominance and submission that PJ and Ruth play out over three harrowing days in the Outback, which concludes with an emasculated yet enlightened PJ surrendering to Ruth, is distinctly queer.

As her characterization makes clear from the start of *Holy Smoke*, Ruth regards herself as apart from her fellow "travelers," who differentiate themselves from "mere" tourists by virtue of their ostensibly fuller cultural immersion and less nakedly consumerist mentality. Yet they, Ruth most of all, are undeniably if ambivalently driven by what postcolonial theorist Ellen Strain calls the *tourist gaze:* "the active process of seeking out, recognizing, and fetishizing difference," suggesting that "at the heart of this fetishization is the basic presumption that the confrontation of difference involves a negotiation of boundaries in order to bolster a sense of self."[13] Travelers are perhaps *more* exploitative than regular tourists, d'Hautserre suggests, for their quest to affirm their own identities through the existential "'other'... [wherein] the penetration of the periphery [of tourist space] is but a continued conquest (even if only at the individual level) rather than a true search for a personal identity through interactive appreciation."[14] Though *Holy Smoke* gives serious examination to these charges, it also puts into question the moralizing binary that Strain and d'Hautserre construct.

David Crouch's observation that "tourist places and services are 'consumed' because they provide pleasurable experiences that are different from those encountered in everyday life" directly evokes the language used to describe not just "bisexual privilege" but (especially mainstream) moviegoing as well.[15] In writing about another white bisexual-bohemian – Diana, as played by Guinevere Turner, in *The Watermelon Woman* (Cheryl Dunye, 1996) is a literal and figurative colonialist who exoticizes the black lesbian body (born in Jamaica, she is "into chocolate") – Mark Winokur observes of the literal white tourist and the figurative white spectator that "tourism is historically hegemonic; it is about the politically neutralized, aestheticized other body. It allows one the feeling of knowing a culture but at a distance, a knowledge of the art without a sense of the colonized anxiety from which it derives."[16] Not just literal tourism but any such encounter with difference, including that intrinsic to the cinematic experience, serves to quell anxiety about the unfamiliar and about one's own incoherence as a subject. The conventional travel film – one in which a foreign culture is displayed and experienced through a Westerner's perspective – typically presents the tourist gaze as disembodied and un-self-conscious. *Holy Smoke*, however, emphasizes its tourist gaze though exaggerated, reflexive visual and aural cues in ways that undermine our comfortable immersion within its voyeuristic perspective. Neither characters nor viewers are relieved of complicity with the tourist gaze, which is depicted as simultaneously seductive and silly from the film's opening sequence of white travelers rapturously dancing to a live performance recording of Neil Diamond's "Holly Holy" on a Delhi rooftop. Though we first see India through Ruth's point of view, subsequently our perspective shifts to see through the eyes of her Mum (Julie Hamilton) as well as through the spoken narration of Ruth's friend Prue (Samantha Murray), and once Down Under we are at significant moments sutured into the American PJ's point of view; this gradual receding of our gaze from Ruth's coincides with her shift to a position of sexual and cultural in-betweenness. Ruth comes to shun the traditional tourist's aversion to impoverished Delhi – displayed by first Prue then Mum, who, suffocated by urban pollution and surrounded by begging children, suffers a hysterical collapse that recalls Adela Quested's in *A Passage to India*. But although she revels in rather than recoils from Delhi's difference, Ruth remains detached from her fellow travelers' "penetrative" exoticism (to use d'Hautserre's sexualized language), longing instead to experience "some of the real stuff," as Ruth says, accessible only to guru Baba's converts. Ruth's conversion predictably provokes panic among her loved ones, who fear that (as she says sarcastically) "I'm going to live in India, marry Baba and commit group suicide." Yet what Ruth justifies as a symbolic marriage ("It's not that literal," she reassures her incredulous girlfriends. "[Baba's] marrying everyone") overlooks the oppressiveness of a practice designed to maintain not just spiritual adherents but gender inequality through polygyny. From her first appearance onscreen, when she brushes away a local man's furtive caress

1.1. The metaphorical conflation of cultural, spiritual, and sexual border-crossing in Jane Campion's *Holy Smoke*.

on a crowded bus, to her subsequent veneration for and desire to pledge herself to the sannyasin (whose honorific "Baba" signifies "wise father"), Ruth struggles to reconcile her Australian traveler's privilege with her female disempowerment. This happens first in "Mother India" then on the Outback frontier, where PJ challenges her appropriation of a patriarchal culture by means of superficially borrowing its costumes and unquestioningly subscribing to its spiritual beliefs, even as he remains very much oblivious to his own sexism.

Ruth's bi-curiosity is metaphorically linked to her exoticizing of foreign cultures, in an early sequence (immediately following that with the rooftop revelers) presenting Ruth's glimpse of her own higher plane as she is visibly captivated by two young women, one also white and with similar coloring and build as Winslet, the "other" Indian, walking past with arms linked and resplendently dressed in saris. Though not necessarily readable as lesbian, their physical intimacy and visible exuberance touches off something in Ruth that sends her seeking similar self-realization in the ashram. This moment foregrounds *Holy Smoke*'s central analogy between Ruth's sexual and spiritual awakenings, conflating the two into a single image of Ruth's ideal self: another white woman who appears to have achieved the enlightenment Ruth craves.

Once resettled in the Outback, a subsequent, similarly entrancing scene positions Ruth in a more earthly ecstasy, as she languorously embraces, to a seductive nightclub cover of "I Put a Spell on You," a woman wearing the black bob hairstyle made famous by Louise Brooks, best known for her own Sapphic dance in *Pandora's Box*, a film well remembered for its bisexual triangle. That Ruth initiates the dance and is positioned to visually mirror the "true" lesbian with whom she dances, but shares Lulu's motive for inciting a man's jealousy, keeps Ruth's sexuality fluid and unfixed. In this moment of ecstasy, Ruth flouts both heterosexual convention and the patriarchal authority exerted by older, macho PJ's surveillant gaze, with consequences as potentially damaging as that of her mystical enchantment in India. Immediately PJ is impelled to rescue his charge from sexual assault by a couple of predatory louts, abruptly yanking Ruth (and we the viewers) from what Hilary Neroni calls "feminist *jouissance*," and which results in a dreadful loss of control that suggests Ruth's near-rape is punishment for her dance floor transgression.[17]

A later, equally climactic sequence has Ruth commandeer a makeover for PJ, who in turn undoes her pretensions with another sort of transformation. Dressed in an ill-fitting frock, his hair fluffed and his mouth painted red, PJ's temporary transvestism as directed by Ruth obliges – or enables – him to see the woman's perspective at the same time as he is forced to confront his own decidedly non-ideal, aged self. The performative nature of gender is signaled through PJ's drag, which itself prompts an appreciation for the other's perspective as PJ's and Ruth's recognition of each other's shared humanity signifies their respective evolution from objectification to empathy. Ruth is likewise not spared her own moment of uncomfortable self-recognition, signaled by the entreaty to "Be Kind" that PJ writes upon her forehead, bindi-style. Finally conceding the falseness of her earlier enlightenment, Ruth gains newfound compassion that allows her to forgive PJ's misdeeds and to see a human being where her disgusted siblings, responding to her distress call, see only "some kind of animal." In the back of a pickup truck that will return them to civilization, the two come to rest in a pietà pose, traveling into a sunset antipodean from the happily-ever-afters of Hollywood.

1.2. Ruth (Kate Winslet) and PJ (Harvey Keitel) riding into the sunset.

David Crouch locates a potentially affirmative tourist gaze, which can encompass "an engaging, connecting, caring content and character of looking, rather than merely a detached, observing, exploitative one."[18] *Holy Smoke* similarly rehabilitates the tourist gaze in portraying Ruth's and PJ's development from exoticizing to empathizing, in relation both to cultural otherness (for Ruth, of India; for PJ, whose cowboy machismo, modeled on too many Hollywood westerns, proves no match for the Australian frontier) as well as to "the other sex." *Holy Smoke* derails the bisexual-bohemian's conventional teleology, leaving her uncontained and more grounded within her chosen culture, working as a social worker in Jaipur at film's close. Shedding her associations with detached exoticism, selfish opportunism, and voracious hedonism, Ruth represents the bisexual-bohemian at her best in establishing a realistic rather than utopian transcultural and bisexual space beyond borders.[19]

Even accounting for the overwhelming norm of whiteness in images produced by the dominant culture industry, there is a disproportionate scarcity of characters of color readable as bisexual in Western film and television narratives. Aside from the Latina women of *Gigli*, *Frida*, and (the subject of my next reading) *Mulholland Drive*, the two most overt examples from contemporary Western cinema are an African American woman (Kerry Washington) in *She Hate Me* (Spike Lee, 2004) and a Chinese American woman (Joan Chen) in *Wild Side*. Both depictions are problematic – *She Hate Me* for its paranoid sendup of queer women as man-hating "sperm stealers" who prove improbably susceptible to male virility, and *Wild Side* for its exoticizing of the sensual, duplicitous "dragon lady," though Chen's character eventually advances beyond her stereotypical trappings. The question of race is often acknowledged by the films themselves, as indicated by instances of the bi-suggestive character's whiteness being explicitly addressed, within my last and upcoming missed moments, as an entitlement – cast off in *Holy Smoke*, adopted in *Mulholland Drive*, or taken for granted in *Girl, Interrupted*. That bisexuality is representationally aligned with whiteness in the Western cultural imaginary seems clear enough, as it is out of that tradition of sexuality discourse that compulsory monosexuality derives. While bisexuality's association with whiteness remains overwhelmingly the norm in English-language television as well, several noteworthy exceptions have recently emerged and will be discussed in chapter 4. Bisexuality's association with socioeconomic as well as white privilege is the subject of chapter 2's bi-textuality, but first there is one additional mode of art cinema to consider, including a missed moment that provocatively investigates the link between bisexual and mixed race identities.

IN OUR DREAMS: BISEXUALITY AS DESUBJECTIVITY IN DREAM FILMS

We need a dream world in order to discover the features of the real world we think we inhabit.

PAUL FEYERABEND, *Against Method*

Is it possible to be two people at the same time?

promotional tagline for *Persona* (Ingmar Bergman, 1966)

At their most ambitious and transgressive, art films engage in a sometimes confounding exploration of what lies beyond compulsory monosexuality. From the silent-era surrealist film *Un Chien Andalou* (Luis Buñuel, 1929) to the contemporary French art film *Swimming Pool*, dream films turn this world inside out, defamiliarizing or "making strange" our naturalized reality by exposing our fantasies – both our erotic desires and our cultural illusions – to the light of (the every)day. With their unfixed character identities, narrative ambiguities, free-floating temporality and spatiality, and exaggerated affect, art cinema's dream films follow a nonlinear, dreamlike (il)logic that calls for flexible subjectivity, sensorial response, and emotional intuitiveness, redolent of a bisexual approach to desire. As perceived from a bisexual subjectivity, the monosexually ordered world appears decidedly *uncanny* – familiar yet strange. Unbound by conventional techniques for clearly delineating dream sequences, dream films' surreal content and uncanny sensibility pervade even ostensibly waking moments, blurring the boundary between fantasy and reality. Writing on the oeuvre of David Lynch, Slavoj Žižek uses the term "ridiculous sublime" to describe dream films' mode of intertwining fantasy and reality to acknowledge how the two invariably inform one another in a symbiotic and overlapping relationship that combines to structure consciousness and hence subjectivity.[20] Dreams and memories often are diegetically foregrounded in dream films, Ruth Perlmutter observes, so as

> to express the tension between remembering and repressing an unacceptable past . . . driven by characters with either hysterical transference (such as an exchange of personalities) or a psychological ailment – amnesia, muteness, paralysis. . . . They hide behind these psychic maladies in an effort to seek a new identity or escape into alternate selves (a desire that often gets expressed by serialization – successive what-if scenarios, parallel worlds, multiple outcome narratives).[21]

Though Perlmutter explicitly links this tension to what she terms "gender confusion," she merely hints at the dream film's emphasis on erotic fantasy and only glancingly acknowledges how substantially non-normative desires provoke this will to escape. Dream films' blurring of fantasy and reality engages a bisexual perspective in that, in dreams as in fantasies, neither subject position nor desire is fixed, and how it makes you *feel* is the chief catalyst for emotional response.

Given their ambiguities, dream films can frustrate our ability not only to identify *with* characters but to identify characters altogether. The recurring tropes of doubling and multiple personality carry associations specifically related to anxieties around queer desire: overly close alliances between same-sex individuals, considered suspect, are thereby imagined as a disconcerting (and disturbing) likeness; a bisexual's troubling attraction to both men and women is rendered as a split self; and same-sex desire is suggested to be narcissistic or imitative, especially when parent-child surrogates are constructed (as chapter 2 will explore further). Whereas these tropes are typically presented as aberrant to a film's otherwise "normal" narrative realism, in dream films they are not so clearly explained diegetically or anchored to individual characters; instead, enigmatic personae and identity-swapping pervade the diegetic world. Frequently, however, dream films will engender what I call the dreamgirl, a figure (like the bisexual-bohemian, nearly always a woman) who exudes and elicits bisexual desire, and whose sexual subjectivity is reflexively signaled through her character's foregrounding of identity construction. For the dreamgirl is, literally and figuratively, a performer: stage actress Elisabeth (Liv Ullman) in *Persona;* seductive muse Anita Pallenberg in *Performance;* magician-performance artist Céline (Juliet Berto) in *Céline and Julie vont en bateau/Céline and Julie Go Boating* (Jacques Rivette, 1974); ethereal Miranda (Anne Lambert) of *Picnic at Hanging Rock* (Peter Weir, 1975), who enthralls her schoolmates through their narrative "dream within a dream"; exotic dancer Christina (Mia Kirshner) in Atom Egoyan's *Exotica* (1994); nymphet Julie (Ludivine Sagnier), conjured by an older woman's lustful imagination, in *Swimming Pool;* the eponymous prostitute (Amanda Seyfried) hired to seduce a married man on behalf of his suspicious wife in *Chloe;* and the soon-to-be-discussed actresses of *Mulholland Drive,* Diane/Betty (Naomi Watts) and Rita/Camilla (Laura Elena Harring). Though this linking of bisexuality to performance is typically embodied in the figure of the capricious bisexual who flits between heterosexual and homosexual "roles," the analogy between bisexuality and performativity in dream films exposes the constructed rather than expressive nature of social performance, and as such the dreamgirl and the bisexual subjectivity she embodies gradually materialize as no longer fantastical but grounded in the everyday.

In *Persona,* young nurse Alma (Bibi Andersson) fantasizes adopting the identity of acclaimed actress Elisabeth, whose ambivalence about her authentic "role" as wife and mother drives her to voluntary muteness. Viewed as pathological by the medical authorities, Elisabeth's refusal to speak – as her doctor speculates, "so that you don't have to lie" – is grounds for her institutionalization and subsequent sequestering in an isolated all-women's community for "resocialization" (making *Persona* a high-art take on the "women's institution" genre of sexploitation films discussed in chapter 2). As in *Holy Smoke,* a willful woman submits to isolation in close quarters with a "healer" sent to cure her of mysterious ailments, only to have the tables reversed in an increasingly volatile struggle for dominance. In both, the process involves a symbiotic, erotically charged central relationship with elements of narcissism, split personality, and conflicted, repressed desires that together serve metaphorically to address bisexual subjectivity. While the metaphor of the split self risks recalling the stereotype of bisexuals as two-faced, less pejoratively it evokes the ambivalence experienced by (and the perception of personal inconsistency attributed to) bisexuals in a monosexual world – a state of being, as the next section will explore, analogous to the experience of racial passing.

Clearly inspired by Bergman, Robert Altman's *3 Women* (1977) features another unhappily married, mute mother-to-be (Janice Rule), who obsessively paints primitive-style murals depicting animalistic males dominating females, symptomatically illustrating the female experience of heteropatriarchy. *3 Women*'s oblique narrative offers a pastiche of bisexual significations: doubling, split personality, mother-daughter surrogates, narcissism, and eroticized hero(ine) worship are all on display. Altman's story, which he claims came to him in a dream, revolves around naif Pinky's (Sissy Spacek) wide-eyed fixation on aspiring domestic goddess Millie (Shelley Duvall), whom the other characters find insufferable and openly mock.[22] Like *Persona*'s Nurse Alma, Pinky occupies a subservient position both socioeconomically and in terms of her reverential admiration of a woman she perceives as an ideal self. Both Alma and Pinky gradually adopt the appearance, name, and increasingly the identity of the women whose class status (or affectation, in Millie's case) and gender presentations they idolize.[23] *3 Women*'s ambiguous epilogue, which creates familial bonds among the three formerly competing women with no men in sight, seems to imagine a matriarchal utopia.

MISSED MOMENT: *MULHOLLAND DRIVE*
(DAVID LYNCH, 2001)

Following a violent automobile accident atop Los Angeles's Mulholland Drive, a raven-haired woman (Laura Elena Harring) stumbles from the wreckage and, drawn by the city lights below, dazedly makes her way to a vacant apartment, where in relief she falls to sleep. When vivacious blonde Betty (Naomi Watts), a newcomer to LA, arrives soon thereafter to the apartment belonging to her traveling Aunt Ruth, she is startled to find the beautiful interloper. Recalling she was in a car accident but unable to remember her name, the distraught woman notices a poster for the film Gilda *and introduces herself as Rita. The only clues to her identity are a purse containing a wad of bills and a mysterious blue key.*

Across town, a cocky young Hollywood director named Adam Kesher (Justin Theroux) is ordered by two sinister men to cast a blonde actress named Camilla Rhodes as the lead in his current project. "It is no longer your film," the men pronounce. "This is the girl." In the next twenty-four hours, Adam's film set is shut down, his bank accounts frozen, and he is forcibly ejected from his house after discovering his wife's philandering. A sensational audition lands Betty a meeting with Adam, from whom she flees to keep a date with Rita. The latter's recollection of a name ("Diane Selwyn") leads the women to hunt down her residence, where they discover her rotting corpse. That night, Betty disguises the spooked Rita with a blonde wig, and the two women fall into an amorous embrace. Awakened later by Rita's cries, the women proceed trance-like to a dilapidated theater called Club Silencio, where they are moved to tears by a female vocal performance revealed afterward to be "an illusion."

Finding a mysterious blue box beside them, the women hurry home to retrieve the blue key when suddenly Betty vanishes. With fright, Rita opens the box to find it empty. It falls to the floor with a thud, and a moment later Aunt Ruth appears to investigate the noise but sees no one. At another apartment, in another bedroom, Diane Selwyn is seen curled up sleeping. A man dressed as a cowboy knocks on her door, saying, "Hey pretty girl, time to wake up."

"A Love Story in the City of Dreams"

promotional tagline for *Mulholland Drive*

What appears above describes the significant narrative action of *Mulholland Drive*'s first two-thirds, apportioned by critics as constituting the film's "dream segment." Revisiting *Mulholland Drive* and the numerous critical analyses it has so far inspired reveals bisexual (in)visibility throughout – evident within the film's representational shifts between bisexuality as specter and as spectacle, as well as in the way that the film's analysts to date advance toward only to retreat from bisexual readings. For these critics and scholars, the point of departure into *Mulholland*

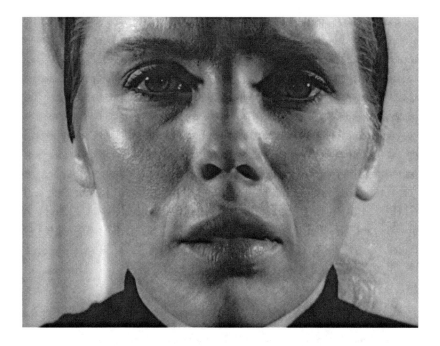

1.3. *Persona*'s famous shot of the merged faces of its leading ladies, Elisabeth (Liv Ullmann) and Alma (Bibi Andersson).

Drive rests on two basic assumptions: first, that Betty/Diane (Watts) is the film's protagonist and as such should be the privileged subject and focal point of analysis; and second, that meaning depends on interpreting *Mulholland Drive*'s dream segment as exclusively Betty/Diane's wish-fulfilling fantasy. These interpretive blinders have led the film's analysts largely to ignore its central narrative engagement with bisexuality, relying instead on a monosexist framework that seems particularly inappropriate given that this is, after all, a film that actually depicts one of its female leads, Camilla (also Harring), as behaving bisexually (acting on both opposite-sex and same-sex erotic desire), and raises the question of the other lead's, Diane's, bi-potential.[24] That Camilla's desire seems predicated on ruthless ambition rather than on romantic/erotic attraction does not preclude her being bisexual so much as it alludes to a particular idea of what bisexuality is like: opportunistic and manipulative. Given the allusion to Carmilla, the female vampire immortalized in Sheridan

Le Fanu's classic story of the same name, even Camilla's revealed name suggests her bloodthirsty drive for "anything that moves."[25] However much her characterization conforms to the stereotypical bisexual, in orchestrating an erotic triangle to suit her own selfish ends, Camilla reveals how considerations beyond gendered object choice are crucial determinants of sexual attraction and behavior.

In the extensive critical literature on *Mulholland Drive,* only David Andrews's analysis ventures to voice bisexuality.[26] Not only do the published readings to date largely ascribe a monosexual identity to a character(s) rendered bi-suggestively, but critics also attempt to stabilize and fix the narrative and characterizations of this radically open-ended cinematic text. In what follows, I explore *Mulholland Drive*'s suggestive ellipses, both in the film itself and in the critical corpus around it, eliciting the film's repressed preoccupation with racial and sexual transgression. In doing so, I shift the focus from Betty/Diane, the central figure for most readings of the film, to the only apparently defocalized Rita/Camilla.

> I just came here from Deep River, Ontario, and now I'm in this dream place!
>
> BETTY, *Mulholland Drive*

Lynch's films continually manifest the fascination with dreamwork characteristic of surrealism; they estrange viewers from the film's reality and from our own in ways that reveal the repressed residing below the surface of what seems natural and normal. *Mulholland Drive* constitutes an exemplary instance of a dream film and one that pays its respects to *Persona* and *3 Women.* The two women who team up to solve a mystery in *Mulholland Drive* are caught up in a role-play fantasy much like that between Elisabeth and Alma in *Persona.* Both films' female fantasists attempt to escape reality by adopting personae conjured in a dream or constructed in a star image. Even as she realizes that were Elisabeth to inhabit her, Alma's "soul would stick out everywhere," Alma fantasizes being Elisabeth no less than Diane desires to be and to have Camilla. These dueling selves, locked in a symbolically schizophrenic battle between repression and exhibition, gradually morph into a united though conflicted ego or split personality – epitomized in *Persona*'s shot (see figure 1.3 above) of Ullman's and Andersson's faces merging, but also

1.4. "Your soul would poke out everywhere," Alma tells Elisabeth in *Persona*.

illustrated in the moments in both films when the heroines compare mirrored reflections.

Like Elisabeth, Rita/Camilla initially seems vulnerable on account of her posttraumatic condition, but she eventually reveals herself to be harboring a manipulative will. Similarly, Alma, like Betty, initially appears a naif enraptured by the "patient" entrusted to her care, but gradually reveals her own highly sexualized nature (in a character reversal as startling and erotically charged as Betty's audition, Alma recounts having taken part in a seaside orgy), and is increasingly driven to vindictive acts by her counterpart's duplicitous betrayals. Indeed both films could be read figuratively as female vampire tales; as Susan Sontag observes of Alma's escalating obsession with and subordination to her emotionally controlling charge, the two are "bound together in a passionate agonized relationship . . . which mythically is rendered as vampirism. We see Elizabeth [*sic*] kissing Alma's neck; at one point, Alma sucks Elizabeth's [*sic*] blood."[27] Through the aforementioned allusion to Le Fanu's "Carmilla,"

1.5. "You look like someone else," Betty (Naomi Watts) tells Rita (Laura Elena Harring) in *Mulholland Drive*.

Mulholland Drive invokes vampire legend in conjuring an exotic seductress who corrupts the "innocent" Betty/Diane, whose transformation from bright-eyed vigor to listless emaciation seems reminiscent of the effects of the vampire's kiss. Ultimately, both films are emblematic dream films for suggesting that a significant portion of the narrative (in *Persona*, the central sequences depicting the two women's convalescence at the beachside cottage) are pure fantasy; as Perlmutter observes, the repeated instances of Alma falling asleep hint that we are "each time descending deeper into dream-states that put external reality and temporal logic into question."[28]

Exhibiting amnesia and schizophrenic symptoms, the female couples in *3 Women* and *Mulholland Drive* also mirror one another, with their mutual interactions conflating hero(ine) worship with same-sex desire. *3 Women*'s Millie initially seems, like *Mulholland Drive*'s Betty, eerily kooky in her self-deluded optimism, while Pinky at first seems as submissive and mysterious as (if far more abject than) Rita. After Millie provokes Pinky's near-fatal suicide (again, shades of *Mulholland Drive*), both women undergo a radical transformation echoed by Lynch's heroines: Millie (like Betty/Diane) becomes self-sacrificing in her guilt-stricken attendance to the now amnesiac Pinky, who (like the "real" Camilla) grows manipulative and selfish. Most resonantly, the amnesia that afflicts childlike Pinky and docile Rita, though again recalling the stereotype of bisexuals as imitative, two-faced, and leading double lives, more affirmatively signifies a "forgetting of oneself," thus suggesting an avenue of escape through bisexuality (however pathologized) from socially constructed monosexuality.

> *Diane's acting career never takes off, and she becomes dependent on the beautiful and successful Camilla Rhodes, with whom she is in love, to get her roles. When she discovers that Camilla is having an affair with her director, Adam Kesher, Diane descends into bitter depression and eventually contracts a hit on the woman who betrayed her. Following the job's completion, a guilt-racked and hallucinating Diane puts a gun to her head and ends her own life. The screen fills up with smoke.*

Despite the film's doubtlessly intentional vagueness about who is dreaming what and when, the bulk of *Mulholland Drive* analyses construct the film's first two-thirds (hereafter "Part 1") as a fantasy sequence dreamt or imagined by Diane, and that which is described above, the film's final third (hereafter "Part 2"), as depicting Diane's waking reality, spotted with flashbacks and hallucinations. Admittedly, *Mulholland Drive*'s emotional poignancy springs predominantly from identification with and sympathy for the tortured Diane – who succeeds, by film's end, in creating such powerful pathos through the immediacy of her suffering (an effect heightened by the raw intimacy of Watts's performance, especially in contrast to the intentional vacancy of Harring's own) that there seems little question of privileging Diane's highly subjective perspective as the surest route to accessing narrative meaning. In the wake of such profuse affect and privileged subjectivity, the consensus view explains Part 1 as Diane's wish-fulfilling fantasy to reconstruct her emotional loss and professional failure through an idealization of what might have been, and to absolve her from the guilt of having arranged Camilla's death. A failure professionally, driven to destroy the woman who rejected her, Diane, acting out of frustration, heartbreak, and fear of exposure, crafts an elaborate revenge scenario that punishes Adam, her main competitor for Camilla's affections, while allowing Diane to realize her professional ambitions *and* get her dreamgirl. Approaching *Mulholland Drive* in this way has produced a rich and persuasive range of readings that I have no wish to discount or cast aside. Yet I remain curious why Lynch chooses, as David Andrews puts it, to

> gently undercut the ideal oneiric reading, creating a thin fissure of indeterminacy in an otherwise closed interpretation.... [The closed reading] dismisses the fact that the film portrays a diversity of sleepers. If the film is a function of Diane's mind, why, near the start of her dream, does the filmmaker so persistently depict Rita falling asleep, sleeping, and waking up? The effect, it appears, is to enclose important scenes within her mind.[29]

Where I differ with Andrews is in his subsequent conclusion that "interpreting these scenes as 'belonging' to Rita leads nowhere." To explore an alternative interpretation by approaching *Mulholland Drive*'s dream segment as Camilla's *desubjectivized fantasy* rather than as Diane's wish-fulfillment may in fact lead us somewhere quite intriguing.

The idea that *Mulholland Drive* hinders viewer identification with Rita/Camilla needs re-examining, for a good deal of Part 1 sutures spectators into a highly subjective point-of-view through Rita's eyes that mirrors the way that Part 2 visualizes Diane's perspective. Rita's amnesia-stricken helplessness makes her the clearer object of compassion in Part 1, especially given the obstacle to viewer identification posed by Betty's Sirkian high spirits and can-do attitude, what one critic wryly refers to as her "vulcanized naïveté."[30] To conclude that the dream "belongs" to Diane with the same finality with which *Mulholland Drive*'s henchmen pronounce "This is the girl" demands that we accept the inducement to overidentify with Diane's Part 2 incarnation, at the expense of taking Rita's sympathetic characterization in Part 1 into account. The crucial point, however, is that the closed interpretation attributes to the dream an unambiguous structure that Lynch purposefully avoids, and the film insists on this ambiguity as a means of preventing any easy delegation of narrative content within a wholly enclosed fantasy realm.

THIS IS NOT THE GIRL.

Ballin (George Macready): Gilda, are you decent?

Gilda (Rita Hayworth): Me? [*pause*] Sure, I'm decent.

GILDA

Mulholland Drive's leading ladies interrupt their initial tryst to ask one another, "Have you ever done this before?" Betty answers only "I want to with you," thereby evading the issue of past experiences. And because Rita is suffering from amnesia, her response ("I don't know") is necessarily vague. That both women articulate their desire as something irreducible to past behavior or identity makes available a space, both on their part and on the viewer's, for the exploration of bi-potential. As Heather K. Love observes, Rita's response "is striking in its insistence that what matters is not memory but desire . . . what we have done and who we are does not count for much – what matters instead is what we are about to do, what we want to do."[31]

This much remarked upon seduction scene serves as a self-conscious sendup of the sexploitation genre cliché of faux innocence that stretches from the coy boarding school romance to hardcore pornographic displays. Both this and *Mulholland Drive's* subsequent sex scene playfully mimic those films' clichéd, wooden dialogue ("What was that you said, gorgeous?" "I said, you drive me wild"), lines that sound not unlike the banal script that the two women practice in advance of Betty's audition. With a tone half-sincere and half-mocking, these scenes comment ironically on customary screen treatments of female same-sex desire even as they similarly aim to titillate. Commenting on this later scene, in which Diane remembers (or perhaps fantasizes) tussling bare-breasted with Camilla, Love notes how Lynch deploys stock characters, narrative scenarios, and male fantasies of what lesbian sex looks like ("very breasty, very kissy") to reveal how "the possibilities for multiple identification and the improvisation opened in the first section of the film are shut down here, as each of the women plays her assigned role in a familiar – all too familiar – drama of lesbian triangulation and betrayal."[32] This scene's lurid tone, and its rapid disintegration into cruelty and resentment, is antithetical to the dreamy sense of erotic discovery in the earlier lovemaking.

This shift in *Mulholland Drive's* sex scenes from tender to tawdry corresponds to the film's juxtaposition of what Love notes are the "two most familiar lesbian plots of the twentieth century": the (initial, comic) adventure of innocent discovery, and the (final, tragic) lesbian triangle "in which an attractive but unavailable woman dumps a less attractive

woman who is figured as exclusively lesbian."[33] But whereas the fantasy
of romantic discovery is revealed to be the wish-fulfilling dream of a
failed starlet fed on fantasies of Hollywood happy endings, Part 2 is
less easily read as a critique of narrative convention in that the dream's
rupture causes the film's tonal shift into the non-ironic and emotionally
wrenching. Yet the conventional lesbian triangle plot lingers: Diane fix-
ates on the impossible object choice, Camilla, who true to form turns
cold and ultimately chooses a man. Nearly any narrative that characterizes lesbianism as a tragic state of suffering provoked by necessarily
doomed desire constructs its nonreciprocating female love object along
bi-suggestive lines. But despite her indispensability to lesbian tragedy,
the female bisexual remains (in)visible. Although she is, in her transformation from malleable, mysterious object of desire to manipulative,
fickle lover, vilified for inflicting suffering of tragic proportions, she is
never endowed with an explicit or continuing bisexual identity – either
in the text or in critical analyses. Love, for one, refrains from naming
Camilla or her behavior bisexual, instead calling it representative of "perverse heterosexuality" that nonetheless carries with it "the glamour of
mobile desire," the latter an almost grudging description of bisexual
flexibility and fluidity.[34]

With the same half-ironic, self-conscious references to classical cinematic tropes, *Mulholland Drive*'s dream narrative inflates film noir conventions to absurdist proportions, replete with shifty gangsters who utter monosyllabic pronouncements and relish sadistic acts of violence,
a slinky femme fatale simmering with duplicity, and her converse, the
idealistic and endlessly efficient girl detective whose insatiable curiosity
will lead her into the dark recesses of the underworld. Rita's chosen name,
visual coding, and mysterious past mark her as a femme fatale and thus
not what she seems – it is only a matter of time before she reveals her
treacherous nature and betrays Betty/Diane, thus precipitating the latter's plunge from chipper ingénue to despondent wretch. That Lynch cast
then-unknown actresses in the lead roles only heightens our dependency
on genre archetypes to shape our initial impressions of these characters
for whom there is no available knowledge of star personae. But whereas
Diane eventually casts off the stereotype that initially characterizes her
(indeed while still in her guise as Betty, for it is during her audition meta-

morphosis that she reveals herself to be not what *she* seems), Camilla grows to inhabit her stereotype – the duplicitous bisexual – fully.

As with romantic/erotic triangle films, film noir possesses a queer potential to "complicate the formerly undisturbed heterosexual coupling," as Chris Cagle notes, "and often [noir] narratives end in deception, distrust, separation, or unceremonious death."[35] *Mulholland Drive* "queers" noir formula by transforming the fall guy – the ambitious, desiring male who falls under the femme fatale's spell and winds up incarcerated or killed – into a woman: Betty/Diane. To stage Part 1's revisionist fantasy within a noir mise-en-scène allows the jilted Diane to imagine herself ensnared within the femme fatale's clutches. However, that this noir re-enactment emanates from Diane's decidedly unreliable perspective raises the possibility that perhaps this femme fatale is *not* not what she seems – a prospect whose plausibility is bolstered by a consideration of the amnesiac's adoptive name.

Camilla's dream-self gives herself Rita Hayworth's name after she catches sight of a poster advertising Hayworth's famous role in *Gilda*. Hayworth's off-screen penchant for professional/personal relationships with powerful men (Harry Cohn, Orson Welles, Prince Aly Khan) parallels Camilla's relationship to her director, Adam Kesher, and evokes the opportunistic stigma often applied to bisexuals. Yet Lynch might have chosen any number of classic Hollywood stars with Pygmalion pasts to reference, and indeed Harring more closely approximates Ava Gardner in her appearance and styling, especially when Harring appears wearing a single-strap black gown that closely resembles that worn by Gardner in her memorable first appearance onscreen in another classic noir, *The Killers* (Robert Siodmak, 1946). Several significant reasons for this particular choice emerge, the first of which being that *Gilda*, despite its customary categorization as noir, is nonetheless an uneasy entry in that canon and its leading lady admissible as a femme fatale only with much qualification. Film noir is a notoriously slippery category, but it seems fair to say that *Gilda* does not straightforwardly embody noir's prototypical attributes. Most importantly atypical is the revelation early in that film that Hayworth's Gilda is *not* a scheming, hard-as-nails femme fatale but is in fact much closer to the lovesick, tormented, traditionally male protagonist who goes to self-destructive lengths (here, marrying a Nazi) in a misguided attempt to "tame" the femme fatale – in this gender-bending queer noir, Glenn Ford's bi-suggestive social climber Johnny. As police inspector Obregon (Joseph Calleia) reassures Johnny, "Gilda didn't do any of those things you've been losing sleep over," a remark that carries dual meaning in light of the implied sexual relationship between Johnny and his benefactor Ballin Mundson. Far from being an arbitrary allusion to Hollywood's golden age, *Mulholland Drive*'s reference to *Gilda* is meaningful both as a refiguring of the femme fatale archetype and for establishing an erotic triangle that, like *Gilda*'s, hinges on an ambitious bisexual with an obscure past. Rita/Camilla is like Gilda (that is, Hayworth) in her suppressed ethnicity, to be discussed below, but is like Johnny in her bisexuality, ambition, and haunted past. Ultimately, the referential recycling of noir tropes serves to frustrate a too easy condemnation of Rita/Camilla as sexual object-turned-villain, while also hiding in plain sight Rita/Camilla's "dark" secret: her Latina heritage. This secret identity, not revealed until two-thirds of the way through the film, rewrites the noir femme as another type of dark woman, serving to displace textual and cultural anxiety about female sexual transgression with an analogous (but safer) representation of ethnoracial transgression.

THE PART OF/FOR A LIFETIME

So imperceptible are her ethnoracial markers that we receive no discernable hint of Rita/Camilla's ethnicity until she is roused from the nightmare that has caused her to speak aloud in fluent Spanish, a language she had shown no previous signs of possessing. Again the allusion to Hayworth becomes relevant, for as Adrienne L. McLean has shown, the classical star's Latina identity substantially constituted the (open) secret of her success.[36] Tellingly, it is a nightmare – that which occurs when the dreamwork fails to sufficiently repress or disguise unconscious thoughts, thus provoking the disturbance of sleep – that causes Rita finally to "speak" her ethnicity and that commands the women (in a voice that seems to be channeling someone from beyond the grave, or from the distant past) out into the night. Also tellingly, it is immediately prior to her nightmare that Rita's fear of being "found out" prompts her to don the blonde-wigged disguise. Here and in the subsequent scene, before she is roused from sleep, Rita is shown in repose alongside Betty with their faces cubistically merged à la *Persona,* suggesting the transformative effect of her passing.

In terms of casting and star-making opportunities, racial minority status is not nearly so disadvantageous in today's Hollywood as during previous eras, though it would be overly sanguine to suggest that mainstream images and industry practices do not still privilege whiteness. Yet *Mulholland Drive,* like a number of Lynch's films, conjures a setting both present and past (specifically the 1950s of Lynch's childhood), and the uncanny anachronism of this classical Hollywood chronotype signals the bi-textual analogy afoot between race then and sexuality now. The ability to pass racially remains of enormous advantage in the acting profession, in which ethnic indefinability allows for flexibility among roles. Similarly, passing as straight (that is, maintaining a public appearance of heterosexuality and gender conformity) deflects the still-powerful threat of stigmatization for actors on the "down low," while concurrently a performer whose publicized lifestyle seems reassuringly straight (heterosexual couplings, preferably married with children) can "safely" play queer because his or her heterosexuality is not in question.

The moment in which Betty tells the disguised Rita "You look like someone else" as they marvel over her transformation evokes, for both women, Lacan's description of the mirror stage, a key moment in the process of self-formation. The dreaming Diane misrecognizes herself both as her alter-ego Betty and as another ego-ideal more successful in love and life: Camilla, who meanwhile imagines her blonde-wigged self as indistinguishable from the authentically blonde Anglo beside her. Taking place in the same physical location (before the bathroom mirror) where she'd earlier named herself impulsively upon glimpsing the *Gilda* poster's reflection, Rita/Camilla's misrecognition is also twofold in its reference to a second ego-ideal: Hayworth, known for her complex negotiation of ethnicity.[37]

At Club Silencio, Rita's repressed Latina identity emerges full force in connection with the distinctly similar-looking Rebekah Del Rio's lip-synced Spanish-language rendition of Roy Orbison's "Crying." Del Rio is introduced as "*La Llorona* de Los Angeles," in Hispanic folklore "the crying woman" said to be a mother who has killed her children in mad-

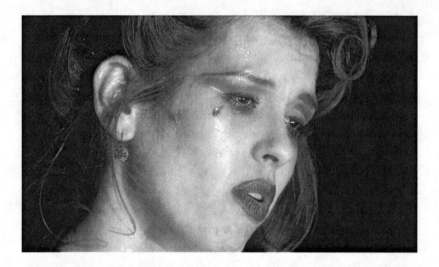

1.6. *La Llorona* of Los Angeles, Rebekah Del Rio.

ness over her abandonment by their father.[38] The atmosphere remains eerily reminiscent of a seance or exorcism, and Del Rio collapses – as if relieved of the demon possessing her – before the song's conclusion. The juxtaposition between this Latina virtuosa relegated to covering popular tunes in midnight performances at a downtown dive and the Anglo actresses seen earlier on a studio soundstage in lip-sync auditions for a nostalgic doo-wop musical illuminates one of classical Hollywood's own darker secrets: that of lower-paid, unseen, and usually uncredited ethnic labor. What is glimpsed at Club Silencio, then, is Camilla's nightmare come to life: the professional dead-end that lies in wait for ethnoracially unassimilated performers. Having yielded to the Hollywood patriarchy by assimilating her ethnoracial and sexual otherness to the anglicized monosexuality it privileges, Rita/Camilla experiences a return of the repressed that rousts her from her "dreamlife" and sends her to Club Silencio to confront her past and herself.

In her study of Hayworth, Adrienne McLean refers to the famous adage attributed to the star, "Men go to bed with Gilda and wake up with Rita Hayworth," as connoting "an ordinary woman who has been engulfed or entrapped by an image ... partly of her own making."[39] Like McLean, Lynch engages the fantasy persona in order to break it down, to reveal how this Rita is hardly an ethnically and sexually malleable blank slate without a past. In taking Betty to Club Silencio, Rita reveals her assumed identity, along with their romantic bliss, to be illusions doomed to failure (presaged by Orbison's lyrics of heartbreak and longing), which provokes in Betty something like an epileptic fit. Jennifer Hudson remarks on the simultaneous breakdown of language (and thus signification) at Club Silencio, wherein foreign tongues intermingle and the (il)logic of intuition takes over. As, in Hudson's words, "words lose their power to inscribe and fix meaning," it becomes the palpable affect conveyed through Del Rio's corporeal presence rather than the actual lyrics (which require a knowledge of either Spanish or Orbison's original) that moves diegetic and nondiegetic audience alike.[40] But in a potent illustration of how Brechtian distanciation techniques can actually intensify identification and affect for the spectator, dream films such as *Mulholland Drive* reveal cinematic artifice through their defamiliarization of "reality" even as they reaffirm the appeal and persuasiveness of screen fantasies as conjured by the powerful audiovisual orchestration of sound/image juxtaposition.

The next section will consider how Rita/Camilla's amnesia works metaphorically to translate the experience of bisexuality and of desubjectivized fantasy. Less affirmatively, perhaps, amnesia also functions as metaphor for the price of making it in Hollywood – the American Dream factory – where success comes at the cost of erasing (via assimilation) or exploiting (via exoticization) one's otherness. Rita/Camilla's ethnoracial passing can be read as analogous to her concurrent "role" as a bisexual passing within monosexist culture, with her success relative to Diane's indicative of her stereotypical invisibility – bisexuals can play it "straight" whereas lesbians are not right for the role. Through this metaphoric connection between bisexuality and mixed-race, played out on the body of Rita/Camilla, *Mulholland Drive* suggests that passing is either a necessary or an opportunistic strategy for survival and success; both the bisexual and mixed-race experiences reveal subjectivity to be, as Pramaggiore describes, "a movement between identities rather than a masquerade concealing an essential identity."[41] In linking Hollywood's dream factory connotations to the actual dreamwork, *Mulholland Drive* reveals the frustrated promise on the part of both to allow for fluid or hybrid identities. But while *Mulholland Drive* has been rightly pegged as an indictment of the American entertainment industry in the wake of Lynch's aborted television series, it aims not to destroy the dream factory altogether but rather to inspire fantasies that are consciously attuned to social realities and that accommodate more diverse spectator positions and desires.[42]

"A WOMAN IN SEARCH OF HERSELF"

By introducing Rita/Camilla with this line, *Mulholland Drive*'s theatrical trailer twists the noir convention of scrutinizing (so as to subjugate) the femme fatale, suggesting she is to retain a degree of authority over her own self-examination. Yet it is Betty/Diane who quickly takes over the investigation and whose "investigative drive harbors a need to control," as Amy Taubin notes. "If she can save Rita, she will have power over her, she will have made herself indispensable."[43] The female bisexual's unknowability is thus tempered in her fantasized transformation from obscure object of desire to her less threatening incarnation as mystery to be solved by plucky girl detective Betty. Predictably, this wish-fulfilling fantasy declaws Camilla, turning the manipulative social-climber with no apparent conscience into a docile pin-up made compliant and needy by her posttraumatic amnesia. The poignant moment in which the mysterious brunette confesses tearfully, "I don't know what my name is, I don't know who I am" has powerful resonance when read bisexually, suggesting the extent to which bisexual identity is deemed unnamable and impossible. Amnesia here holds the potential of fantasy (in its Lacanian formulation, as described by Todd McGowan) to "offer subjects respite from the incoherence that plagues their daily experiences."[44] Like McGowan, Jennifer Hudson points to the metaphorical connection between amnesia and fluid subjectivity but stops short of naming it bisexual:

> As a tabula rasa, Rita has no identifying markers . . . her preexisting identifying markers have been erased and thus left questionable, open to the flexibility and potential of being without a self. . . . However illusory Rita's attempt at becoming a self may appear, she seems to be the most real character in the film, in the sense that, as an amnesiac, she must be reactive. In other words, Rita's genuineness comes from her trust in her own emotions and intuitions.[45]

In language that continues tacitly to invoke bisexuality, Hudson goes on to describe Rita as "exud[ing] the fluidity and promise that comes from not having a fixed self . . . without conceptual borders surrounding her identity, Rita disrupts traditional either- or logic."[46] With the amnesiac Rita embodying bisexuality, Part 1 fantasizes an intensely fraught – but ultimately liberating – escape from the "trauma" of monosexuality (in which past experience dictates identity) that simulates the experience of unfixed subjectivity that bisexual desire and desubjectivized fantasy (as in cinematic spectatorship) so richly engage.

Thus the individual fantasies that Diane and Camilla conceive are attempts to free themselves from their respective prisons of desire: Diane's wish-fulfillment fantasy imagines that Camilla is alive and attainable; Camilla, entrapped by monosexist subjectivity, fantasizes her release from its confinement of her. Amnesia provides an imperfect route to independence, however; Camilla is made vulnerable and dependent on the nearest available caregiver, Betty, with whom she forms a surrogate mother-child relationship. The metaphorical bisexuality envisaged as flexible and reactive is, on its flip side, subject to stereotypical connotations of imitativeness, suggestibility, and parental fixation. "Rita attempts to invent herself by responding to her stimuli," Hudson writes, first through the *Gilda* poster and later by becoming "dependent upon Betty to supply her with an identity. The irony is that Betty turns Rita into a spitting image of herself": blonde and sapphically inclined.[47] Just as the brunette takes Hayworth's lead in passing as white, her corresponding impulse is to identify herself sexually through Betty, suggesting the pressure for bisexuals to "pick a side." One additional reason to leave open the possibility that Rita/Camilla is also a dreamer is so that she may conjure her own dream place complete with the obliging Betty, as McGowan suggests, "in order to help Rita solve the enigma of her desire."[48] To whomever it "belongs," the drive of *Mulholland Drive*'s dream is to discover and secure the mysterious brunette's "real" identity, alluding to the perception of bisexuality as something furtively and only temporarily concealing one's "true" nature.

Given that the dream also constitutes Diane's wish-fulfillment fantasy, there is a lesbian determinism to the narrative drive that is foreshadowed by the scene in which Rita tearfully confesses her memory loss,

1.7. Betty urges Rita to open up to her.

prompting Betty to suggest a search of Rita's belongings. Their subsequent discovery of an ominous wad of cash and a blue key in Rita's purse is scripted and composed in such a way to emphasize its sexual import. Rita sits on the edge of the bed, Betty kneels at her feet and places the purse (the contents of which will surely illuminate her identity, Betty says) in Rita's lap. When she hesitates to open it, Betty asks "You want to know, don't you?" "Yes, but . . . ," Rita answers and fearfully slides the zipper open. Reaching into its depths, her eyes meet Betty's with the same close-up intensity of the aforementioned Lynchian shared gaze between couples (see note 24), as the two women marvel wide-eyed over the riches contained within. Their suggestive posture and wording, accompanied by the purse's Freudian significance as a symbol of female genitalia, indicates that this (rather than the explicit sex scene to follow later) is Rita's primary initiation, guided by Betty's firm insistence, into the pleasures of lesbian eroticism.[49] Having discovered the "key" to unlocking Rita's identity (though it remains wholly a mystery what exactly it opens), Betty enthusiastically propels them onward in the investigation by suggesting they venture out in search of news of "Rita's" accident. But before departing, Betty insists upon hiding the evidence of their discovery, both purse and money, away from view – and where else but in that proverbial (bedroom) closet. Continuing to steer the investigation toward her preferred outcome, Betty encourages Rita's subsequent retrieval of the name "Diane Selwyn" from her amnesiac haze. When an inconclusive recorded voice answers their phone call to the listed number, Betty proposes hunting her down in person: "If it is Diane Selwyn," she says confidently, "she could tell you who you are."

"JUST LIKE IN THE MOVIES, WE'LL PRETEND TO BE SOMEONE ELSE."

With this line, Betty convinces Rita to continue their investigation into Rita's unknown past and mysterious identity – though Betty herself seems the one most eager for answers. Their search leads them to a shocking confrontation with Diane Selwyn's fetid corpse, and as the two women flee in horror, their images are visually rendered as fanning out and overlapping – at once signaling the illusory surface of the cinematic image, the women's comparably illusory, fraying identities, and their overlapping and fused interconnectedness. Whereas the search up to this point has been for Rita's identity, the discovery of the corpse initiates, as Martha Nochimson notes, the "beginning [of Diane's] discovery of her own identity," which turns out to be no less elusive and unstable.[50] Much as Bergman sets the film strip itself aflame in *Persona*, Lynch orchestrates the breakdown of cinematic "reality" here and with the subsequent revelation at Club Silencio that "it is an illusion." That dream films frequently culminate in this self-reflexive narrative "breakdown" leads Perlmutter to speculate that "the text itself may respond to repression and the denial of reality by collapsing; that is, suffering a textual trauma that parallels mental breakdown."[51] In *Mulholland Drive*, what precisely is being broken down is each woman's fantasy (Diane's of her dream girl, Camilla's of her dream self), seen visibly to fray as Diane loses her assurance of fixed subjectivity, that in which Camilla is paradoxically finding herself encased.

As reality increasingly permeates the narrative's dream space, each woman's fantasy self destabilizes and they become closer to their waking selves. The first intimation comes in the moment of identity conflation/conversion as Betty remarks "You look like someone else" when assessing the newly blonde Rita's disguise; from here on out it will be Diane who is lost and Camilla who is successful. As they then begin making love, Betty twice confesses her devotion to Rita ("I love you . . . I love you") with only carnal exchange offered in return – a portent of how we will soon see Camilla to be the emotionally withholding partner. Once into Part 2, another scene inverts the earlier "mirror stage" shot that had Rita misrecognizing herself as her Anglo ego-ideal. In this subsequent sequence, Lynch constructs a series of shots that disrupt the 180-degree line that spatially orients the spectator – a "radical" formal technique anathema to mainstream film style – in order to place Camilla where, in the logic of filmic space, Diane herself should be standing. Positioning Camilla in this impossible space conveys that her appearance is merely Diane's hallucination that Camilla has "come back" to her, while simultaneously jarring the viewer with a visual suggestion of Diane looking at herself. The effect serves to visualize Diane's fantasy of both *having* and *being* Camilla, even as that fantasy is ruptured by what is essentially a breakdown of the "mirror phase" as Diane fails to maintain her illusory self-image as her ego-ideal, recognizing herself for the disheartened depressive she actually is.

In the party scene that follows, Diane and the viewers also are forced to see Camilla as she really is. Rendered more acutely through Diane's perspective than any other sequence in the film, it is the crucial point at which she firmly seizes viewers' sympathy and thus their allegiance to her over Camilla. The latter's insensitivity in inviting Diane to her new lover's home, the lure of brief hope she gives Diane in leading her up the idyllic wooded shortcut, Camilla's failure to defend Diane (indeed, she appears to enjoy watching her squirm) when chastised for her tardiness, her feigned obliviousness to Diane's misery as Adam protractedly announces their engagement, and her provocative kiss with a sultry blonde unfurl a veritable rogues' gallery of pejorative connotations chained to bisexuality. The blonde whom Camilla kisses – as with her on-set clinch with Adam, she clearly enjoys doing so under Diane's tortured gaze – is the "Camilla Rhodes" (Melissa George) of Part 1 seen auditioning for her assured part in the doo-wop musical. It is the ultimate performance of bisexual privilege and exhibitionism: publicly kissing a woman as she gives her hand to a man for reasons implied to be opportunistic – a resounding reaffirmation of the cliché of the sexually adventurous but socially conservative bisexual. But while *Mulholland Drive* may grant access to a bisexual perspective of reality in Part 1 only to reproduce familiar bisexual stereotypes in Part 2, this does not necessarily constitute a capitulation to reductive conceptions of bisexuality. Though her characterization is not pitched in the highly ironic register of most of the film's other allusions (to lesbian exploitation films, to film noir), in so exaggeratedly embodying bisexual stereotypes, Rita/Camilla clearly signifies cultural constructions of bisexuality. Denied the fleshed-out characterization that Diane receives in Part 2 (and that Hayworth's Gilda and Ford's Johnny acquire by Act 2), Camilla is cut off from viewer sympathy and identification – she remains the obscure object of desire.

Here it becomes essential to consider how *Mulholland Drive* cleaves between dream and reality, for the way that Part 2 returns us (Diane, Camilla, and the viewers) to harsh wakefulness with the same deadening thud of the mysterious blue box dropping to the ground and the neighbors' knocks that rouse Diane. Whereas Part 1 conjured a dreamworld in which Diane and Camilla were freed temporarily from their prisons of desire, Part 2 returns them and us the viewers to a world resembling far more closely that which exists off the screen and outside our minds (though the film draws as permeable a border between Parts 1 and 2 as human perception is wont to do). While *Mulholland Drive* brings to the screen a supremely convincing and compelling representation of bisexual desire and subjectivity, its refusal to keep that fantasy alive at film's end is precisely what guarantees its import as both art film and bisexual text. To do otherwise would be, in Paul Schrader's formulation, to solve the problem rather than to probe the dilemma of compulsory monosexuality.

In closing, one final facet of *Mulholland Drive*'s bisexual (in)visibility calls for closer examination: the film's publicity campaign and the careful, muted way in which bisexuality was mobilized within it. It is surprising to note how inconspicuously the film's lesboerotic angle was acknowledged and how indirectly queer audiences were targeted in official, first-wave promotional materials. Same-sex desire was only obliquely alluded to in its tagline ("A Love Story in the City of Dreams") and was wholly absent from its trailer, and yet went on to be invariably referenced in critical reviews and through other channels not dictated by the film's U.S. distributor, Universal Focus Features. 1996's *Bound* (directed by first-timers the Wachowski Brothers and produced by Dino De Laurentiis and

1.8. Lesbian eroticism used to advertise *Mulholland Drive*.

Aaron Spelling), a comparable if more audience-friendly neo-noir art film centered around a lesbian love affair, widely publicized its transgressive status through unmistakable butch/femme references in its still images and trailer, and consequently found a substantial following among queer women spectators. *Mulholland Drive*'s distributor and publicists made little overt effort to foreground its lesbian representation in the official promotional materials released domestically, preferring to emphasize its genre markings, romantic Hollywood locale, and the Lynch brand. The teasing still image depicting the kiss Camilla gives the blonde at the dinner party is frequently displayed alongside reviews in European publications but is absent from the domestically released press packet and from mainstream U.S. press coverage.[52] While the "family values" specter may have been a factor in the domestic marketing campaign's choice to downplay the film's lesbianism, it was likelier the case that *Mulholland Drive*'s distributor did not wish to confine it to a niche audience (the gay ghetto), especially one thought to prefer positive role models and lighthearted stories. In any case, *Mulholland Drive*'s lesbian content was hardly kept secret; critical reviews predictably pounced on the provocative angle, while co-stars Watts and Harring played it up in media profiles by describing the sex scenes' filming and, though it also speaks to the double standard in gender representation, posing provocatively in magazine spreads.

The film brought Lynch his first overwhelmingly positive critical reviews since the first season of *Twin Peaks* (Lynch and Mark Frost, ABC, 1990–1991), broke through to a more mainstream audience than Lynch's previous films, and even was nominated for an Academy Award. These positive results were perhaps helped along – though certainly not hindered – by *Mulholland Drive*'s particular thematic transgression, lipstick lesbianism being more commercial than other sensational topics previously exploited by Lynch (torture, incest, psychogenic fugue). This strategy of "officially" oppressing the film's transgressive qualities, including not only the queer angle but its art film narrative and aesthetic more generally, in favor of emphasizing its more traditionally appealing elements, was used to market the film to mainstream ticket buyers while drawing only the thinnest of veneers over the film's non-normative elements still legible to in-the-know audiences. Chapter 3 to come describes the similar strategy deployed to make what was billed as Hollywood's biggest risk in years a box office and cultural phenomenon: selling "gay cowboys" to America.

A *NEW* NEW QUEER CINEMA?

To conclude this chapter, I examine a final noteworthy case of how art cinema's narrative ambiguity and complex characterization engender characters highly readable as bisexual. If dominant conventions of screen narration often seem guided by a need to resolve queerness or pin down its exact nature, then art cinema's aim to resist these conventions may provide an opportunity for less monosexualized versions of identity and desire to emerge. We can see this clearly across the oeuvre of Taiwanese filmmaker Tsai Ming-liang, in whose work characterization consistently resists traditional psychologization and sexual motivation is never clearly mapped onto a stable identity. Tsai populates his films with the disaffected youth of contemporary Taipei for whom it seems sexual relations are but half-hearted attempts at human connection – as indicated by the title of his *I Don't Want to Sleep Alone* (2006). These characters end up ultimately no more fulfilled than do the ennui-stricken leisure class of Tsai's modernist forebears Antonioni, Bertolucci, and Fellini. Upon introduction to the recurring character and Tsai alter ego Hsiao-

Kang (Lee Kang-sheng) in *Rebels of the Neon God* (1992), the first entry
in Tsai's early "Taipei Trilogy," we are invited to view the reticent youth
as almost presexual, though strangely fixated on an insolent male thug
encountered while "cruising" the arcade. By Tsai's second feature *Vive
L'Amour* (1994), homoeroticism is allowed greater narrative expression,
while actor Lee (whose brooding reticence is redolent of James Dean) is
repeatedly displayed in scantily clad poses that established Tsai's muse
as a gay icon of global art cinema. It comes as a surprise, then, when the
trilogy's final installment, *The River* (1997), begins with Hsiao-Kang's
sexual encounter with a female classmate, and more startling still when
Hsiao-Kang drifts into the gay sauna his closeted father frequents and
the two have what begins as an anonymous sexual encounter.

Because Tsai's films are not self-contained but linked through a tacit
narrative progression, their stories unfold at a pace more akin to that of a
television series – or of real life. The temporal component that typically
hinders bisexual representability in the feature-length format allows for
more expansive story and character development in Tsai's diegetic world.
In his recent films – *What Time Is It There?* (2001), *The Wayward Cloud*
(2005), and *I Don't Want to Sleep Alone* – Hsiao-Kang's and other characters' ongoing opacity calls us repeatedly to reevaluate the nature and context of erotic drives. Because we have been given none of the accompanying signifiers typically employed in mainstream cinema (which identifies
nonheterosexual characters primarily by their sexual preference), displays of same-sex desire come as a surprise and force us to reappraise
heterosexist viewing assumptions. For all their outward appearance of
taciturn indifference, Tsai's characters shield complex, even tormented,
inner lives; in this sense they are not so much depsychologized as kept
at a distance, with sexual preference (like other conventional markers of
background, family, and profession) left obscured. Denied unproblem-
atic identification with would-be protagonists, we are forced to observe
Tsai's characters from a remove, as if meeting them in life. The import
this has for bisexual representability is significant: not only is their erotic
potential kept from being immediately definable and self-defining, but
these recurring characters and their accumulated episodes across films
enable a cumulative appraisal of sexualities in continual flux.

Tsai joins the ranks of other contemporary art cinema auteurs such as Pedro Almodóvar, François Ozon, and Apichatpong Weerasethakul in presenting queerness unapologetically and matter-of-factly. In so doing, these filmmakers can be said to have initiated a *new* New Queer Cinema, one less overtly politicized than the 1990s incarnation but arguably more progressive in its movement beyond a limiting obsession with issues of identity hyperconsciousness and the imperative to define the world in terms of the binary "us vs. them." The New Queer Cinema put queers at the center of the story, but those characters often achieved self-definition only by reacting against the straights left just offscreen. Immersed in the cinematic worlds of Tsai and his confrères, one gets the impression that queerness is the norm. This is not to say that politically we cannot still benefit from identity coalitions, or that everything, sexually speaking, is dandy in the queer worlds constructed within postmillennial art cinema. Indeed, the sexual turmoil that Mark Hain notices in Ozon's work pervades the collective consciousness of these new queer auteurs:

> Ozon's work explores bourgeois culture as an oppressive and deadening construct, which enforces a stifling repression. This surplus repression, which prevents the subject from realizing the liberating potential of sexual expression, including alternative sexualities derided as "perverse" by the dominant culture, can burst through in horrible ways, including murder, suicide, unhealthy sexual behavior, and insanity.[53]

By drawing narrative attention not only to alternative sexualities but to the consequences of their repression, these art films achieve something more deeply affirmative than campaigns for positive images and visibility. In addition to suggesting *why* we must attend to our culture's binary trouble, these more genuinely "queer" filmmakers and the art cinema legacy that influences them reveal *how* we might unthink, and undo, compulsory monosexuality. The solution, it seems, lies in the distinction between art cinema and conventional Hollywood cinema: as put rather more judiciously by David Bordwell than by Paul Schrader, art cinema's "commitment to both objective and subjective verisimilitude."[54] Etching its transcription of reality to show us what our world and ourselves are actually like, art cinema reveals the degree to which we all already do experience desire beyond the "straight" and narrow.

[O]ur popular representations – themselves consumers of our collective wishes, anxieties, and fantasies – are speaking us in a way that we don't seem quite ready to claim, or even to own up to. If we want the pleasure of the ride they offer us, we need an analysis of fantasmatic identifications that is up to speed with these representations. And this involves the violence and the pleasure of imagining sexual identity not as cause but as effect."

SHARON WILLIS,
"Hardware and Hardbodies: What Do Women Want?"

TWO

Power Play/s: Bisexuality as Privilege and Pathology in Sexploitation Cinema

EVEN MORE OPEN – EFFUSIVELY SO – TO EROTIC EXPLICITNESS and excess than art cinema, sexploitation films use the titillation of female bisexual desire as a primary narrative conceit. As a mode of filmmaking, sexploitation traverses historical eras, national cinemas, genres, aesthetic movements, and even industrial sectors. Historically, exploitation cinema refers to low-budget, independently produced features which compensate for their lack of brand-name talent and production value with sensational subject matter, attention-grabbing promotions, and saturation booking intended to generate profit in a quick theatrical run. This strategy's success was noted, and duly exploited, by major studios hoping to attract youthful audiences during the late-1960s downturn, when soft-core European and Japanese imports and subsequently their American knockoffs proved consistently appealing to art house and cult audiences looking for occasionally high-minded yet more often prurient thrills. Sexploitation is often maligned as art cinema's unrefined cousin and seen as one step away from hardcore pornography, and for a brief time in the 1960s and 1970s, these three overlapping modes – art cinema, exploitation cinema, and pornography – even shared exhibition venues; the "art house" and the "grind house" occupied the same physical and cultural space. As is inevitably the case with oppositional binaries, highbrow art cinema and lowbrow sexploitation turn out to have quite a bit in common – not least in their propensity for establishing bisexual spaces, in which bisexuality acquires legibility even as it continues to be displayed as an exoticized, eroticized spectacle of social deviance and sexual decadence. Since the brief craze for porn in the mainstream, sex-

ploitation tropes have migrated into the big-budget erotic thrillers populated by what Lynda Hart calls the "fatal women" and Chris Holmlund
terms the "deadly (lesbian) dolls" of contemporary Hollywood.[1] But
sexploitation films continue to inhabit diverse formal and commercial
realms, encompassing what's left of "official" sexploitation, from big-
budget Hollywood productions like *Basic Instinct* to European art films
like *Swimming Pool* to U.S. "indie" films like *Wild Things,* all discussed in
this chapter. Such films regularly receive straight-to-video sequels and
knockoffs that, freed from the restrictions associated with mainstream
theatrical distribution, substitute cut-rate actors for the original cast
and up the ante on nudity and sex.[2] As indicated by Holmlund's use of
parentheses around "lesbian," the tantalizing promise that sexploitation
offers up is more precisely "girl-on-girl" eroticism, and such films rarely
articulate any well-rounded (much less politicized) lesbian orientation.
Rather, as we will see, female same-sex desire is first spectacularized
and then "spectralized," or obscured – though telltale traces remain, as
ever, (in)visible.

ALL'S FAIR IN BISEXUALITY: RICH BITCHES, DEPENDENT DOUBLES, AND TRIANGULAR DESIRE

> I never thought of Catherine as bisexual or even sexual.
> Sex is just the currency she uses to get what she wants.
>
> SHARON STONE on her character
> in *Basic Instinct,* Catherine Tramell

Sexploitation films often construct dual discourses on privilege – socioeconomic and bisexual – whose simultaneous negotiation at the narrative level implies a relationship between them. This bi-textual form of
narration repeatedly enacts a power play of alternating dominant and
submissive roles between an independent(ly) wealthy female character whom I call the *rich bitch* and her disadvantaged female dependent
double (again lesbian desire proves admissible where male same-sex desire does not). Bisexuality operates as the primary weapon of the characters' dual (and dueling) economic and sexual showdown, wielded on
one hand as a spoil of affluence by the rich bitch and on the other as a
leveraging device for socioeconomic empowerment by her dependent

double. This bi-textual mode compulsively reproduces a metaphor of class privilege under perceived threat to allay those anxieties provoked by economically (and thus sexually) self-sufficient women and opportunistic, "two faced" bisexuals by relating them to and negotiating them through other, class-related anxieties: paranoia about the disruption of moneyed complacency versus frustration about class immobility and conspicuous consumption. Thus the resultant insight to arise from this metaphor concerns that of the elsewhere disavowed connection between sexuality and (late) capitalism.

Relationships and scenes presenting female same-sex desire in sexploitation films are infused with an eroticism of aggression, competition, envy, and personal gain – gender-unspecific significations that invoke bi-stereotypes of predatory opportunism and selfishness. This section considers how a number of sexploitation films negotiate the rich bitch's bisexual and bi-textual significations, asking how these films take up the stereotype of "bisexual privilege" and whether their narratives work to contain or promote female social-sexual agency. What I aim ultimately to determine is the degree to which each film endorses or resists hegemonic strictures on gender roles and sexuality, and in so doing maintains or disrupts the discursive masking, through the concept of romantic love, of late capitalism's inextricable relationship between pleasure and profit.

Keeping in mind that sexploitation is produced largely by and primarily for straight males, my inquiry into textual motivations will be accompanied by consideration of how queer appropriations and cult fandom perform "pleasurable negotiations" of sexploitation, and how these oppositional readings too can subvert or resist heteronormative as well as socioeconomic structures.[3] While mainstream triangle films grant heterosexuality greater visibility, sexploitation cinema challenges heterosexual primacy by emphasizing same-sex relations. Furthermore, alongside these films' destabilization of heteronormativity is a potential critique of capitalist exploitation, wherein social constraints on upward mobility may be addressed and the sources and uses of wealth play a crucial factor in determining who will come out "on top." More demonstrable than bisexual privilege, class privilege *does* ensure economic security, a sense of entitlement, and ease of movement through the world even for those inhabiting marginalized sexual identities. Sexploitation narratives repeatedly stage a dialectical battle between haves and have-nots, wherein the dependent double's disenfranchisement leaves her vulnerable to exploitation by her benefactress, at the same time that it drives her impulse to revolt. In striving for a way out of her subordinate status, the dependent double seduces (or allows herself to be seduced by) the rich bitch in hopes of accessing social empowerment, and often will adopt the appearance, name, and increasingly the complete identity of the rich bitch to whose class status she aspires. Female sexuality and social agency are therefore represented as active, mimetic, and even predatory, wherein both women have something the other does not but desperately desires. For the rich bitch, it is the not-yet-possessed body of the dependent double, who in turn desires the wealth and (associated) agency enjoyed by her benefactress.

What seems uniquely bi-suggestive about sexploitation is that it privileges neither opposite-sex nor same-sex couplings. Moreover, within these romantic/erotic configurations, gendered object choice – that which is deemed the primary determinant of sexual desire and identity in our culture's monosexist paradigm – is replaced by other, specifically material, determinants driving characters' desires and relations. Like the industry personnel shaping sexploitation's plot contrivances and demographic targets, these characters also have money on the mind when it comes to making decisions about sex. While this might not immediately register as a progressive move beyond conceptualizing sexuality in terms of gendered object choice, it lays bare the unavoidable but underacknowledged economic determinants of desire. If identity and subjectivity are constituted by our lived experiences of and perceived alliances to categories of gender, sexuality, class, race, and vocation, among others, a consideration of sexuality cannot be disengaged from a consideration of accompanying material and contextual factors. As Scott D. Paulin notes of *Single White Female*'s (Barbet Schroeder, 1992) sexually ambiguous rich bitch, Ally (Bridget Fonda), "Her sexuality is never simply a given, nor does it progress smoothly on a trajectory; it is de-essentialized, placed in the context of social and personal relations."[4] Such contextualization acknowledges, as Paulin suggests, "a mobility and fluidity between [sexual] states, motivated by specific relational, cultural, and historical imperatives."[5]

As Rosemary Hennessey has shown, sexual identity "has been fundamentally, though never simply, affected by several aspects of capitalism: wage labor, commodity production and consumption."[6] Alongside which, as Gayle Rubin has demonstrated, women's positioning as
property and commodities of exchange historically has fueled heteropatriarchal capitalism's self-perpetuating production and distribution of
wealth.[7] Just as capitalism produces an insatiable desire for commodities,
the socialized subject constructs unrealizable desire in the realms of
sexuality and identity. Independent women don't just disrupt heteropatriarchal capitalism but also threaten monogamy, which even before
its connection to sexual orientation implies property and is the foundation for capitalist society's construction of the nuclear family as emotional buffer against the hyperrationalized market and heartless free
labor system.

The sexploitation narrative provokes anxiety in two ways: by the capacity of the independent(ly) wealthy rich bitch to threaten the ideological stability of the nuclear family and woman's socially constructed role
as nurturer, and by the female dependent double's struggle (often violent)
to gain access to economic security and emotional support by infiltrat-
ing a surrogate family or creating a nontraditional family. Occasionally,
as we shall see in the discussion of the female vampire film below, the
narrative even concludes with the (re)creation of a matriarchal structure
and/or the same-sex "marrying up" that heteropatriarchal capitalism
seeks to prevent. More often, sexploitation films characterize bisexuality
as ensnaring and imitative – given the opportunity, any impressionable
individual would fall into it – whose result is a loss of love and cohesive
identity. Both rich bitch and dependent double are depicted as cutthroat
capitalists who sacrifice their own humanity and that of others in their
drive for material wealth. The sexploitation text persistently questions
whether, as Valerie Traub asks about Black Widow's (Bob Rafelson, 1987)
scheming Catharine (Theresa Russell), the bi-suggestive female "is capable of love or desire at all."[8] This textual anxiety stems from paranoid
perceptions about bisexual opportunism as potent enough a force to
render an individual's "real" emotional and sexual constitution opaque
and even nonexistent. As depicted in sexploitation films, bisexuality becomes inextricably joined with the capitalist appetite for accumulation,

whereby the latter as a socially sanctioned form of rapacity becomes tainted with the "pathology" associated with bisexuality, and vice versa.

In film noir, a criminal investigation runs parallel with the (often more memorable) investigation of the femme fatale, with both hinging on the discovery of a "true" identity – that of the criminal perpetrator in the whodunit plot, and that of the fatal woman's authentic nature (whether or not she can be redeemed as a "good woman" fit for domesticity) in the romantic plot. Inevitably, the metaphoric association between criminality and female sexuality comes to seem an identity, with the implication that the femme fatale's criminality inheres less in whatever lawbreaking she may have performed than in her social and sexual deviance. To set into motion the power play of class competition, sexploitation cinema in the postclassical era revives and updates classical film noir's femme fatale, by endowing her with the New Woman's financial self-sufficiency and sexual freedom. While noir's conservative impulse to contain female "deviancy" lingers, Celestino Deleyto notes that because narrative containment "can no longer be produced from a safe and justifiable moral and ideological position," it "becomes discontinuous, contradictory, full of fissures."[9] In postclassical cinema's more lenient climate for screening sexuality, the rich bitch's deviance is figured as decadence, resulting in her ambivalent signification as both, Deleyto continues, "the ultimate object of desire and the ultimate threat to [the male's] already precarious status in patriarchy."[10]

To further update and "bisex" film noir, the emasculated male dupe who typically falls under the femme fatale's spell is now joined or occasionally replaced altogether by the disadvantaged female dependent double, with whom the rich bitch plays games of material, emotional, and sexual dominance and submission. This dependent double becomes the "other woman" as well as the Other, whose outsider status leads to her victimization, exploitation, and ultimate drive to revolt against the rich bitch. Where the male is retained, he becomes an ineffectual and uncharismatic "man-object" (as Claude Chabrol referred to one such would-be patriarch, Paul [Jean-Louis Trintignant], in his film *Les Biches* [1968]), a plaything for the rich bitch and sometimes sugar daddy for the dependent double. Of *Black Widow*'s man-object Paul (Sami Frey), Traub notices that "in inverting the male homosocial system by which women are exchanged between men, Paul's body becomes a courier, communicating indirectly those desires that [the leading women] cannot express."[11] With the male improbably relegated to a conduit for lesbian desire, the resulting erotic triangle further feeds the narrative atmosphere of envy and competition, wherein, as Lucille Cairns observes, "the male third term invades and often destroys the lesboerotic dyad – thus reflecting male 'revenge' fantasies stemming from their decentering as the locus of all desire."[12]

The sexual paranoia narrative that thrived in 1980s and 1990s Hollywood hit films including *Basic Instinct, Disclosure* (Barry Levinson, 1994), *Fatal Attraction* (Adrian Lyne, 1987), *The Hand That Rocks the Cradle* (Curtis Hanson, 1992), and *Single White Female* identifies the threat to male privilege not simply in "woman," as Scott Paulin points out, but in those women who are so masculine that relationships with them are practically homosexual, making it more difficult – but doubly imperative – to vigorously police the hetero/homo divide.[13] The rich bitch presents a similar threat that according to Paulin's schema is bisexual in two senses: in her not-exclusively-heterosexual desire and in her resistance to classification as either masculine or feminine by insisting on the privilege of both. As noted in the introduction, on its initial entry into the medical and psychiatric lexicon, *bisexual* referred to a biological duality of male and female traits. Consistently conflating bisexuality's relation to both object choice and gendered behavior, Freud ultimately perceived female bisexuality as an inability to fully repress phallic, masculine ambitions. Steven Cohan describes how this correspondence between masculine agency and bisexual desire becomes written on the body of one such phallic female, Sharon Stone's character in *Basic Instinct*:

> [Catherine's] power to destabilize the ground of masculinity is epitomized by the film's insistence on her opacity as a bisexual body. Catherine's avowal of her bisexuality marks out her erotic disengagement from a phallocentric fantasm of the female that underwrites male heterosexuality through the gaze. She disrupts that gaze through her performativity – not only in the interrogation scene but also in her manipulation of the narrative, which . . . grants her an incomprehensible agency . . . one that openly affronts the heterosexual regulation of desire according to the binary that polarizes "straight" against "queer." A perceived threat to the sovereignty of normative straight white masculinity makes itself evident in both the indeterminate narrative *and* the "indecipherable" (which is really to say, bisexual) figure of Catherine Tramell.[14]

Though her intelligence and looks are certainly no hindrance, it is Catherine's class status as an independent(ly) wealthy woman that enables her sexual freedom and licenses her contempt for legal authority and middle-class morality as well as her commandeering of narrative authority.[15]

Wealth and the agency it affords are what seem most threatening about Catherine to the film's ineffectual male authorities. Privilege is also the primary factor that drove female audiences to embrace her, bitch or not. Despite public protests by lesbian and bisexual activists against what they considered to be the film's homophobic depiction of queer women, Thomas Austin's reception study of female viewers in the United Kingdom demonstrates the considerable appeal of Catherine for women.[16] It is overwhelmingly, Austin shows, her wealth and the resultant autonomy and flagrant disregard for authority that Catherine displays which respondents cited as desirable qualities – but desirable as a figure of identification (i.e., a role model), or as an object of sexual desire? Did Austin's interviewees want to *be* Catherine or to *have* her? Both, suggests Jackie Stacey in her meditation on women's spectatorship: "The love of the ideal . . . may express a desire to become more like that ideal, but this does not exclude the homoerotic pleasures of a love for that ideal."[17] Against claims that she was de-eroticizing lesbian desire, Stacey insisted that she sought not to de-eroticize desire but to eroticize identification. This, precisely, is what constitutes a bisexual viewing practice: one that refuses to choose between identification and sexual desire. Less fortunate than the rich bitch in multiple ways, the disenfranchised dependent double upon initial appearance possesses neither phallic agency nor full womanly appeal. Thus her desire is bisexual as well as "bi-sexual" in that it is directed at the rich bitch's access to both masculine and feminine privilege. This is not to subscribe to the notion that female same-sex desire is predicated on wanting either to be a man or exclusively upon identification with the other woman, but rather that desire is indivisible not only from identification but also from notions of social and economic privilege.

1970s feminist film theory's attempts to theorize gendered spectator positions and patterns of identification and desire were much challenged on the grounds of their unquestioned assumption of the spectator as white, heterosexual, and middle-class. Subsequent work on cinematic spectatorship would pay closer attention to how racial difference and sexual orientation influenced spectator practices, positing a more fluid and multivalent dynamic at work than was previously recognized.[18] Yet the question of how characters' social class may inhibit or encourage their *and* our willingness to identify and desire remains largely unexamined, and the spectator continues to be the same trans-class construct that Christine Gledhill observed in 1988. In sexploitation films, the female dependent double frequently acts as a surrogate for the spectator – both are placed in a fantasmatic position of identification with and desire for the rich bitch, wherein the fantasy of being/having arises as much from class envy as from erotic longing. Analogous to early cine-feminism's formulation of female spectatorial pleasure as gender transvestism, sexploitation's class transvestism allows both the female dependent double and the spectator to fantasize by "trying on" socioeconomic privilege.[19]

In representation as in fandom, the inextricable interlacing of desire and identification and of bisexual and class privilege offers rich possibilities for hiding queerness in plain sight, suggesting but never making explicit the female dependent double's queer sexuality; as Paulin observes of *Single White Female*'s ability to "have it both ways": "Hedy's [Jennifer Jason Leigh] potential desire for Ally may be disguised since it is always concretely tied to Hedy's identification with her."[20] Hedy's desire/identification constitutes a wish not just to "have" Ally sexually but to have Ally's rich life: handsome fiancé, chic wardrobe, head-turning hairstyle, successful business, swanky apartment, and poised self-presentation. "Look at yourself," a bitterly envious Hedy tells Ally as the two compare reflections in one of the film's recurring mirror shots. "We're not in the same league." What finally threatens Ally's sense of self is the ease with which Hedy performs what Ellen Brinks calls "mimetic identity theft," one that "undermines Ally's fantasmatic class stability" and "displaces and jeopardizes the idea of the subject as private or as property."[21] The superficiality of the means by which Hedy appropriates Ally's identity – borrowing her clothes, mimicking her personal style, appropriating her boyfriend – further reveals the illusory nature of social roles. To mimic, writes Luce Irigaray, is to "assume the . . . role deliberately . . . so as to make 'visible,' by an effect of playful repetition, what was supposed to remain invisible."[22] But where this revelation might prove effective in destabilizing gender norms (as in Judith Butler's theory of the subversive potential of drag), socioeconomic divisions are not so easily overturned.[23] Whereas Ally guards her possessions with a vengeance, as Brinks notices, "Hedy's communal approach to bodies and things marks a political commitment to a leveling of class distinctions. It ends up wildly exacerbating Allie's [sic] proprietary instincts." Because Hedy's class transvestism, Brinks continues, "represents the potent threat of communally held, circulating property and class mobility," so her inevitable murder provides a "(temporary) sacrifice that would recuperate stable distinctions between classes and sexual identities."[24]

Although Ally has not yet attained socioeconomic security (and so is not quite a legitimate rich bitch), her upward mobility allies her with wealth and promises entry into the privileged class. Her all-but-assured success is particularly evident in contrast to the dead-end prospects for Hedy, whose attempts at secondhand mimicry are never wholly convincing and prove ultimately futile, her queerness and subordinate status combining to relegate her to second-class citizenship. Whereas Ally is able to leave her comfortably middle-class if provincial upbringing behind for a glamorous Manhattan existence, Hedy's ongoing economic dependency seems inescapable, as Brinks points out, by her working-class Southern origins revealed in her unshakable accent and insecure demeanor, her transient employment as a bookstore clerk, and the division of labor established immediately upon Hedy's arrival, when she sets about a routine of cooking, cleaning, and generally serving as a domestic laborer to and slavish admirer of Ally's career girl.[25] Notably, *Single White Female* begins by insinuating that the upwardly mobile woman's quest for class status has the ultimate goal of attaining a husband and forming a nuclear family (for the newly professional woman, money lands husbands rather than the reverse), but ends with a conspicuous absence of men – perhaps owing to the alarmist premonition that women who prioritize professional accomplishment end up as *single* (white) females.

Most often the rich bitch's income is inherited or, if earned, is earned by means that do not constitute traditional labors. Catherine Tramell is both an heiress *and* a best-selling novelist, doubly establishing hers as a life of privilege and relative leisure. Another Catharine, Theresa Russell's character in *Black Widow,* is a gold-digger eventually trapped

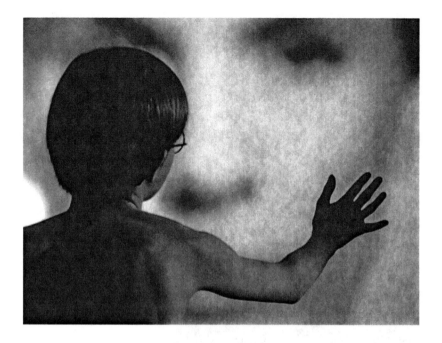

2.1. The child examining the maternal image in *Persona*.

by the dogged efforts of butch Justice Department agent Alex (Debra Winger) – though she does not go down without provoking Alex and us into a reassessment of the femme fatale archetype. Rather than rely on the conventional positioning of the femme fatale as unknowable Other, both Winger's investigator and the viewer are encouraged to identify with and desire this rich bitch. Breaking from the investigation plot's typical alignment of the spectator's gaze with that of the investigator (making our access to knowledge dependent on his or her own), *Black Widow* alternates between its two female leads' subjectivities. We thus receive considerable insight into the femme fatale's mindset, witnessing her apparently genuine remorse over committing murder and her panic at learning that the authorities are on her trail. The unknowable Other is thereby humanized, her criminal deeds rationalized as an opting out of unrewarding "woman's work" or Alex's hardscrabble attempts to make it professionally in a man's world, where she is consistently hindered by sexual harassment and her own lack of feminine wiles.[26]

2.2. Federal agent Alex (Debra Winger) searching for clues to the elusive identity of mystery woman Catherine (Theresa Russell), in *Black Widow*.

Black Widow directly addresses the labor of female beauty and its value as capital when Catharine tells Alex that she thinks of it as her job to make herself appealing. She proves to be exceptionally good at this calling: her expertise in feminine performance allows her to impersonate each new husband's ideal woman, and her charm enables her to control men's emotions (and consequently their bank accounts). Significantly, it is the female investigator Alex's ability to "see through" Catharine that finally traps her, yet Alex's motivation in doing so – much like the feminization she undergoes in her attempt to "become" Catharine – is never wholly convincing. In the crucial final scene, we are positioned on the same side of the jail bars with Catharine when she refers to her victims, saying, "I loved every one of them." Her ultimate incarcera-

2.3. A vampiric embrace in *Persona* . . .

tion is as unsatisfying as Alex's transformed appearance (in the film's final shot) wearing a flowered dress upon leaving the jail is bewildering. Though the revolutionary potential their partnership posed is ultimately suppressed by the law's authority, we are left with the sense that justice was not done.

As these stills (figures 2.1–2.4) indicate, sexploitation films will often mimic art cinema as well as other sexploitation films in their visual and narrative motifs, creating a dense web of intertextual allusions that fuel bisexual readability in any individual text. While the sexploitation films discussed thus far do not explicitly feature vampires, there is frequent allusion made to the iconography and attitude of vampire legend. Indeed it is such films' mimicking of the 1970s sex-and-schlock vampire cycle (the focus of my next missed moment, discussed in the section to come) that determines my placement of them in this chapter rather than among

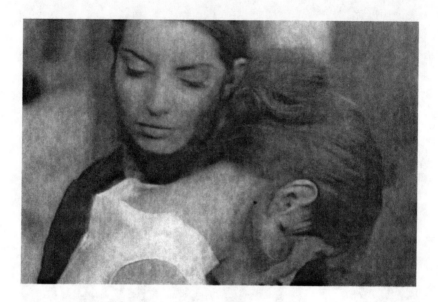

2.4. ... echoed in Chabrol's *Les Biches*.

the art films previously discussed; while there are art cinema attributes on display, titillating content and near-camp excessiveness characterize these films. Such references are particularly prevalent when depicting close female bonding, commonly characterized as unnatural, ill-fated, and even perverse. The literal threat that vampires embody becomes figurative: a predatory "true" lesbian drains the vitality and femininity out of the newly converted woman. The opening scene of Chabrol's *Les Biches* (variously translated as *The Does, Bad Girls,* and *Girlfriends*) conjures a Gothic atmosphere and macabre stylings to depict rich bitch Frédérique's (Stéphane Audran) cruising and pickup of a street artist named Why (Jacqueline Sassard), so called by Frédérique when the younger woman deflects her request to give her name. As this opening scene illustrates, Frédérique's class privilege buys her the prerogative to pass touristically between elite and marginal worlds, first to exploit and then to colonize the disadvantaged Other. First seen literally crouching at the rich bitch's feet, Why succumbs to Frédérique's seduction and gradually is incorporated into her opulent, idle existence in off-season St. Tropez, financed by the lucrative family business under Frédérique's control.

2.5. Aristocratic Frédérique (Stéphane Audran) cruises street artist Why (Jacqueline Sassard) in the opening scene of *Les Biches*.

Repeatedly remarked upon as being "lucky" (at cards, *les boules*, even the lottery), butch Frédérique dominates what Robin Wood and Robert Walker have called "the Chabrol triangle, [in which] envy usually plays a central role. . . . But an essential aspect of the relationship between the envier and the envied is the pleasure that the latter derives from the admiration."[27] Chabrolian triangularity implies, significantly, that the roles of "envier" and "envied" are constantly shifting. In one particularly loaded scene that demonstrates how envy (for love, money, and youth) suffuses this triangular dynamic, Why sits trapped between Frédérique's possessive grasp as her benefactress knowingly dangles money at her, while on Why's other side new admirer Paul (the aforementioned man-object) devourers a chicken leg while eyeing her hungrily. As a way out of this objectified status, Why proceeds to make herself into a cheap copy of Frédérique. "Using other people's things is like changing your skin," Why says, and her class transvestism is ultimately more effectual than the revolutionary rhetoric spouted by the connotatively queer couple who are parasitic hangers-on in Frédérique's circle until Why effects their ouster. Chabrol is quick to concede the political bent of his film,

2.6. Lucky in cards, unlucky in love? Why stares down man-object Paul (Jean-Louis Trintignant) as Frédérique wins big at poker.

released in 1968, whose subject he says "isn't really a power struggle. It's a revolution: the replacement of one class by another," while his interviewer Guy Austin notices that

> the film thus becomes a political vampire narrative about the appropriation of Frédérique's bourgeois values by the innocent and impoverished "receptacle" that is Why. The brilliance of *Les Biches* lies in this portrayal of the *embourgeoisement* of the working classes through the metaphor of a vampire breeding new vampires.[28]

A genuinely political revolution is abandoned, then, in favor of Why's violent appropriation of the wealthy Frédérique's property and values – as in *Single White Female,* mimicry in itself is not enough to change one's class status or to dismantle class distinctions. As Chabrol himself noted, "Why replaces Frédérique, but she does it by *becoming* Frédérique."[29]

Why's inscrutable motives and implacable demeanor – we are never sure with whom her allegiances or desires lie – prevent full resolution even with her murder of Frédérique at film's end. This sudden act of violence can be read as purely psychotic, or as revenge for Frédérique's theft of Paul, or – given that it immediately follows Frédérique's contemptu-

2.7. Frédérique staking her claim on Why as Paul looks hungrily on.

ously telling Why "your love disgusts me" – as punishment for her rejection of Why. Still another possibility, since this bisexual triangle is also a family of sorts, is that the childlike Why has successfully modeled herself on the mother figure and so takes Frédérique's place with the father. But just as *Black Widow*'s love triangle seemed lopsided, with the relationship between the women most charged, *Les Biches'* Paul exudes an ineffectual colorlessness that keeps the intensity firmly between the leading women and emphasizes the forced quality of rich bitch Frédérique's drastic reversal to heterosexual bliss and feminized, domesticized appearance with Paul. Why's motives remain as ambiguous, but are unmistakably connected to her lower class status. Both Why and *Single White Female*'s Hedy share the subtle yet intensifying rage exhibited by a closely related queer female character type whom Christine Coffman calls the "murderous maid," after her study of two films fictionally based on the Papin affair, *Murderous Maids* (Jean-Pierre Denis, 2000) and *Sister My Sister* (Nancy Meckler, 1994). Coffman notes the narrative connection between such a character's sudden, seemingly inexplicable violence and her professional servitude, which "deftly points to the role that class oppression may play in her psychosis. . . . Though she aspires to escape servitude, her attempts to master her circumstances come to nothing" and thus propel her to violence.[30] As with the (fictional and nonfictional) Papin sisters, Why and Hedy along with their disenfranchised queer female counterparts in films such as *La Cérémonie* (Claude Chabrol, 1995) and *Poison Ivy* (Katt Shea, 1992) direct their murderous rage at the privileged benefactresses who serve as representatives, in the subordinated women's lives, of the class structure that oppresses them.

As follows from her desire for and identification with the Other and the concomitant notion of the dual self, the female dependent is habitually characterized as the rich bitch's double. The double, as Robin Wood notes in his writing on horror cinema, is a recurring figure in Western culture used to connote "the relationship between normality and the Monster."[31] Read bisexually, these films' doubling signifies a blurring of the lines between the sexually normative individual and the queer Other, ultimately suggesting the presence of both within everyone. Again *Basic Instinct* serves as a consummate – if hyperbolic – example. Never one to be outdone, Catherine has *four* doubles, all of whom are comparatively disadvantaged: her near-identical but more butch lover Roxy (Leilani Sarelle); the older, also blonde Hazel (Dorothy Malone) with whom Catherine appears to share a not-quite-platonic mother-daughter bond; psychiatrist Beth (Jeanne Tripplehorn), who was obsessed with Catherine and copied her appearance during their college years; and even Detective Nick Curran (Michael Douglas), who increasingly emulates Catherine's confident demeanor, contempt for authority, and defiant retorts ("What are you going to do, charge me with smoking?") as his erotic obsession with her develops. But as Austin's *Basic Instinct* reception study and the following section on vampire films argue, even in her most monstrous incarnation the bi-suggestive rich bitch is rarely depicted as totally unsympathetic. Rather, she often serves as the film's emotional center, and despite her inevitable violent destruction at film's end she uniformly proves to be the most memorable and exciting character. The dependent double, with whom we share a sense of fascination with the rich bitch and who therefore acts as our surrogate, possesses agency that drives our perceptions rather than the plot. It is the rich bitch's sexually *and* textually expressive force, as perceived by her envious double (and admiring audience alike) which overcomes the horror film's "superficial project [which] is to insist that purity-normality can be separated from contaminating eroticism-degradation" and hence reveals "its deeper project [which] is to demonstrate the impossibility of such a separation."[32]

To exaggerate this doubling, or what Lucille Cairns calls the "(con) fusion-of-identity" motif, still further, sexploitation films frequently feature mirrored reflections that emphasize their female leads' physical resemblance.[33] Read bisexually, these shots' significations relate to anxieties about queer women: overly close alliances between women, rendered suspect, are thereby imagined as a disconcerting likeness; a bisexual woman's troubling attraction to both opposite-sex and same-sex partners is thus imagined as her having a split self; and female same-sex desire is thought of as narcissistic or as substituted desire for the mother. This motif is often read through Freud's theory of female homosexuality as narcissistic pre-Oedipal fantasy, and sexploitation films themselves often seem to suggest misplaced mother-love by showing dependent doubles in films such as *Les Biches, Poison Ivy,* and *Single White Female* playing "dress up" much as a girl might do with her mother's makeup and clothes, but deliberately styling herself in imitation of the privileged woman and exhibiting no shame when caught at her "game." This attempt to explain female same-sex desire as narcissism and the love object as surrogate mother ultimately reveals less about lesbian fetishizing of gender similitude than it does about our cultural festishizing of sexual difference *and* opposite-gendered object choice. What seems more significant in sexploitation's excessive deployment of doubles and mirrors is its construction of a screen for misrecognition (in the Lacanian sense of subject formation) by the dependent double, who sees in the rich bitch's reflection an ideal self apparently, but only fantasmatically, attainable.

Sexploitation's "(con)fusion of identity" motif and its preoccupations with bisexual (in)visibility and anxiety receive particularly excessive treatment in the 1994 slumming studio sexploitation feature *The Color of Night,* directed by Richard Rush. The plot involves New York psychologist Dr. Bill Capa (Bruce Willis), who travels to Los Angeles – the place where dreams are manufactured – to recuperate from the trauma of a patient's recent suicide for which he feels responsible. When the old friend and colleague he is visiting is brutally murdered, Dr. Capa takes over as leader of his highly dysfunctional therapy group (any one of whose members, it is evident, could be the killer) and soon begins an affair with an elusive young woman named Rose (Jane March). At the utterly delirious denouement, it is revealed that not only has Rose been carrying on simultaneous affairs with every member of the group *and* Dr. Capa – altering her appearance and personality to fit each person's ideal fantasy – but she has actually been a member of the group all along, in the guise of a preoperative male-to-female (MTF) transsexual. The all-too-Freudian impulse behind Rose's multiple masquerades and duplicities is attributed to abuse by an unhinged sibling (he, not Rose, turns out to have been the murderer) but this exorbitant projection of bisexual *and* transgender anxieties remains an astounding amalgamation of stereotypes: promiscuity, capriciousness, schizophrenia, mutability, exhibitionism, and deceit. Rose's stupefying volte-face becomes slightly less astonishing after recalling that director Richard Rush had previously orchestrated what might be the most overblown obliteration of the "queer threat" in American film history, when a transsexual assassin gets annihilated by James Caan's macho cop in *Freebie and the Bean* (1974). As in *The Color of Night,* character motive remains cloudy (the assassin's only apparent crime was whacking the mob boss that the cop himself was attempting to prosecute), but it could well have something to do with exorcising the rampant homoeroticism all too apparent between the cop and his partner on the force. As *The Color of Night* makes clear, bisexual and bi-suggestive characters are depicted as possessing a threatening and (self-)destructive sexuality, dangerous for its refusal of monosexual containment. The only figure perhaps more spectacularized in this way is the female vampire. Although, as I argue in the next section, the two are in fact one and the same.

MISSED MOMENT: IMMORTAL, INSATIABLE,
INVISIBLE – THE STRANGE CASE OF THE
VANISHING BISEXUAL VAMPIRE

Copious scholarship (not to mention celluloid) is devoted to cinema's female vampire.[34] That critical discourse, however, for the most part brings

to bear a lesbian framework of understanding on works whose representations and logic of desire are often complex and ambiguous. While these
lesbian readings offer a great deal of illumination on the female vampire,
fully capturing this figure's embodiment of fluid desire and subjectivity demands a bisexual reading. Challenging compulsory monosexuality and compulsory monogamy, the female vampire's polymorphous
pleasure-seeking exemplifies an experiential, nonteleological view, as
Pramaggiore puts it, "of sexuality beyond gender and sex [wherein] desire becomes an all-pervasive rhythm of sex, blood, and satiation rather
than courtship, coupling, and conclusion."[35] Possessing appetites for
which the limiting binary of monosexuality does not suffice, the vampire additionally defies the gender binary with her phallic femme body.
Moreover, neither alive nor dead but undead, the vampire's *being* itself
is queer, Sue-Ellen Case asserts, in "employing the subversive power of
the unnatural to unseat the Platonic world view."[36] Certainly the female
vampire figure represents transgressive sexualities on the whole; her
relocation of the primary erogenous zone from the sex-differentiated
genitals to the sex-indiscriminate neck, her phallic authority, the invisibility of the queer desire hidden behind her deceptively femme exterior,
and her insatiable, indiscriminate taste for initiating both fair virgins
and unsuspecting males into her blood pact – anyone warm-blooded will
do – all invoke specifically bisexual stereotypes.

The late 1960s and 1970s were the golden age of female vampire films,
as England's Hammer Studios shifted from Bela Lugosi–anchored fright-
horror shtick to a female-centered sexploitation treatment of the vampire legend. In *Vampires and Violets: Lesbians in Film*, Andrea Weiss observes that the female vampire has been cinema's most persistent image
of (what she terms) lesbian desire, with the exception of that contained
within straight male pornography.[37] But not until the Hammer trilogy
The Vampire Lovers (Roy Ward Baker, 1970), *Lust for a Vampire* (Jimmy
Sangster, 1971), and *Twins of Evil* (John Hough, 1971), produced in quick
succession, did female vampire films become explicitly erotic and their
formerly suggestive lesboeroticism emerge unambiguously.[38] European
and American exploitation filmmakers quickly followed Hammer's lead,
cranking out a cycle of B movies in response to the increasing popularity
of soft-core pornography (made possible by relaxed censorship codes

commencing in the mid-1960s). The Hammer trilogy's self-applied X
rating capitalized on the new freedoms granted by the waning of censorship (and the temporary legislation that permitted self-rating), with
second installment *Twins of Evil* casting *Playboy*'s first twin playmates
in the title roles. Whether aesthetically cut-rate like the Hammer films
or glossily upmarket like *The Hunger*, vampire films are consummately
sexploitative in echoing porn's repetitive, threadbare plots, with narrative progress subordinated to erotic titillation and ultimate payoff. Yet
the most noteworthy discrepancy between soft-core vampire films and
hardcore porn is that the latter's so-called money shot – privileged above
all else in porn for rendering male sexual pleasure hypervisible (as Linda
Williams has theorized) – is displaced by vampire films' privileging of
the (oral) consummation of female same-sex desire, metaphorically rendered as bloodsucking.[39]

Following Sue-Ellen Case's formulation of the queer vampire as positioned in an ontological territory of betweenness, Barbara Creed notes
that this figure "represents abjection because she crosses the boundary
between the living and dead, the human and animal."[40] Associated in
legend with hematophagous bats, vampires are repeatedly represented
through imagery of wild animals – depicting them as nonhuman and
enslaved by their instinctual urges – much as bisexuals are characterized as predatory and undiscerning in their appetite for sexual partners.
The Hunger (Tony Scott, 1983), *The Vampire Lovers*, *Vampyros Lesbos*
(Jess Franco, 1971), and *The Velvet Vampire* (Stephanie Rothman, 1971)
all use highly stylized intercutting of animal shots (lab monkeys, cats,
scorpions, and bats, respectively) during scenes of vampires preying on
their victims, while *Nadja*'s (Michael Almereyda, 1994) vampire calmly
handles her imminent victim's pet tarantula that "scares most people."
Tellingly, horses and dogs (both domesticated species) frequently show
extreme fright in the presence of vampires, with the perverse bond between vampires and wild animals redoubled by reference to yet another
taboo transgression: incest. *Blood and Roses*' (Roger Vadim, 1960) Carmilla (Annette Vadim) is in love with her Karnstein cousin and childhood playmate, Leopoldo (Mel Ferrer). Parodying the inbred lineage of
filmic vampire ancestry, the Andy Warhol–Paul Morrissey take on the
Dracula legend, *Andy Warhol's Dracula* (1974) has as its titillating center-

piece two sisters, called "a couple of tramps" by their manservant Mario (Joe Dellasandro), who sleep with each other, among others. *Nadja's* brother and sister vampires, Nadja (Elina Löwensohn) and Edgar (Jared Harris), share an unusually close bond – one which is consummated when Nadja transmigrates into the body of Edgar's fiancée, Cassandra (Suzy Amis). The film closes on the couple's union at city hall – implying there is something intrinsically perverse about the institution of marriage, something that (I will discuss) vampire films frequently dare to suggest.

"Given their undetectable ubiquity," comments Marjorie Garber, "it was perhaps inevitable that bisexuals would assume a mythic identity in popular culture."[41] As vampire hunter Dr. Van Helsing (Peter Fonda) warns in *Nadja*, "These creatures are everywhere. The streets are full of them – any major city – they just blend in." Like the vampire, the shadowy specter of the bisexual, simultaneously everywhere and nowhere, was seized upon by politicians and media in the late 1980s and 1990s as a particularly insidious embodiment of the threat of AIDS, "even more heinous than the out gay man with AIDS," notes Garber, "because he (or sometimes even she) could 'pass' as straight – and thus pass on the deadly virus to an unsuspecting victim."[42] The AIDS epidemic made bisexual women specifically a target of suspicion in the lesbian community, where fear of contaminated sperm (and women who come into contact with sperm) motivated a safer-sex edict against "intermingling."[43] Depicting the horrible consequences of relations with the nonhuman, vampire films could be read as endorsing the prudence of sleeping only with "one's own kind."

The critical silence on the bisexual significations of the female vampire seems all the more curious given how explicitly the vampire herself often articulates bisexual desire. "Look how perfect *they* are," croons the Countess Elisabet Bathory (Delphine Seyrig) to her "assistant" Ilona (Andrea Rau) in *Daughters of Darkness* (Harry Kümel, 1971), upon glimpsing newlyweds Valerie (Danielle Ouimet) and Stefan (John Karlen) sharing their conveniently deserted Ostend hotel one midwinter's evening. Because their temptations are so often adulterous (witness their particular craving for newlyweds), vampires violate the social and marital order that binds female desire within heterosexual marriage. Deromanticizing the bond that sustains heteropatriarchy, these films depict marriage not as blissful but as ineffectual or even perverse, in forms ranging from the unsatisfied couples in *Vampyros Lesbos, The Hunger,* and *Nadja* to the sadistic brutality enacted by *Daughters of Darkness*'s Stefan toward his worshipful bride (we later learn, in an exceedingly curious reveal, that the unseen mother from whom Stefan shields Valerie is a middle-aged homosexual man by whom Stefan is apparently kept).

If read through Lacan's formulation of the mirror phase, the vampire's lack of a reflection suggests that she circumvents inscription within the Symbolic Order and so remains unsubordinated to the Law of the Father – as unnamable and (in)visible as the bisexual. Indeed, the female vampire is the hyperbolic embodiment of everything threatening about sexploitation's bisexual rich bitch: in her aristocratic and single (thus financially as well as sexually independent) status, in the power play she performs with her dependent double, and in the metaphorical associations of vampirism with economic exploitation. The ease with which blushing brides are lured away from the "straight life" is predicated both on the contrast between their phlegmatic grooms and the bewitching vampire, and on the riches and life of leisure in which the vampire luxuriates. "You have so many beautiful things," Dr. Sarah Roberts (Susan Sarandon) exclaims to Upper East Side maîtresse Miriam (Catherine Deneuve) in *The Hunger,* upon touring her exquisitely appointed townhouse as foreplay to seduction. The subsequent standoff between Old World epicureanism and New World ingenuity culminates in the patrician European being taken down by the enterprising efforts of the driven American scientist, who at film's end stands among the plundered antiquities furnishing her newly sequestered domain. (Fittingly, *The Hunger* was a Hollywood revamping, directed by British import Tony Scott, of the Euro-sexploitation tradition it borrowed from.) The decadent, perverse, old-money aristocrat who reaps benefits from but does not add to the production of capital, threatened with dying off if she does not continue to feed on the disenfranchised, figures "bloodsucking" as capitalist exploitation.

Nearly always portrayed with long hair, curves, luscious red lips, and pale skin, the female vampire creates an unthreatening fetish object for these films' primary target audience – heterosexual males – yet also alludes to the bisexual's and the femme's deceptive ability to pass as straight. Conversely, the initially heterosexual female initiated into the blood pact (and, with it, same-sex desire) usually has a noticeably butch appearance of short hair, mannish clothes, boyish body, and assertive demeanor – witness Sarandon's short-haired, chain-smoking doctor's seduction by vampires Deneuve and Bowie in *The Hunger* as well as the studiously tomboyish Lucy (Galaxy Craze) taken under vampire Nadja's wing. In the recent German vampire reboot *We Are the Night* (Dennis Gansel, 2010), after becoming undead, punked-out baby butch Lena (Karoline Herfurth) transforms into a gender-conforming femme when a trio of vampire vixens first take her mortality, then take her shopping for a wardrobe suitable for the seduction of male victims.

The self-reflexive foregrounding of erotic role-play and gender performance in vampire films, which so often achieve camp (whether or not they were aiming for it), encourages reading them as deconstructive drag. *Andy Warhol's Dracula* opens on a shot of the Count (Udo Kier) applying makeup before a dressing-room mirror (in which his reflection cannot be seen) as if preparing to go onstage for a performance that never actually materializes; *he* is the performance. *Vampyros Lesbos* stages a ritualistic sex show/performance piece in which two women act out a bondage/submission fantasy for a diegetic and nondiegetic audience of (bi-)curious onlookers. *The Hunger* begins in an underground nightclub populated by denizens of Goth-punk subcultures, posing alongside rockers Bauhaus performing "Bela Lugosi's Dead." Taking them all down a notch, *Interview with the Vampire*'s (Neil Jordan, 1994) Claudia (Kirsten Dunst) remains unimpressed by a vampire cabaret troupe that performs as humans performing as vampires, sniffing, "How avant-garde." Vampire lore is steeped in ritual – from vampires' appearance to the specific way in which they must be killed – and vampire films exhaustively execute these ritualistic practices as high (if never highbrow) performance. But what these recurring references within vampire films to playing roles also do is encourage thinking about sexuality itself as a performance.

The female vampire's challenges to gender and sexuality orthodoxies in combination with her enigmatic charisma function to fetishize anxiety about bisexuality. She typically winds up impaled upon a large

(phallic) stake, defusing her excessive threat and reaffirming patriarchal order, and yet as the most fascinating character by far she is resur-
rected as readily as noir's femme fatale in viewers' minds. Having already
been dead – or undead – to begin with, killing her off seems ineffective.
Moreover, a newly transformed female vampire is almost always ready
to take her place. The incredibly close – bound by blood – bond which
these women share even suggests an internal struggle between a split
self, in which the stiflingly straight self is inevitably seduced by the in-
finitely more enticing, immortal queer self. Finally, the excessive delay
and intervention needed to reestablish the heterosexual monogamous
couple in these films undermines our sense of its normalcy, and denatu-
ralizes – occasionally even defeats – its (re)production.

Perhaps the cycle's most subversive instance of the latter is a low-
budget 1970s film out of the U.K., *Vampyres* (José Larraz, 1974), also with
a self-applied X rating and a tagline promising "very unnatural ladies."
Though its numerous brightly lit sex scenes framed from a diegetic male
voyeur's perspective conform to porn's aesthetic conventions, viewer
identification is deflected from this faceless sadist to the leading ladies
he is implied to have murdered upon finding them in bed some years
earlier. In a twist on vampire legend, it is suggested that immortal lovers Fran (Marianne Morris) and Miriam (Anulka) became undead to
avenge their murders. *Vampyres* further frustrates the conventional gaze
of straight porn by denying it any climax – sex scenes are obscured from
view and abruptly cut away from in a manner too self-conscious to be
explained by censorship or ratings concerns. Equally interesting, the
vampire's inflicted wound – typically displayed as a two-pronged bite
mark – is refigured in *Vampyres* to more closely resemble female genitalia. The women feed on their latest male victim Ted (Murray Brown) by
inflicting a long, narrow slit wound which they periodically re-bleed – effectively rendering his a feminized, nurturing body upon which they
consummate the desire that their killer sought to destroy. "What are
you?" Ted asks the enigmatic Fran. "You wouldn't believe me if I told
you," she answers. After Fran has taken Ted to bed but has also explained
her relationship with Miriam ("She's my girlfriend. We have a lot in common. We get on great together"), Ted voices his anxiety: "You intrigue
me – and you worry me – because I don't understand you." What the un-

imaginative Ted fails to understand is Fran's bisexual desire. Ultimately, rather than a conventional conclusion in which patriarchal order is reaffirmed by impaling the vampires upon phallic stakes, *Vampyres* allows its (noticeably unfanged) women to survive, making this a radical pairing of two women into eternity and a celebratory female-revenge scenario.

More conventional depictions of the female vampire abound with worried declarations of "She's not herself lately, Doctor" and "You seem like a different person," recalling Victorian-era anxieties that diagnosed female non-normative behavior as hysteria and schizophrenia. Such allusions and their import for bisexual discourse are examined in depth in the next section's discussion of promiscuity-as-pathology within the sexploitation trope of "institutional bisexuality." A prominent example from the vampire cycle is sexploitation impresario's Jess Franco's *Vampyros Lesbos*, which too pays homage to *Persona*. Beset by nightmares and beckoned by a disembodied female voice calling her name, Lynda (Ewa Strömberg) abandons her unsatisfying married lifestyle to travel alone to a private Mediterranean island (shades of Sappho) where, she is warned, "something horrible happens" to women who dare to venture. There she finds the Countess Nadine (Soledad Miranda), the glamorous heiress to Count Dracula's legacy, who initiates her into the pleasures of nude sunbathing, rich red wine, and lesbian sex. *Vampyros Lesbos* immediately distinguishes itself visually from vampire legend by substituting for the traditional Gothic accoutrements (dark empty castles, mist-shrouded forests, fair maidens) an updated mise-en-scène of mid-century modernism. The film's principal locations – a cavernous white beach house on an otherwise isolated island and a similarly stark medical clinic – mirror *Persona*'s settings. *Vampyros Lesbos*' two female characters, the initially mortal blonde Lynda and the brunette vampire Nadine, are positioned repeatedly as converse images of one another, evoking *Persona*'s famous shots of the women comparing mirrored reflections and later their visages fusing. Also akin to *Persona*'s use of what I described in chapter 1 as art cinema's bi-suggestive dream narration, *Vampyros Lesbos*' narrative nonlinearity and trippy sensibility maintain throughout the possibility that Nadine is merely a figment of Lynda's imagination. The latter is diagnosed a schizophrenic by her physician and her emotional longings dismissed as hysterical symptoms by her psychoanalyst. Even if not necessarily based in reality, her fantasy of Nadine (prompted by witnessing the erotic stage show in which the beguiling brunette appears) is what seems most real and affective in an otherwise sterile existence. Lynda's (and the film's) last line, "You exist in both my fantasy and my real life," is uttered twice: once to her husband and once to the "woman of her dreams" – an ambiguous resolution *and* articulation of desire, but one that forcefully refuses monosexual closure.

The female vampire's unquenchable thirst for blood conjures up cultural anxieties about insatiable female sexuality and the myth of the promiscuous bisexual, unsatisfied by relations with just one sex and willing to go with "anyone who moves."[44] Particularly in her post-AIDS-era incarnations the female vampire is characterized by her cruising, indicating contemporary apprehensions surrounding casual sex. The bloodthirsty women of *The Addiction* (Abel Ferrara, 1995), *The Hunger, Nadja, Vampyres,* and *We Are the Night* locate their victims by prowling nighttime streets, scouring after-hours venues, or hitchhiking, luring their prey home for one-night stands, of a sort. They do so effortlessly, possessing bewitching skills of seduction, and as bisexuals ostensibly do they threaten to lure their pickups away from the straight (or lesbian) and narrow. Just as bisexuals allegedly perform their seductions under a cloak of monosexuality – straight or lesbian – the vampire's cape hides her giveaway pallor while lush lips conceal her deadly fangs and sweeten her deceptive words. *The Hunger's* Miriam Blaylock secures companions by promising them immortality, when in truth they live only two hundred years before succumbing to a rapid aging and an eternity spent decaying in an attic coffin. In an atypical acknowledgement of the female vampire's bi-suggestibility (albeit under the title "Lesbians Who Bite"), Ellis Hanson observes that

> bisexuality becomes the preferred mode of this betrayal, not the least because it is already popularly associated with hedonism, with narcissistic gratification, and with a promiscuous prowling from lover to lover and from gender to gender. In [*The Hunger*], bisexuality represents the wish to be the subject of the promise, to be the alluring locus of an everlasting life.[45]

In *Eternal* (Wilhelm Liebenberg and Federico Sanchez, 2004), the female victims are neither uncorrupted nor passive; a bisexual wife of a cop meets Elizabeth Kane (née Bathory) in an internet chat room and, after making a date, arrives at the countess's Montreal mansion for a casual encounter. The second victim is the cop's (also) married mistress, who shares his penchant for BDSM sex and is a dead ringer for Elizabeth. Lest it seem that *Eternal,* and the vampire cycle generally, have adopted the slasher film's "final girl" convention to reward only virginal women with (albeit not everlasting) life, even the flirtatious but virtuous teen-age babysitter who lives next door falls prey – as do a dozen vestal Venetian partygoers whose unsullied blood Elizabeth bathes in for immortal beauty in the film's denouement.

One of few female-directed vampire films, Stephanie Rothman's *The Velvet Vampire* (financed by exploitation maestro Roger Corman), generally follows formula in surrounding her female vampire with all the accoutrements of social and sexual liberation and privilege: a beautiful woman of independent means lures a curious "swinging" couple to her Palm Springs pleasure dome. Yet Rothman notably desexualizes the vampire's customarily titillating conquest of her prey; instead, the predatory woman morphs into a bat before administering the initiatory bite to her unsuspecting victim, and furthermore relegates the action to offscreen space as if to deny us the anticipated visual pleasure of Sapphic seduction. When girl-on-girl action does materialize, it is both less deadly and exploitative than the norm: in the first, the aptly named Diane Le Fanu (Celeste Yarnall) suggestively sucks snake poison out of the thigh of twice-bitten Susan (Sherry Miles), and subsequently the two enjoy an idyllic romp in a utopian dreamspace imagined by a peacefully slumbering Susan.

As a foreign woman, often accented, who hails "from the East," the female vampire is easily read as a racial or ethnic Other as well as bisexual. Both associations are played with in *Irma Vep* (Olivier Assayas, 1996), which uses its film-within-a-film (an updating of Louis Feuillade's 1915 *Les Vampires,* shooting in modern-day Paris) to comment on the vampire legend even as that legend is brought to life within the off-set narrative. Lead actress Maggie Cheung (playing herself), outfitted in a form-fitting black latex "vampire suit" (purchased in a bondage shop), takes to prowling after dark to get in character and finds her screen role gripping her in an alluring fantasy that begins to overtake reality. Entrancing en masse the film-within-a-film's cast and crew but particularly

attracting the affections of a female costume designer, Cheung finds
both her private and public personae being gradually engulfed by her
eroticized alter ego. At the film's close, however, Cheung sheds her latex
costume and with it the fantasy of seduction and transgression comes
to an abrupt halt.

My bisexual appropriation of the vampire is by no means exclu-
sionary, given that she can be read as embodying cultural myths about
nearly any category of Other. Like every eroticized celluloid spectacle,
the vampire is an icon, a fetish, an image – made up to represent what we
desire (and fear), yet ultimately only screen-deep. It is not so much the
vampire herself who has changed as the various modes of reading her,
influenced by shifting cultural anxieties throughout the past century,
whether of dangerously aggressive heterosexual female "vamps," gay
men and lesbians, Jews and other ethnoracial minorities, AIDS carriers,
or bisexuals and the transgendered. "If the vampire myth is about insid-
ers and outsiders, endogamous and exogamous sexual relations," writes
Garber, "then its timeliness and ubiquity today sort with current fears,
and current desires."[46] Assuming Garber is correct, that in its most recent incarnation – the Stephenie Meyer–penned tween-lit turned screen
franchise *Twilight* – the vampire myth stands in for anxiety about sex
itself is dismaying but not surprising given the abstinence-preaching
culture wars of our times. "Dominant representation has made of the
vampire a horror story," writes Case, and more recent films *Let the Right
One In* (Tomas Alfredson, 2008), *Near Dark* (Kathryn Bigelow, 1987),
and *Trouble Every Day* (Claire Denis, 2001) have downplayed the vampires' allure (if not their humanity) in favor of sermonizing on the hor-
rors of immortality in a contemporary world depicted as starkly dysto-
pian.[47] Another recent trend has revisionist narratives (Jewelle Gomez's
The Gilda Stories, for instance) attempting to recast the female vampire
in a more feminist light, devoid of irony or camp inflection, which Ellis
Hanson disparages as "sentimental, moralistic, and sweet."[48] Everything
we love about the female vampire – her violence, her fetishism, her voy-
eurism – flies defiantly in the face of such deflating efforts. Rather than
spurning the vampire for her sexual (mis)behavior, I prefer to focus on
her spectacular power to remain defiantly undead in viewers' minds.
If one considers that vampires rarely suffer a final and complete death,

then the conflict set up by these films never finds a stable monosexual resolution.

> One "camp[s] up" ideology in order to undo it, producing knowledge about it: that gender and the heterosexual orientation presumed to anchor it are unnatural and even oppressive.
>
> CAROLE-ANNE TYLER

Sexploitation films' excesses of signification – their iconic characters, symptomatic plots, and hyperbolic tone – qualify them as queer camp, in that they work to denaturalize, through those performative exaggerations, gender roles and sexual binaries. The irony and dramatic ambiguity generated by bi-textuality creates levels of interpretation available to naive *and* knowing viewers, much as the complexities of Elizabethan drama, in Empson's account, satisfied "both groundlings and courtly critics."[49] Accordingly, sexploitation engages mainstream viewers (i.e., straight men) along with image-starved queer spectators, who produce fan cults to embrace such rich bitches, fatal femmes, and female vampires as Theresa Russell in *Black Widow*, Sharon Stone in *Basic Instinct*, and Catherine Deneuve in *The Hunger*.[50] Such fandom is often forged in defiance of criticism by the gay press and the misogyny and homophobia legible in the texts; fans choose instead to read these images as celebrations of female power and same-sex desire. As Paula Graham notes,

> forms of parody in which "feminine excess" (i.e., feminine power) signifies an il-legitimate form of power are usually an index of tensions within the heteropatri-archal order . . . [and] efforts to contain fears of female power (often symbolized by lesbianism) are readable in many camp classics.[51]

Such queer camp spectatorship produces resistant or oppositional readings of the rich bitch as a commanding and compelling diva of female agency, empowerment, and non-normative desire. Confirming Ellis Hanson's formulation that the most affecting performances of camp contain not just humor and exaggeration but "a disturbing sexual fantasy and a genuine identification with the parodied figure of abjection," queer cult fandom is frequently fueled by casting rumored real-life lesbians or bisexuals – Barbara Stanwyck in *Walk on the Wild Side*, Delphine Seyrig

2.8. Self-reflexive surveillance of lesbian desire in *Wild Things*.

in *Daughters of Darkness* and *Johanna d'Arc of Mongolia* (Ulrike Ottinger, 1989), David Bowie in *The Hunger* – providing a wink of complicity to in-the-know audiences.[52]

Still alive and kicking at the millennium, thanks to demand from premium cable and DVD rentals, sexploitation has grown more sexually explicit even as its production values gain gloss. The bi-textual discourse on class also still surfaces, energized by the depredations of free-market capitalism and by increasing inequality in the division of wealth. In *Wild Things*, dependent Suzie's (Neve Campbell) social invisibility alongside her bisexual (in)visibility to her wealthy partners-in-crime (and would-be double-crossers) as well as to the educational and legal institutions they control, ultimately allow her to triumph. *Wild Things* sets its socioeconomic/sexual struggle within a milieu of late American capitalism and postfeminist sexual politics, yet does so in a camp mode that might be considered political for denaturalizing and critiquing oppressive structures around class and female sexuality. Both female and male bisexuality are suggested within the diegesis, but sexuality itself is portrayed as highly exhibitionistic, performative, and overdetermined by power relations. The tantalizing commercial lure of bisexuality is knowingly sent up (even as it is gleefully exploited) by the film's self-aware genre play, in which the noir thriller's standard elements (role reversals, convoluted plot, subjective point of view) are exaggerated into parodic excess to match the film's gluttony of visual pleasure.

Treated with similar irreverence, though suggesting a sharper critical stance, is the film's depiction of the various institutionalized means (especially within American educational and legal systems) of privileging the rich, prosecuting the poor, and regulating female sexuality. Even as *Wild Things* glamorizes the affluent enclaves of South Florida, it addresses the American class divide by juxtaposing well-groomed estates with trailer park backwaters and their disenfranchised, sympathetic, but not sentimentalized residents. While *Wild Things* may be more accurately described as mainstream camp – which Paula Graham describes as a "permissible form in which sexual deviance may be displayed as spectacle for heterosexual consumption (and its threat neutralized)" – its homoerotic titillations are always playfully but probingly tied to its examination of how privilege ensures civic and sexual agency in contemporary American society.[53]

Moreover, though its parodic tone and sexual self-indulgence bracket any claims to serious social critique, *Wild Things* does conclude with the female dependent's triumphant redistribution of wealth. Having double-crossed all her accomplices – shady lothario Sam (Matt Dillon), sadistic cop Ray Duquette (Kevin Bacon), and mother-daughter rich bitches Kelly (Denise Richards) and Sandra Van Ryan (*Black Widow*'s Theresa Russell, in homage casting) – by hiding her intelligence and faking a "tragic lesbian" obsession, Suzie ultimately winds up rich and contentedly alone, commandeering her newly acquired sailboat across the Caribbean while her trusted collaborator, an ambulance-chasing lawyer (Bill Murray), ends up at an exclusive country club, much to the dismay of its blueblood membership. With none of the regret or loneliness shown to nag at other femmes fatales who get away with it – Kathleen Turner's character in *Body Heat* (Lawrence Kasdan, 1981) comes to mind – Suzie's triumph and resulting independence, flush with cash and alone in the middle of the ocean, is portrayed as liberating and empowering.

The corollary to this sexploitative and often violent rich bitch–dependent double dyad is the female "friendship" film, in which bi-suggestiveness is contained by opposite means – rather than rendering it excessive and destructive, it is relegated to the realm of gentle opacity and playful experimentation. *Personal Best* interestingly conflates these two strains, depicting how a sexual and emotional relationship between two female Olympic pentathletes challenges their individual competitiveness. Here the older and butcher Tory (Patrice Donnelly) – the more established athlete and (the film implies) the more committed lesbian – though not literally a rich bitch, occupies a dominant if nurturing position over the younger, more femme Chris (Mariel Hemingway). While it substitutes athletic success for wealth and socioeconomic status as the element structuring the woman-woman power dynamic, *Personal Best's* outcome remains divisive: only as friends and teammates – *not* as same-sex mates – can each pursue her *personal* best. Chris's eventual choice to throw Tory over for lanky swimmer Denny (Kenny Moore) is only obscurely reasoned within the narrative, which, in the manner of the vampire films, renders the "man-object" characterless and oafish, and suggests it is his aptitude as surrogate coach/father (someone decidedly *not* a threat professionally) that makes him attractive to Chris. The final scene shows Chris and Tory, reunited as friends after having both qualified for the Olympic team, standing side by side on the dais and joined by the third qualifier, an African American woman. As the American flag waves and the national anthem is played, the ethos seems clear: women competing against women serves to solidify friendships (even helping to surmount racial boundaries) *and* to forward patriotic aims, but *too*-close female relationships corrupt individual *and* national success.

(UN)COMMITTED WOMEN: PATHOLOGICAL BISEXUALITY IN FEMALE INSTITUTION FILMS

> Marriage is a fine institution, but I'm not ready for an institution yet.
>
> MAE WEST

Freud's "Dora: An Analysis of a Case of Hysteria" recounts his psychoanalytic sessions with a young female patient whose father seeks treatment for what he feels is her socially unacceptable and embarrassing "hysteric" behavior, which Freud diagnoses as the symptoms of repressed bisexual desire.[54] This young woman, Freud concludes, suffers from an unresolved Oedipal process whereby her attachment to an emotionally withholding mother found an outlet in her idealized recreation of that love for another older married woman, Frau K., nurse and lover to Dora's syphilitic father. Dora, meanwhile, experiences feelings of disgust in response to the sexual attentions concurrently paid her by Herr K. Freud attributes her disgust to repressed desire for Herr K., his prognosis engendering a bisexual triangle and a substitute family much like the one presented in Chabrol's *Les Biches*. When Dora ends treatment prematurely, Freud believes the lack of resolution has left her in a "dangerous" bisexual state. The case of Dora, which comprises Freud's most significant work on bisexuality, constructs much of the signification assigned (especially female) bisexuality as a liminal, temporary phase that, if left unresolved, festers into a pathological state.

I begin with this reference to Dora as a means of linking contemporary conceptions of bisexuality to turn-of-the-twentieth-century psychiatric discourse's still influential construction of female sexual pathology. Alternately diagnosed as repressed, frigid, promiscuous, hysteric, neurotic, and eventually lesbian and bisexual, female sexual pathology was attributed to the patient's "presumed failure not only to follow the Oedipal narrative of psychosexual development to its heterosexual finish," Christine Coffman describes, "but also to establish a stable distinction between self and object, self and other."[55] In his conception of the mirror stage, Lacan posits that subject formation, if thwarted by a refutation of the heteropatriarchal order, results in psychosis – that is, the refusal or inability to integrate oneself within the discursive social realm (Lacan's aforementioned Symbolic) makes one unable to function as a social subject.[56] To explain gender nonconformity and nonheterosexuality as symptoms of psychosis conveniently attributes them to individual pathology rather than to a breakdown in the heteropatriachal order, a key strategy in Western modernity's regulation of sexuality, Gayle Rubin observes:

> When medicine and psychiatry acquired extensive powers over sexuality, they were less concerned with unsuitable mates [as were earlier religious sanctions on kinship forms of social organization] than with unfit forms of desire. . . . Psychiatric condemnation of sexual behaviors invokes concepts of mental and emotional inferiority rather than categories of sexual sin. Low-status sex

practices are vilified as mental diseases or symptoms of defective personality integration. In addition, psychological terms conflate difficulties of psycho-dynamic function with modes of erotic conduct. They equate sexual masochism with self-destructive personality patterns, sexual sadism with emotional aggres-sion, and homoeroticism with immaturity.[57]

Rubin's wariness of employing psychiatric frameworks is shared by a good many feminist and queer theorists, but it seems to me that precisely because of the link psychiatric discourse maintains between nonhetero-sexuality and psychosis, closer examination is demanded of how power and knowledge shape our cultural logic of desire.

Toward that aim, this chapter's final section considers the construc-tion of another bi-textual archetype, the *(un)committed woman,* as a means of negotiating these associations of female bisexuality with promiscu-ity and mental illness. This archetype primarily appears in narratives set within all-female communities, institutions that can exist both for the purpose of and as a respite from gender socialization. The bi-textual metaphor thus constructed reveals how female ambivalence about or re-sistance to heteropatriarchy is pathologized and policed by prescriptively confining women within gender-ordered "institutions" of heterosexual-ity, marriage, domesticity, motherhood, and sexual propriety. Bisexual-ity and other forms of "deviant" female sexuality are likened to mental and criminal deviance (variously diagnosed as abnormal, antisocial, and insane), and the women thus charged suffer both legal and moral condem-nation. Yet the bi-textual link constructed within these female institution films repeatedly serves to trouble, and thus to acknowledge the spaces between and beyond, the oppositions between hetero- and homosexual-ity and between sane and insane (or normal and abnormal, or social and antisocial).

Many studies of lesbian representability in fictional texts draw on this narrative connection between female same-sex desire and mental and criminal pathology; one need only view Lady Gaga's "Telephone" video from 2010, which makes reference to women's prison films, *Thelma & Louise* and the rape-revenge genre, and lesbian cult favorite *Bound,* not to mention the twin peaks of Madonna's and Britney Spears's bad girl incarnations (the song itself is a defiant declaration of women's sexual independence). In her examination of lesbian desire in French and Fran-

cophone cinema, Lucille Cairns identifies criminality and psychopathol-
ogy as "the two most salient lesbian paradigms in the corpus."[58] This (un)
committed woman, then, shares a sisterly bond with another pervasive
archetype, the *psychotic lesbian;* both are figures of fascination and anxiety, borne of curiosity and paranoia over the disruption of the heteropatriarchal order. The rich bitches and dependent doubles discussed in this
chapter's first section quite clearly align with the psychotic signification
heretofore assigned (exclusively) to the filmic lesbian, for the way their
desire mutually hinges on aggression and identity fragmentation. The
(un)committed women discussed below, however, are more accurately
characterized as sociopathic, defined by attitudes and behavior deemed
antisocial – namely their (bi)sexual independence.

> Isabel Archer: I always want to know the things one shouldn't do.
>
> Mrs. Touchett: So as to do them?
>
> Isabel: So as to choose.
>
> HENRY JAMES, *The Portrait of a Lady*

By their very premise, female institution films put women's relationships, and with them female same-sex desire, at their center. Fittingly, the
female Gothic tradition weighs heavily on such films even when they are
set in the contemporary era, suggesting ongoing Freudian and Victorian
repressiveness around female sexuality but also emphasizing the subversive release that female relationships and communities provide. These
(un)committed women are not endowed with the rich bitch's wealth
and agency or the hippie chick's countercultural freedoms but rather are
subject to control by rigid authority figures (parents, teachers, and doctors), much as the European women who were Freud's contemporaries
and patients were bound by social mores that limited their options largely
to heterosexual marriage and the "romantic friendships" that BGLQT historian Lillian Faderman chronicles.[59] By the late Victorian period, however, these romantic friendships were on the wane, under attack by a new
policing of women's intimate relationships, as Richard Dyer observes:

> Where earlier periods had conceived of "romantic friendships" between
> women (which might or might not have involved sexual relations), by the early

twentieth century the medical and psychological profession had started to
think of such relationships in terms of "lesbianism," as, in other words, defined
by the sexual element. Faderman sees this as springing from men's desire to
prohibit the possibility of women forming important attachments to each other
separate from and even over against their attachments to men. The notion of
"lesbianism," seen as a sickness, was used to discredit both romantic friendship between women and the growth of women's political and educational
independence.[60]

As compulsory monosexuality became increasingly entrenched as a result of this sexualized and pathologized othering of (too-)close female
relationships, the binary line dividing "lesbians" from "just good friends"
was firmly established. But as Alexander Doty rhetorically asks, "Is there
an erotic component in certain friendships, even if it's not sexually acted
upon?"[61] Female institution films, in constructing a "safe space" for female friends to explore bisexual possibility, imagine how our logic of
desire might be reconceived along a more fluid range.

The context in which the term *liminal* (from *limen*, Latin for *thresh-
old*) was first used, by anthropologist Arnold van Gennep in his studies
of rites of passage in traditional societies, is particularly pertinent for
films dealing with so-called "environmental lesbianism" (or bisexuality) among adolescent females in single-sex communities.[62] Such social
spaces present a challenge to normative processes such as compulsory
monosexuality. In encouraging women's alliances and bonding, and in
delaying that which our society deems a (if not *the*) principal female
rite of passage – heterosexual courtship and marriage then, heterosexual
intercourse now – the all-female institution undermines the importance
of this social ritual. The "deviant" female's resistance to or violation of
heteronormativity thus serves as catalyst for what Victor Turner calls
the *social drama* of breach, crisis, and resolution, "at which point the
wider sense of social order is also restored, indeed reaffirmed."[63] The bisexual figures and bi-textual narratives discussed below ritually restage
sexual identity development in an attempt to allay anxieties about monosexuality's social constructedness and hence precariousness. Like the
all-female institution, bisexuality, insofar as it functions as a refusal to
"choose sides" in the compulsory monosexuality paradigm, constitutes
a permanently liminal space in that alternative forms of social order may
be imagined, even if they cannot be enacted.[64]

Am I gay? Am I straight? And then I realized, I'm just slutty.
Where's my parade?!

MARGARET CHO

From early sound films *Mädchen in Uniform* (Leontine Sagan, 1931) and *The Wild Party* (Dorothy Arzner, 1929) to classical Hollywood's *Lilith* (Robert Rossen, 1964) and *The Snake Pit* (Anatole Litvak, 1948), to global art films *Persona* and *Picnic at Hanging Rock,* to sexploitation flicks *Caged Heat* (Jonathan Demme, 1974) and *Therese & Isabelle* (Radley Metzger, 1968) to female-directed indies *Foxfire* and *Lost and Delirious* (Léa Pool, 2001) to contemporary U.S. specialty cinema *Girl, Interrupted* and *Mona Lisa Smile* (Mike Newell, 2003), the female institution in its various permutations (boarding school, mental hospital, prison, gang) and depictions (as oppressive reformatory or utopian refuge from an oppressive external world) provides an enduring setting for negotiating and occasionally subverting those social forces generative of heteronormativity. As will be discussed below in regard to *Girl, Interrupted,* the female institution film often rejects the stigma attached to female promiscuity. Particular female institution films may contain or promote female social-sexual nonconformity, and may capitulate to or challenge stereotypes of female promiscuity. Taken together, these films expose just how tightly the assessment and treatment of female psychiatric conditions – including nymphomania, lesbianism, bisexuality, abuse-related traumas, eating disorders, mythomania, dissociation, depression, addiction, and anxiety – are tied up with gender roles and rules. Before considering in depth some missed moments for bisexual readings of female institution films, I would like to contemplate one performer who emerged out of this genre of sexploitation, and whose overpowering star persona is charged with some of the same associations as her characters. Just as female institution films look with fearful fascination at sexually and socially transgressive young women, so the public has responded to actress Angelina Jolie.

JOLIE AS BISEXUAL "BUTCH-FEMME"

A prayer for the wild at heart, kept in cages.

TENNESSEE WILLIAMS (*quotation tattooed on Angelina Jolie's left forearm*)

Jolie, who won the triple crown of Academy Award, Golden Globe, and Screen Actors Guild (SAG) Award for Best Supporting Actress for her role in *Girl, Interrupted*, offers a rare instance of a woman in the contemporary public sphere who (at least initially) openly and consistently identified as bisexual in promotional discourse.[65] Mapping this early proclamation as it was then disseminated in her film performances and public activities and appropriated by publicists, journalists, and fans offers an illuminating case of how "real life" bisexuality is interpreted and translated through a star text. In interviews Jolie gave during the breakout phase of her career in the late 1990s, she frequently claimed to have dated both men and women, and publicly acknowledged that she was for a time involved in a relationship with model-actress Jenny Shimizu, her *Foxfire* co-star. (Of course her marriages to Jonny Lee Miller and Billy Bob Thornton and her current partnership with Brad Pitt have been widely documented in the press.) Jolie first gained widespread attention after portraying the bisexual fashion model Gia Carangi in the HBO biopic *Gia* (Michael Cristofer, 1998), and, as I will demonstrate below, her roles in *Foxfire* and *Girl, Interrupted* are inflected with bi-suggestive elements. In her insightful essay on Jolie, Cristina Stasia adds that Jolie's role as car thief "Sway" (note the suggestive name) in *Gone in 60 Seconds* (Dominic Sena, 2000) offers another bi-suggestive characterization.[66] Moreover, Stasia argues, Jolie serves as a "bicon" of queer/third-wave-feminist culture in her "both/and" convergence of erotic signifiers formerly treated as either/or designations – most blatantly, by troubling the monosexual binary through identifying as bisexual. Additionally, Stasia continues, the butch/femme binary commonly used in pre-queer-theory discourse and lesbian culture to designate opposite but inseparable identities within a relationship becomes, within Jolie's star text, an inbetweener identity (the *butch-femme*) within a single individual. Neither clearly butch nor clearly femme in style or attitude (in either her film roles or her role as "Angelina Jolie"), the actress's resistance to aligning herself along conventional binaries of gender presentation combines with her defiance of monosexuality to make queer female sexual identity hypervisible.

This identity is not always portrayed or received positively by Jolie's public, however, and it is interesting – though more than a little dismaying – to see how Jolie's "indecipherable" sexual persona is perceived as threatening and subject to all the typical bisexual stereotypes: predatory, manipulative, opportunistic, exhibitionistic, etc. The relationship with Pitt has provided endless fodder in this regard, as the tabloid press has presented her as a home wrecker and dragon lady (or, perhaps, vampire) who lured Pitt away from his long-term relationship with actress/"victim" Jennifer Aniston. The ostensibly irresistible powers of seduction that Jolie was alleged to wield (and the passivity attributed to Pitt) during this drawn-out media episode significantly colored and then overshadowed her other publicly reported activities at the time, adopting orphaned children and working as a UNICEF ambassador. Her early career persona as a bisexual "wild woman" who enjoyed blade play and sported multiple tattoos has been tempered by these more staid recent interests in mothering, philanthropy, and most recently, writing and directing her first film, *In the Land of Blood and Honey* (2011). Yet the public's perception of her as a sexually unrestrained adventuress – one that she courted in early interviews, then endured during the Aniston-Pitt episode – has changed its tone distinctly. A crucial turning point came during her on-stage admission to being "in love" with brother James Haven at the 2000 Academy Award presentation, which prompted rumors of an incestuous relationship and shifted the tide of opinion toward its current estimation of Angelina the perverse, rather than Angelina the adventurous.

Nevertheless the notion of the queer continues to inflect Jolie's star persona, and with increasingly pejorative overtones, based on these highly mediatized accounts or displays of non-normative desire. Where this seemed to work in Jolie's favor during the breakout phase of her career, it has increasingly alienated her from her mainstream audience even as the roles she gravitates to since becoming an A-list performer target the very viewers inclined to shun her. The audience with whom she remains popular as a symbol of pansexual desirability and rebel ethos – a figuratively and often literally queer audience of more offbeat taste and liberal standards – are hardly the chief demographic for her recent work, which oscillates between big-budget action films such as *Salt* (Phillip Noyce, 2010) and *Wanted* (Timur Bekmambetov, 2008) and liberal dramas like *A Mighty Heart* (Michael Winterbottom, 2007) and *Changeling* (Clint Eastwood, 2008). Though Jolie's reputation and professional clout among mainstream audiences can be said to have faltered in recent years (while still bankable enough to open a movie), her presence in a film is enough of a reason for some Aniston loyalists (my mother, for one) to skip it, she remains an important commodity whose worth stems substantially from her enigmatic bi-suggestibility and the power it holds over men and women.

What is perhaps most interesting about Jolie's early roles is just how preoccupied her female institution films were with the queer female gaze. The two Jolie-starring features discussed below construct powerful structures of desiring and looking that are oriented almost exclusively around women's pleasure, power, and self-knowledge, and are focused on bi-suggestive female relationships and women's communities. While both films contain marked sexploitation elements – sensational subject matter and promotional tactics, titillating scenes of same-sex desire, melodramatic tone, outsized characterization and performance that open them to a camp reading – they are also studio-produced specialty division projects based on popular works of female-authored fiction and memoir. In cleaning up (somewhat) the sexual explicitness and "girl on girl" prurience of female institution films, *Foxfire* and *Girl, Interrupted* reshape the genre's motif of female deviance to be palatable to a general audience but remain critical of sexploitation's complicity in constructing and maintaining the female "sex fiend" stereotype.

MISSED MOMENT: ANGELINA JOLIE'S EARLY FILMS

Independent feature *Foxfire,* based on the novel *Foxfire: Confessions of a Girl Gang* by Joyce Carol Oates and directed by first-time director Annette Haywood-Carter, associates its characters with rebellion in its tagline ("It took them 17 years to learn the rules. And one week to break them all") and riot grrrl sensibility (set in Portland, Oregon, and with a soundtrack featuring The Cramps, L7, and Patti Smith).[67] The film's opening sequence initiates an arresting reversal of the typical male gaze by depicting young protagonist Maddy (Hedy Burress) photographing her boyfriend posing nude in the outdoors. Their subsequent exchange makes it clear that Maddy controls the gaze as well as her emotional agency, and is the one less consumed by the relationship. Shortly thereafter, the arrival in town of Legs (Angelina Jolie) throws Maddy's safely straight (if it ever was) life into upheaval. An orphaned drifter mistaken for a new student at Maddy's high school, Legs's first appearance on-screen establishes her butch self-presentation (boyish haircut, leather jacket, undershirt, and motorcycle boots) and causes her to be mistaken for a "young man" by a hall monitor. (In a later scene, Legs's arrival at a new friend's house will be announced by a mother who says, "There's a girl, or whatever, here to see you.") Legs stages her first rebellious act against her new community by freeing a frog seconds before it was to be dissected in biology class. Inciting others to do the same, pandemonium quickly breaks out. The incident foreshadows Legs's next and more violent coup: beating up a teacher who has been sexually molesting several of his female students.

In addition to underlining Legs's seditious sway over her peers, this early scene sexualizes the relationship between Legs and Maddy from the moment the former sits down across from the latter and reaches over to suggestively stroke the trembling frog on its dissection tray. Later that night, Legs arrives at Maddy's bedroom window and asks for a place to sleep for the night and a dry shirt. "I'm kind of wet," Legs announces just as suggestively, proceeding to disrobe in front of Maddy, who looks away uncomfortably but not before stealing a quick glance. While walking together to school the next morning, Maddy pauses while crossing the bridge that will continue to feature significantly in the story, christening it an evocative locale with her light-of-day acknowledgment of having been disarmed by this stranger. "I don't even know your name," she says, to which Legs responds with an arch " . . . she says the next morning."

As her attraction to Legs develops, Maddy feels increasingly alienated from her boyfriend and more drawn into the newly formed girl gang – rounded out by the two girls whom they rescue from the teacher's sexual abuse as well as by a fellow outcast and baby butch Goldie (Jenny Shimizu) – who sets up headquarters in an abandoned house. It is here that *Foxfire*'s most overtly erotic scene of metaphorical same-sex initiation takes place, when Legs again disrobes (provoking the same discomfort and stolen looks) and tattoos a burning flame on her chest as her new friends look on wondrously. Maddy impetuously flings off her own shirt and requests that Legs "Do it to me," and to the ethereal tune of Mazzy

Star's "Into Dust," Legs proceeds to "initiate" each of the all-too-willing girls in turn. It is intriguing to imagine how this scene would have differed under a male filmmaker's direction; while the scene certainly milks the erotic appeal of this ritual of surrender, it has little of the lewd tinge of analogous girl-on-girl scenes in *Wild Things* or the blood-sister pact in the female vampire films. Instead, the scene's charged emotions and ritualistic atmosphere are conveyed with such solemnity that it mostly avoids the feminine excess and parodic register that Paula Graham terms "girls' camp."[68]

While the increasingly charged bond between Maddy and Legs is never explicitly consummated onscreen, the following exchange on the eve of Legs's planned departure makes clear the nature of their feelings and their unspeakability:

Maddy: Would you take someone with you?

Legs: Is that someone sure? Is she cut out for the unknown? Sometimes the unknown will disappoint you.

Maddy: If I told you that I loved you would you take it the wrong way?

Legs: What do you mean by wrong?

Maddy: It's just that I'm not ... and you're ...

Legs: I'll take it however you want me to, Maddy.

Despite the film's focus on what is clearly a love story between Legs and Maddy, *Foxfire*'s DVD cover imagery (at least in its U.S. distribution) downplays the homoeroticism of the tattooing scene with a still photograph of Maddy looking petrified rather than aroused as Legs probes her with the needle (fittingly, the still that accompanies this image is one of Maddy kissing her boyfriend, who goes largely unseen following the film's opening sequence). For the movie's marketers, *Foxfire* was very much a "film about female *friendship* [italics mine] and rebellion," as the DVD cover proclaims. Though this promotional strategy appears to depart from sexploitation's embrace of opportunities to highlight bi-suggestive elements, films featuring queer teenage sexuality tend to soft-pedal such elements in their marketing with oblique (and rather trite) references to "loss of sexual innocence," "a journey of self-discovery," and the like. Symptomatic of a cultural uneasiness about teenage sexuality, especially of the queer variety, these equivocal marketing campaigns (perhaps by design) rarely succeed in keeping queer content below the radar, and in-the-know viewers recognize codes or references that signal queer readability within adolescent female friendships, whether implicit as in *Foxfire* and *Times Square* (Allan Moyle, 1980) or explicit as in *All Over Me* (Alex Sichel, 1997) and *Lost and Delirious*. All but the latter reference the riot grrrl movement and construct butch/femme pairings, while queer Québecois filmmaker Léa Pool's *Lost and Delirious* is set in a girls' boarding school and makes repeated allusion to gender-bending performances from Peter Pan to Macbeth ("Come, you spirits that tend on mortal thoughts, unsex me here").

Of course this canny strategy of "having it both ways" can work both ways, in the sense that promotional materials may hint at subversive desire only to evade and even censure it within the narrative. Released in the same year as *Foxfire* and following a superficially similar plotline, *The Craft* (Andrew Fleming, 1996) offers a useful counterpoint for demonstrating how queer themes can be compromised when given "straight" treatment. As in *Foxfire*, *The Craft*'s girl gang is united by their shared outcast status and desire to combat the injustices suffered by social-sexual gender nonconformists, with the thematic dyad of oppressive coed high school versus liberating all-female space restaged. Yet *The Craft* offers a more sensationalized and considerably less queer variant on *Foxfire*'s themes, starting with the basis for these girls' difference. Their shared otherness and the power they engender in one another stems from a fantasy phenomenon (witchcraft) rather than an actual activist movement (riot grrrl). Furthermore, the mostly femme styling of the female leads and the lack of even a hint of sexual chemistry among them makes *The Craft* appear almost paranoid in its repudiation of gender nonconformity and same-sex desire. The film's only progressive element is its critique of petty high school hierarchies, which subject two of the gang's members – an African American and a burn victim – to harsh treatment for their racial difference and physical irregularity. Target of first her classmates' then the film's greatest scorn and most blatant double standard is the gang's Goth-styled leader Nancy (Fairuza Balk), initially reviled as a "slut" while her male partners enjoy a boost to their social reputations.

In its latter half, however, *The Craft* ends up subscribing to the same high school mentality that the film spends its first half rebuking. Nancy develops into an increasingly monstrous figure while the primary male antagonist, date-raping jock Chris Hooker (Skeet Ulrich), is treated as ever more sympathetic. With the male villain softened, it comes as little surprise when the women turn on one another, and less surprising, but no less disappointing, that the showdown between "good witch" Sarah (Robin Tunney) and "evil witch" Nancy turns on both women's baffling desire for the feckless Chris. Though *Foxfire*'s gung-ho grrrlpower may stray too far into earnestness at times, it is much preferable to *The Craft*'s spectacle of two formerly self-assured women competing to claim the football player who sexually assaulted and emotionally humiliated them both.

> Guidance counselor: Women today have more choices than
> [ending up like their mothers].
>
> Susanna (Winona Ryder): No they don't.
>
> *Girl, Interrupted*

Although produced, like *The Craft*, by Hollywood power mogul Douglas Wick, *Girl, Interrupted* is primarily a female-authored venture. Adapted for the screen as a personal project of actress Winona Ryder, from the memoir by Susanna Kaysen, its story of a would-be romance between two female patients in a psychiatric institution aspires to present a serious if still sexploitation-tinged treatment of the female institution film, targeted to a mainstream audience.[69] After scandalizing her family and community with an affair deemed inappropriate, the film's narrator and protagonist Susanna (Ryder) is incarcerated on a women's ward for what is diagnosed as a sexually promiscuous borderline personality. As is typical of the film's genre (the female institution film) and setting (a mental hospital), *Girl, Interrupted*'s Claymoore is simultaneously depicted as a repressive environment and a refuge from an even more repressive (for women) external world.[70] Films set within mental hospitals and narrated from the point of view of the institutionalized often employ this narrative conceit – that it is the inmates who are sane and the world that is "crazy." In *Girl, Interrupted*, this structure is reframed to suggest a less rigid delineation of mental status and to point out how gender is inextricably tied up with society's conception and treatment of psychiatric conditions. The chief transgression that provokes Susanna's forced commitment to Claymoore is having swallowed a bottle of aspirin to cure a headache, but her ancillary offense – undoubtedly more offensive to her elders – was having had sexual relations, considered age-inappropriate, with a married older man and friend of her parents. That cradle-robbing Professor Gilchrist (Bruce Altman) is perceived as nothing worse than a philanderer testifies to the double standard that treats both heterosexual men's desires and older man–younger woman pairings (unlike younger man–older woman pairings) with marked leniency.

Girl, Interrupted makes explicit the pathologizing of "deviant" female sexuality, and investigates its multiple manifestations as personified by Susanna and the ward's other inhabitants: butch lesbian, incest victim, anorexic, pathological liar, burn victim, and the seductive sociopath Lisa, played by Jolie. In each case, the patient's malady is one linked specifically to gender performance – as either a refusal or inability to act and look the proper lady, as in the case of the butch Cynthia (Jillian Armenante), the scarred Polly (Elisabeth Moss), and the aggressive Lisa, or as an excessive internalization of cultural expectations for women, in the case of emaciated Janet (Angela Bettis), the literal "daddy's girl" and disturbingly domestic Daisy (Brittany Murphy), and the overeager-to-please mythomaniac Georgina (Clea DuVall).

Girl, Interrupted's opening shot of Susanna cradling Lisa in her arms is presented out of temporal sequence – it actually occurs later in the film's diegesis – but immediately signals a close and affectionate relationship between the two, and Simon and Garfunkel's overlaid lyrics ("It was a time of innocence . . . ") emphasize the transformative instance of both these girls' adolescence and of mid-1960s America. As Susanna's opening voiceover goes on to speculate, "Maybe I was really crazy, maybe it was the sixties, or may I was just a girl . . . interrupted," her mental status gets bound up with its cultural determinants – social mores, gendered socialization, sexual development – just as her elders diagnose and treat her for a condition defined as a result of her gender. In repeatedly making reference to the 1960s milieu, more than a mere backdrop, *Girl, Interrupted* connects its predominant subject – female mental and sexual pathology – to the cultural transformations occurring in contemporary America: the burgeoning (second-wave) feminist movement and other nonconformist mobilizations (draft-dodging, race riots, the hippie counterculture). "We live in a time of doubt," a newscaster is heard to say. The bourgeois conformity evident in the prosperous Boston suburb where Susanna lived and to which she will ultimately return is directly juxtaposed with the budding counterculture glimpsed when Susanna and Lisa escape from Claymoore, hitch a ride in a vw bus, and spend the evening with hippies reveling in acid rock and mind-altering substances (the latter not so unlike the meds forced nightly on Claymoore patients). Tellingly, it is en route to this party when an exuberant Susanna kisses Lisa on the lips; in this liberating personal moment and transformative cultural moment, same-sex desire is one more taboo to be broken and new experience to be embraced.

The civil rights movement and racial politics are also indirectly but repeatedly referenced, both through a televised broadcast of a speech by Dr. Martin Luther King Jr. that the girls gather to watch and through these upper-middle-class white patients' relationship to their working-class African American head nurse Valerie (Whoopi Goldberg). Though Valerie is for the most part the stock African American character whose role it is to dispense sage advice to the white folk, Goldberg's impudent screen persona surfaces to make Valerie edgier than she might otherwise have been. Responding in one instance to an irate Susanna's racist taunts (which she delivers in a mammy voice), Valerie aggressively takes Susanna to task for being a spoiled rich girl indulging herself by acting crazy. Also important is that Goldberg's star persona is informed by some spectators' knowledge of the performer's queer identity. Because four of the film's leads (Goldberg, Jolie, DuVall, and Vanessa Redgrave) are actresses known for identifying as and/or playing queer women, *Girl, Interrupted* seems to be inviting in-the-know audiences to speculate on the blurring of boundaries between performance and the performer's "real" self.

Still another supporting character who integrates 1960s countercultural politics into the narrative foreground is Susanna's pre-Claymoore boyfriend and Vietnam draft-dodger Toby (Jared Leto). At film's start Susanna expresses urgent sexual desire for Toby; learning that she has had premarital relations, Susanna's doctor asks her, "Is there something about sex that lifts your feelings of despair?" to which Susanna responds "Have you ever had sex?" Yet as her stay at Claymoore and her relationship with Lisa develops, Susanna increasingly shies away from linking her life up too exclusively with Toby. When he appears at the hospital en route to refuge in Canada and urges Susanna to accompany him, she tells him, "I want to leave but not with you." Though draft-dodging and breaking out of Claymoore are here equated as means of escape from an intolerable situation, Susanna will all too eagerly run away soon thereafter – but with *Lisa*. To leave with Toby – even under lawbreaking circumstances – would be, for Susanna, the safe choice: an escape, but one leading back into a life of heteronormative conformity.

During the half hour of screen time preceding Lisa's first appearance in the film, Susanna is shown to be enormously curious about this magnetic personality about whom she has heard much and who appears to exert such influence over the ward's residents. Upon her arrival, Susanna learns that she is to occupy the room of a former patient, recently departed. Inquiring as to her whereabouts, Susanna is told that "Jamie was sad last week after Lisa ran away, so she hung herself with a volleyball net." From this comment we can gather that the dead girl, however mentally unstable, had been in love with Lisa. As the new occupant of Jamie's room and bed, Susanna, it is suggested, will become her replacement – in every sense. When Lisa is found and brought back to the ward, Susanna sneaks out of her room to steal a look through the narrow window of Lisa's isolation cell. The point-of-view shot that we are shown is blurred (the effect of Susanna's sleeping pill kicking in), and from this moment on Susanna's vision – of life and of the hospital, and of her place in both – grows still cloudier.

The scene in which the patients sneak into Claymoore's basement bowling alley after lights-out serves as an instance of illicit nighttime activity among women much like the tattooing scene in *Foxfire*, and here again it is staged and presided over by Jolie's character. Throughout the raucous midnight match Lisa remains on the sidelines, gazing upon the other women and especially the initially hesitant Susanna (whom she encourages to participate) to the soundtrack's accompaniment by Ray Charles crooning, "Night time is the right time for being with the one you love." The intense gazes that Susanna and Lisa share here, in another loaded moment as the two pass along a stairwell, and in the number of stares they exchange through the barrier of Lisa's locked isolation chamber, are charged with longing. Yet that this couple are never permitted to share the frame in such moments signifies their forced separation.

Strapped to a gurney on her way to the emergency room, close to unconsciousness after swallowing a bottle of aspirin, Susanna mumbles, "Sometimes it's hard for me to stay in one place." When one doctor initially diagnoses Susanna as suffering from borderline personality disorder, Susanna's response is "Borderline between what and what?" Telling her the condition is "not uncommon, especially among young women," the doctor goes on to describe the symptoms as "uncertainty about self-image, goals, types of friends or lovers to have and which values to adopt." The uselessly imprecise way in which Susanna's alleged condition is defined is reasserted when the girls sneak into the hospital chief's office to read their personal files. Susanna consults a psychiatric manual she finds there:

> Susanna [reading]: "Borderline Personality Disorder. An instability
> of self-image, relationships and mood ... uncertain about goals,
> impulsive in activities that are self-damaging, such as casual sex."
>
> Lisa: I like that.
>
> Susanna: "Social contrariness and a generally pessimistic attitude
> are often observed." [pauses] Well that's me.
>
> Lisa: That's everybody.

This exchange echoes an earlier one between Susanna and the cab driver who deposits her at Claymoore. Curious why she should be checking into a mental hospital ("You look normal," he tells her), he inquires as to what is wrong with her. "I'm sad," says Susanna. "Well, everyone's sad," he responds. When the same cabbie improbably picks Susanna up upon her release from Claymoore at film's end, she has earned a new diagnosis: "recovered borderline." "What that means I still don't know," Susanna muses in voiceover. "Was I crazy? Maybe. Maybe the world is."

Susanna's diagnostic relegation to a psychological borderland signals a bi-textual correlation between the film's construction of two types
of inbetweenness – in mental status and in sexual desires. Bi-suggestiveness remains implicit but nevertheless highly perceptible during the
scene in which Susanna is finally summoned to meet with Claymoore's
head psychiatrist, Dr. Wick (Redgrave). Up to this point, the topic of
female adolescent sexuality has repeatedly been referenced with regard
to heterosexual desire – patients are forbidden from leaving the grounds
with visiting boyfriends (Susanna is later caught pleasuring Toby in her
room on visitors' day) as well as from consorting with male orderlies (she
manages to break this rule as well). In this realm as in others, Lisa presents a threat to the doctors' and administrators' attempts to curtail their
patients' burgeoning sexuality. When one girl, soon to be married, asks
Lisa's advice about premarital sex, Lisa tells her to "fuck his brains out.
Use a rubber." Lisa's perspective, representative of the nascent sexual
revolution outside Claymoore's walls, poses an alarming alternative to
the philosophy of abstinence (for women, anyway) preached within.
As their populist-cum-fascist leader, Lisa threatens to lead these young
women astray – or so the doctors suspect – in the ways of desire. All ways,
because while it is only heterosexual relations that are directly articulated in the "house rules" and in the film's dialogue, the topic of female
same-sex desire remains present if silenced. The girls are under strict
surveillance and are subject to bed checks every night – since no visiting
boyfriends or male orderlies are present after hours, the implication as
to what is being checked for is self-evident. As with the earlier revelation
that Lisa's absence had driven a girl to suicide, what is left unspoken carries great significance.

The topic of Susanna's heterosexual promiscuity (on which her
other doctors dwell obsessively) is never brought up during this initial
consultation with Dr. Wick. Instead, Claymoore's chief proves herself
worthy of the nickname bestowed by her patients ("Dr. Dyke") by immediately honing in on Susanna's developing relationship with Lisa.
"Does it feel bad [to be friends with Lisa]?" "No," Susanna answers. Dr.
Wick goes on, suggestively: "Did you have many girlfriends before you
came here?" In what ascends into an even more loaded monologue, Dr.

Wick corrects a common misconception about the word "ambivalence" that, in the definition she provides, meaningfully establishes Susanna's bi-potential.

> Susanna: I'm ambivalent. In fact that's my new favorite word.
>
> Dr. Wick: Do you know what that means, ambivalence?
>
> Susanna: I don't care.
>
> Dr. Wick: If it's your favorite word, I would've thought you would . . .
>
> Susanna: It *means* I don't care. That's what it means.
>
> Dr. Wick: On the contrary, Susanna. Ambivalence suggests strong feelings in opposition. The prefix, as in "ambidextrous," means "both." The rest of it, in Latin, means "vigor." The word suggests that you are torn . . . between two opposing courses of action.
>
> Susanna: Will I stay or will I go?
>
> Dr. Wick: Am I sane . . . or, am I crazy?
>
> Susanna: Those aren't courses of action.
>
> Dr. Wick: They can be, dear – for some.
>
> Susanna: Well, then – it's the wrong word.
>
> Dr. Wick: No. I think it's perfect.

In suggesting to Susanna that she alone possesses control over her mental status and subsequent destiny, Dr. Wick acknowledges the often arbitrary nature of psychiatric diagnoses that essentialize divisions between sane and insane. Urging Susanna to consider "how much will you indulge your flaws? Are they flaws?," Dr. Wick undermines that which Susanna's other authority figures have consistently maintained, when she suggests that sexual desires and behaviors deemed socially inappropriate may not in fact constitute personal flaws or pathologies. Still another telecast given prominent placement in *Girl, Interrupted*'s story world is the film *The Wizard of Oz* (one patient obsessively rewatches it, reciting the dialogue by heart). As my earlier quotation ("Of course, people do go both ways") indicates and as Alexander Doty has persuasively argued, it is a story pregnant with bisexual meaning.[71] For Susanna, the lesson learned – and, like Dorothy, "she had to learn it for

"Played with dangerous edge and show-stopping verve by
Angelina Jolie. A touching performance by Winona Ryder."

Peter Travers, ROLLING STONE

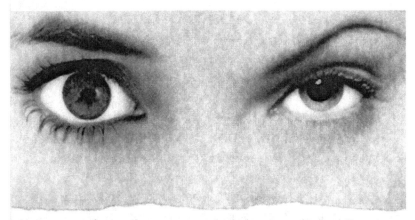

GIRL, INTERRUPTED

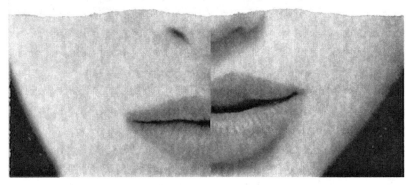

2.9. An homage to *Persona* in *Girl, Interrupted*'s promotional campaign.

herself" – is that her heart's desire is to be found in her own backyard, at Claymoore.

An image prominently displayed in a good deal of the film's marketing depicts Susanna's face overlapping with Lisa's, presumably inspired by *Persona*'s famous shot of its leading women's faces fusing. In *Girl, Interrupted*, the significance of this doubling motif appears related to my (and the film's) point that psychiatric diagnoses pathologize gender and sexuality nonconformity among female adolescents. As noted, the residents at Claymoore are remarkably alike in that gender socialization is the collective origin of their respective conditions.

> Lisa: We are very rare and we are mostly men.
>
> Janet: Lisa thinks she's hot shit cause she's a sociopath.
>
> Cynthia: I'm a sociopath.
>
> Lisa: No, you're a dyke.

Though Lisa's rebuttal here is a sobering indicator of how, in the 1960s, homosexuality and gender nonconformity were treated with institution- alization, her comment also serves to draw a clear line between "sane" and "insane" where it is otherwise blurred – as in Dr. Wick's remark to Susanna that she possesses agency over her mental status, as one instance. The character of Lisa is, in all ways, presented as exceptional – she seems able to surmount gendered norms along with hospital secu- rity and the naggings of conscience. Though the film acknowledges that the institutionalized regulation of psychiatry and sexuality frequently judges mental status in binary terms and according to gendered norms, *Girl, Interrupted* ultimately suggests that those like Lisa are "just plain crazy." When Lisa tells Susanna, "You're a lifer, like me," her comment can again be read bi-suggestively, as an observation that Susanna's "per- verse" sexuality is not curable, that she will disobey Dr. Wick's urgings and give in to her "insanity." The more transparent meaning, of course, is that Lisa recognizes in Susanna the same refusal to accept confor- mity – in sexuality, mental status, or otherwise – that would permit ei- ther their release from Claymoore or their ability to function in the repressive external world. As Lisa says of her own condition, deemed too dangerous to allow her her independence, "It's a gift – it lets you see the truth." Without being too glib about the seriousness of sociopathic behavior and other psychiatric disorders, it seems to me that what the film offers here is a Foucauldian assessment of the ways in which modern discourses around mental status and criminality (as well as sexuality) have been constructed by systems of power and knowledge. "That's why Freud's picture is on every shrink's wall. He created a fuckin' industry. You lie down, confess your secrets, and you're saved," Lisa cynically remarks, in a way that implicates psychiatry with other "value" regimes of capitalism and religion.

Yet the film, and Susanna, eventually take sides against Lisa and her cynical understanding of the psychiatric industry. While not entirely revoking its intimations throughout that the division between "sane" and "crazy" is a construction of a repressive medical and cultural establishment, *Girl, Interrupted* does finally issue its diagnosis on Lisa, voiced through Susanna's final words to her friend: "I'd rather be fucking out there [in the world] than down here with you." Again the wording has suggestive connotations, especially given that Lisa is strapped to her bed as Susanna issues her indictment, continuing on mercilessly: "Your heart is cold. You need this place to feel alive." Read bi-textually, one is left with little recourse but to conclude that upon her departure from Claymoore, Susanna has come to see her relationship with Lisa as perverse. The tone of this closing dialogue is strangely incongruent with the film up to this point, and ultimately does little to dispel the potency of earlier scenes between Susanna and Lisa. This discordant ending strikes me as the type of recuperative resolution necessarily imposed on characters such as Lisa – who may well demonstrate sociopathic tendencies and is indirectly responsible for provoking the suicides of at least two of the female characters. To narratively grant her a clean reprieve would be problematic, clearly. Yet in much the same way as the sexually and criminally deviant is viciously contained or improbably redeemed to (however shakily) restore the status quo, Lisa emerges as the most memorable character – and Jolie as the most arresting presence – in *Girl, Interrupted*. This combustible energy of screen characterization coupled with star persona can overcome narrative attempts to douse its powerfully suggestive effects for alternative readings and spectators.

Just as the love triangle discussed in the previous section invites bi-suggestive eroticism, so does the female institution film by providing an environment for women to consider same-sex relationships more than is possible "on the outside." This bi-suggestive eroticism is further encouraged by such films' female-led ensemble casts, which typically include male characters but nearly always relegate them to marginal roles as curious interlopers (and stand-ins for the audience). Yet not for nothing are these films also known by the moniker popularized by Karen Hollinger, "female friendship films."[72] Perhaps more than in any other realm of bi-suggestive representation, the female institution film occupies a liminal or borderline space that calls for reading bisexually but that is complicated by the friendly affection and supercharged emotiveness shared by its virginal if hormonal female characters and the close quarters in which they live. And yet, given that its protagonists often are adolescents and are frequently under surveillance or even incarcerated, female institution films are often less excessive than most sexploitation in their display of same-sex eroticism. Not surprisingly, critical analyses of these films have echoed this restraint, and much of the cinematic content which I read as having specifically bisexual meaning has been or could also be identified as (proto-)lesbian or, alternatively, "just good friends." But as the next chapter demonstrates, the perennial but newly reinvigorated male buddy film, or bromance, continues to challenge sexual and representational boundaries. To see bisexually requires an understanding that same-sex desire need not be shown onscreen explicitly to register powerfully within the social and erotic imagination.

Males do not represent two discrete populations, heterosexual and homosexual. The world is not to be divided into sheep and goats.

ALFRED C. KINSEY,
Sexual Behavior in the Human Male

THREE

Of Cowboys and Cocksmen: Bisexuality and the Contemporary Hollywood Bromance

ONE OF THE TOP-GROSSING U.S. FILMS OF 2005 . . . CREDITED with transforming the U.S. film industry . . . a queering of Hollywood genre . . . a romance between two all-American dudes . . . I refer not only to *Brokeback Mountain,* but also to 2005's *other* blockbuster male love story: *Wedding Crashers,* which in grossing $285 million worldwide substantially rejuvenated the R-rated comedy and popularized what has come to be called the bromance, by updating and hybridizing the male buddy film and the "comedy of remarriage."[1]

Wedding Crashers is the story of longtime friends Jeremy (Vince Vaughn) and John (Owen Wilson), Washington, D.C., divorce mediators who infiltrate strangers' nuptials to take advantage of the amorous feelings that weddings elicit in female guests. Like *Brokeback Mountain*'s "gay cowboys," *Wedding Crashers*' male duo came branded with a similarly reductive label: "buddies," thus presumed to be straight. Just as *Brokeback Mountain* thwarts efforts to categorize its protagonists monosexually, *Wedding Crashers* makes bisexuality legible by depicting same-sex and opposite-sex couplings as equally indispensable and also (though tacitly) romantically and erotically charged. While Hollywood films still rarely imagine, let alone endorse, a stable bisexual identity or a non-monogamous arrangement, *Brokeback Mountain* and *Wedding Crashers* do both. In putting into question and even rejecting compulsory monosexuality and monogamy, *Wedding Crashers* ultimately endorses a realistically complex conceptualization of sexuality that is queer-friendly, feminist, and sex-positive. In league with these affirmations, *Wedding Crashers* defamiliarizes and thus destabilizes the monolithic "marriage myth" that naturalizes and romanticizes compulsory monogamy, revealing how marriage is institutionalized and commodified through church and state sanctioning, Western cultural imperialism, and what Gayle Rubin terms "the traffic in women" – "a systematic social apparatus which takes up females as raw materials and fashions domesticated women as products."[2]

Brokeback Mountain, itself industry-changing in proving that a same-sex relationship drama was a risk worth taking for its producers and A-list cast, stacked the deck for its success by rendering its queer content "tasteful" to a fault, in the opinion of many critics. This mainstreaming impulse undoubtedly informs the ambiguity I notice in *Brokeback Mountain's* veering from seeing sexuality as constructed and determined by social, historical, and material factors to adopting the essentialist position that "love is a force of nature," as its tagline proclaims. At the textual level, this oscillation results in an indeterminate assignment of sexual identity to both male leads, reminding us of sexuality's complexities and ambiguities. Yet the film's massive promotional campaign (at a cost of $30 million, it was twice as expensive as the film's relatively modest production budget) ultimately reinforced rather than complicated the sexual binary by emphasizing a "love is universal" message that effaced the leading couple's queer specificity even as it claimed that Ennis Del Mar (Heath Ledger) and Jack Twist (Jake Gyllenhaal) are fundamentally gay, ultimately serving not to complicate the sexual binary but to reinforce it. The collusions and compromises, both textual and extratextual, made by *Brokeback Mountain* determined to significant degree the film's success in eliciting sympathy among straight viewers for queers' oppression and the rights of same-sex couples. Nonetheless, *Brokeback Mountain* remains preeminently concerned with how sexual identities are negotiated through emotional alliances and material circumstances – factors that go beyond gendered object choice.

At the outset of this project I had intended to focus solely on representations of *female* bisexuality, which I rationalized with the (it occurs to me now) paradoxical excuses that I needed to maintain a manageable scope of study and that, at least representationally, female bisexuals vastly outnumber male bisexuals. Midway through my undertaking, however, I could not help but notice that one new theatrical release after another was dealing with male bisexuality in ways too intriguing to ignore. Most curious of all was that these films were emanating from what would seem to be the unlikeliest of sources: they were fairly large-budget, avowedly mainstream studio productions that would go on to be bona fide blockbusters.[3] Moreover, given their success, a market niche coalesced around these so-named bromances, the development of which I trace to Hollywood's 2005 releases *Brokeback Mountain, The 40 Year Old Virgin* (Judd Apatow, 2005), and *Wedding Crashers.* While it may seem an odd fit within this threesome, *Brokeback Mountain* of course is a bromance in the literal, unironic sense. Furthermore, despite its relatively restrained production budget and art house veneer, and for all its truly significant homosexual candor, *Brokeback Mountain* is undeniably a commercial mainstream film that toes the homonormative line in its representational politics.[4]

With a few exceptions (*Basic Instinct, The Hunger, Single White Female*), the female bisexual corpus has overwhelmingly comprised highbrow art films and low-budget sexploitation – aesthetically and industrially fertile ground for bisexual spaces. Hence the bisexual representations and meanings that I have been assessing up to now are drawn from films aimed for the most part at marginal audiences of various "queer" breeds of spectators (BGLQT persons, art house patrons, cult film fans). Bisexuality's crossing over to commercial Hollywood productions is significant in several ways: in the shift from art house and exploitation to mainstream modes of sexual representation, in the financial incentives and risks involved in producing more expensive and high-profile films dealing with bisexuality, and in the different audience being targeted and reached. My purpose here, in analyzing three of the biggest box office hits of 2005, is to demonstrate how accustomed we already are to representations of sexuality as irreducible to assignment as *either* heterosexual *or* homosexual. Examining these queer preoccupations in American popular culture against contemporaneous orientations in BLGTQ activism reveals a common trend that suggests the extent of our ongoing cultural disavowal of bisexuality. The past decade's prioritizing of marriage equality risks enabling a "separate but unequal" doctrine (as San Francisco Mayor Gavin Newsom termed civil unions in an appearance on *Charlie Rose*) that sustains otherness, rewards "family values" while punishing sexual "deviants," and ignores the variety of nontraditional households.[5] The rise of the Hollywood bromance coincides with marriage equality advocacy and the reactionary politics mobilized against it and thus suggests mutually informing discourses over the question of marriage in twenty-first-century America. As queer sexualities are increasingly articulated and negotiated through a normalizing model that reinforces monosexuality, monogamy, gender conformity, and the nuclear family, what role does the bromance play?

BEYOND MARRIAGE, GAY OR OTHERWISE

BGLQT political activism in the United States since the turn of the twenty-first century has taken as its principal cause the struggle to achieve those civil and legal rights granted to opposite-sex couples in recognition of the marriage decree, a struggle that in recent years has witnessed both wrenching setbacks and exhilarating victories in two of the nation's most populous states, New York and California. Pragmatists in BGLQT circles argue for prioritizing marriage equality, viewing it as a highly palatable goal that is appealing to liberal voters, and perhaps even capable of rousing sympathy in enough conservative voters to be "winnable" (as evidenced by the Republicans in the New York legislature who voted "yes" on gay marriage). Yet elsewhere marriage equality has proven to be a "co-belligerency issue" that solidifies political alliances among social conservatives who share an aversion to this and other divisive issues (abortion, for instance) and who are willing to show up at the polls in force to vote down what is for most liberal voters not a deciding issue.[6] Alongside this tendency, another element of the marriage equality agenda considered worrisome by some is its ideological and institutional endorsement of marriage itself, viewed as a repressive tool of assimilation that rewards monogamous same-sex couples while stigmatizing singles and the non-monogamous. Moreover, same-sex marriage as a rhetorical and practical concept forces bisexuals, transgenders, and queer-identified individuals to self-define by one's gender or the gender of one's partner (if you have one, or only one), even as resistance to such self-identification is a driving force in claiming these queer identities. There is also an economic argument to be made against prioritizing marriage equality; Lisa Duggan and Richard Kim claim that BGLQT activists also have played into the hands of fiscal conservatives' "small government" agenda by

> push[ing] economic and social responsibility away from employers and government and onto private households. . . . By limiting recognition and benefits to a declining number of married families, marriage advocates are able to appeal to fiscal conservatives who might otherwise be wary of such moral legislation. . . . The "threat" of gay marriage enabled [pro-marriage conservatives] to portray marital households as under assault (from homosexuals and judges) without addressing any of the economic factors that put marital households under stress and without directly attacking any of the related legal and social transformations (no-fault divorce, new reproductive technologies, women in the workplace) that most Americans would be reluctant to reject.[7]

If its reinforcement of conservatism is not reason enough to resist marriage's deeper entrenchment in American society, consider the liability of promoting a strategy that, Ellen Willis points out, "will force homosexuals, as it now forces heterosexuals, to sign on to a particular state-sponsored, religion-based definition of their relationship if they want full rights as parents and members of households."[8] Yet another danger zone in the push for gay marriage is its programmatic reliance on positioning homosexually identified individuals as "born this way," therefore deserving civil rights protection; witness the public outcry over actress Cynthia Nixon's recent comment that her lesbianism was a "choice."[9] Though obviously, and not unproblematically, taking its cue from African Americans' anti-discrimination action, this twenty-first-century move for BGLQT equality works on the same premise as the established medical model at the turn of the twentieth century, which used lab-coated posturing to socially construct and scientifically justify the cultural understanding of homosexuality as the congenital or early childhood "disease" of an isolated few – thereby cementing its control through medicalization, as explored in chapter 2, while relieving the self-proclaimed straight majority of concerns about its own susceptibility.

Revisionist thinking on marriage equality holds that BGLQT activism should downplay "marriage" in favor of "equality," with the goal of framing the issue in a way that allows Americans inclined to oppose gay marriage to understand that they and their loved ones have a stake in broadening the kinds of relationships that can receive legal and social sanction. Conservatives may not *think* they know any queer people personally, but odds are that they count among their familial/social circle some other domestic arrangement(s) that goes governmentally unrecognized. Though it risks effacing queer visibility, however temporarily and provisionally, redefining marriage equality legislation in broader terms would make it relevant and thus appealing to more Americans by recognizing household diversity of all sorts – not just same-sex but opposite-sex nonmarital cohabitation, single parent families, companionate nonconjugal unions, multigenerational households, *and* singles, all of whom are currently denied benefits granted to married opposite-sex couples.[10]

Shoring up the institutionalized heterosexism that sanctifies "traditional marriage" as a smokescreen for state-sanctioned favoring of certain citizens over others is the culturally pervasive myth of "true love." Although "capitalism has almost certainly enabled more people to marry for love than ever before," as Donna Minkowitz reminds us, the marriage myth of which Hollywood is one of the chief purveyors promotes the myth of true love leading to marriage is one of the chief supports of a capitalist social organization that reproduces class and gender stratification.[11] Historian John D'Emilio has demonstrated how modern capitalism's "free-labor system" (however deceptive the term) first made possible a publicly recognizable gay identity, only to find in gays and lesbians the ideal scapegoats to take the blame for capitalism's ills, namely the disintegration of the family.[12] Aggressively promoting traditional marriage while granting same-sex couples such half-measures as civil unions reinforces compulsory monosexuality and encourages BGLQT assimilation only so far as it suits neoliberalism's need to promote "family values" without taking responsibility for compensating what has traditionally been called "women's work"; indeed, the hoopla around gay marriage serves to distract Americans from this continuing devaluation of what is more accurately described today as the unpaid labor of parenting.

Returning to *Brokeback Mountain* and *Wedding Crashers,* how can we explain the success in 2005 of two films that respectively melodramatize and poke fun at the instability of our society's heteromasculine infrastructure, and what are we to make of the textual and extratextual obfuscations complicating any determination of their political stance? *Wedding Crashers* less overtly invoked its connection to contemporary debates over same-sex marriage than did fellow bromance *I Now Pronounce You Chuck & Larry* (Dennis Dugan, 2007), the Adam Sandler–Kevin James vehicle about two male firefighters who get married for the healthcare benefits. Yet neither was *Wedding Crashers* as defensive in its reassurances of the "we're not gay – not that there's anything wrong with that" variety, a form of pseudo-tolerance that *I Now Pronounce You Chuck & Larry* commences with a tagline ("They're straight as can be but don't tell anyone") that reeks of its "don't ask, don't tell"–era ethos of compulsory monosexuality. Even if mainstream BGLQT activists are less complicit in establishing than in maintaining the primacy of the gay marriage debates, that these debates have come to dominate gay rights discourse bears on the genesis and popularity of the bromance. In their engagements with pro-marriage and pro–marriage equality discourses, *Wedding Crashers* and its bromance brethren *The 40 Year Old Virgin, Anchorman: The Legend of Ron Burgundy* (Adam McKay, 2004), *Blades of Glory* (Josh Gordon and Will Speck, 2007), *The Hangover* (Todd Phillips, 2009), *The Hangover Part II* (Todd Phillips, 2011), *I Love You, Man* (John Hamburg, 2009), *Old School* (Todd Phillips, 2003), *Superbad* (Greg Mottola, 2007), *You, Me, and Dupree* (Anthony and Joe Russo, 2006), and many others released in the past decade alternately endorse and contain queer images and attitudes. At its most conservative, the bromance sells marriage at the same time that it works to restrict the definition of marriage and reconcile male buddies to compulsory monosexuality. At its most progressive, the bromance works against the gay marriage movement's reinforcement of sexual binaries. In one way or another, marriage is at the center of cinematic crises of male bonding; the question of marriage is what holds these films together and makes them speak to one another. Certainly that case can be made for *Brokeback Mountain*, which though it qualifies as a bromance was inaccurately labeled "the gay cowboy movie" by the popular media.

THE BISEXUAL SHEPHERD MOVIE

In the deluge of reviews that greeted *Brokeback Mountain*'s U.S. theatrical release in December 2005, it became de rigueur for jaded film critics to point out just how inaccurate it was to refer to the film as the first gay

Western. At that year's Academy Awards ceremony, where *Brokeback Mountain* received several nominations, a montage riffed on the (not so) subtextual moments of cowboy camaraderie in classic Hollywood westerns such as *Red River* (Howard Hawks, 1948) and *Johnny Guitar* (Nicholas Ray, 1954). (Unsurprisingly, Andy Warhol and Paul Morrissey's anything-but-subtextual *Lonesome Cowboys* from 1968 went unmentioned.) Even co-president of Focus Features (which produced *Brokeback Mountain*) James Schamus admitted it was nothing new: "Since all cowboy movies are gay," Schamus said, "I don't see what's so special about that label."[13] What *is* special – that is, unique – about these "pardners" is that they finally are out of the connotative closet, yet with their traditional masculinity intact and embraced by a broad segment of the American audience. Jack and Ennis have far more in common with actual figures of the historical West than with the countless deviants, saintly victims, and witty confidants that historically comprise the majority of queer male characters in mainstream American films – from Peter Lorre's perfumed dandy in *The Maltese Falcon* (John Huston, 1941) and Clifton Webb's snobbish aesthete in *Laura* (Otto Preminger, 1944), to the rough trade in *Cruising* (William Friedkin, 1980) and the doomed martyr in *Philadelphia,* to Rupert Everett's gay best friend who lives to serve Julia Roberts's character in *My Best Friend's Wedding* (P. J. Hogan, 1997) – even if that unshakable code of heteromasculinity, in themselves and their society, proves Jack and Ennis's undoing, and indicates Hollywood's own unshakable code when it comes to male screen heroes who may have sex with one another but are still (whew!) gender-conforming and suitably manly. Much as Hollywood in 1982 dared to represent *Making Love's* (Arthur Hiller, 1982) homosexual couple as "real men" (although the film came affixed with a warning statement to viewers), the queer male character's screen transformation from effeminate to macho threatens to privilege the "manly man" even as the queer male character's contours are reconfigured to accommodate those manly men who love men. Yet make no mistake; that Jack and Ennis have sex – rather than just comparing guns or sharing whiskey – onscreen in multiplexes across the United States is what makes *Brokeback Mountain* groundbreaking, in that the film presented the relationship between the protagonists as undeniably sexual. But most radical of all is *Brokeback Mountain*'s refusal to represent Ennis or Jack as simply monosexual, provoking us to ask how their sexual identities, desires, or behaviors would have been different had they not discovered their attraction in the rarefied utopia atop the eponymous peak in 1963. Against *New York Times* cultural critic Frank Rich's claim (in a column titled, natch, "Two Gay Cowboys Hit a Home Run") that the film "dramatizes homosexuality as an inherent and immutable identity," *Brokeback Mountain* instead attests to how substantially social and material circumstances dictate desire.[14]

Brokeback Mountain's christening as "the gay cowboy movie" is wrong on both counts. As was frequently pointed out in exasperated letters to the editor and other oblivious city folk written by Americans familiar with rural ways, Jack and Ennis are shepherds, hired to watch sheep. Despite carrying a fair amount of jest, the "gay cowboy" moniker also perpetuates an oversight or simplification pertaining to the historical myopia that clouds our conceptions of sexual identity. "You know I ain't queer," Ennis proclaims to Jack following their first tryst, on a moonlit night atop Brokeback. "Neither am I," Jack responds defensively and a bit wearily, as if not for the first time. As George Chauncey and other historians have shown, in the years predating the emergence in Euro-American society of a public gay identity, homosexual acts were rarely perceived as queer when committed "out of necessity" (among isolated male communities such as the military, prison, or the Western frontier). Nor was the "active" (i.e., penetrating) partner likely to consider himself or be considered queer, a label reserved primarily for the "passive" partner and gender nonconformists.[15] Jack and, especially, Ennis are unlikely to have been labeled – much less to have labeled themselves – "gay," because in 1963 use of this label constituted an assignment or acceptance of identity rather than a description of behavior or desire, even more so than it does now.

Even allowing for a substantial degree of historical and cultural variance, I would argue that *Brokeback Mountain* works energetically to establish these men as what we would today call bisexual. How (and how intentionally) does *Brokeback Mountain* arrive at this bisexual space? The relationship between Jack and Ennis clearly is depicted as their deepest and most significant, even as the narrative prevents us from interpreting this prioritization on the basis of either man's preference for members of one sex over another. This implication that same-sex desire could "be-fall" anyone folds into the film's universalist "love is a force of nature" rhetoric, while at the same time suggesting that sexual orientation is continually in flux. Preventing any conclusive sense that Jack and Ennis were "gay all along," *Brokeback Mountain* depicts same-sex love and lust that does not stem from same-sex preference, and that does not preclude opposite-sex attraction.

> If two cowboys, male icons who are 100 percent all-man, can succumb, what chance do I have, half to a quarter of a man, depending on whom I'm with at the time?
>
> LARRY DAVID

Eight years in the making, *Brokeback Mountain*'s journey to the multiplex was reportedly slowed by the skittishness with which studios and actors shied away from signing on to the project. Screenwriting partners Larry McMurtry and Diana Ossana bought the screen rights to author Annie Proulx's short story soon after it was published in the October 13, 1997, issue of the *New Yorker,* but producer Schamus was "trying repeatedly to get a studio to give it the go-ahead, but none of them would . . . [and] no actors would commit," including one who would later go on to star in the film: Jake Gyllenhaal.[16] "At the time, I was a teen, so it wasn't a realistic prospect," is the diplomatic explanation, given in a studio publicity sound bite, for why Gyllenhaal initially passed on the project, though he expressed it more bluntly to the *New York Times:* "I remember going, 'No way, no way. . . . All I'd heard was that it was a gay cowboy movie. I was 16 and couldn't even think about it."[17] A revolving door of potential directors (including Pedro Almodóvar and Gus Van Sant) also came and went, prompting critic B. Ruby Rich to state the following:

> I don't believe they would have ever allowed an openly queer director to make this movie, nor do I believe that actors of this caliber would have signed on. In a long line of ironic outcomes, it took these guys with impeccable heterosexual credentials to make this kind of breakthrough.[18]

The director whom they finally settled on, Ang Lee, possessed an oeuvre replete with characters whose emotional desires run counter to their society's constraints, from *Sense and Sensibility* (1995) to *The Ice Storm*

(1997) to *The Hulk* (2003), and so seemed to offer a queer sensibility of sorts despite his "impeccable heterosexual credentials." Surely it did not hurt that Lee's breakout film, 1993's *The Wedding Banquet,* was a light comedy about a young gay man who fakes marrying a woman to placate his traditional Chinese parents.[19]

Not only in their choice of director did *Brokeback Mountain*'s creators execute elaborate rope tricks designed to lasso mainstream *and* marginal audiences; the film's publicity strategy succeeded in unleashing a opening weekend stampede that was subsequently carried along by word of mouth. Schamus reportedly told Lee early into the film's production schedule that their marketing campaign would target one core audience. "Yes, of course," Lee said. "The gay audience." No, said Schamus, "women."[20] Marketing to women involved poring over posters of "fifty of the most romantic movies ever made, and deliberately choosing to evoke one in particular: *Titanic* (James Cameron, 1997)."[21] The gay audience *was* targeted heavily, but the film aimed at and achieved a far more ambitious reach. *Brokeback Mountain* first opened in coastal urban centers (though not necessarily in gay neighborhoods), relying on word of mouth and critical acclaim to carry it along, and so they did. An illustration that ran in the *New York Times* alongside Frank Rich's aforementioned op-ed, depicting people lining up from all directions outside a cinema located at the intersection of Middle America, referenced the perfect storm of broad audience compatibility and profitability, and only minimal controversy, which greeted *Brokeback Mountain*'s arrival.[22] *Brokeback Mountain*'s official publicity, which relied on euphemistic references to Jack and Ennis, who, "hunger[ing] for something beyond what they can articulate . . . gravitate towards camaraderie and then a deeper intimacy," testifies to its makers' vigorous attempts to be "tasteful" and "universal." What is troubling about this vagueness is that it subtly shifts the source of the "complications" hindering the men's "lifelong connection" from an external to an internal realm.[23] That their hunger goes unsatisfied is likewise attributed to their not having the ability or knowledge to name their desire, rather than to the variety of social factors preventing them from realizing their desire.

3.1. Taking a cue from the highest-grossing love story of all time.

Brokeback Mountain adheres to the generic conventions of melodrama, fittingly the genre of choice for camp appropriation by queer
spectators, who identify with its stock characters (social misfits, star-
crossed lovers), situations (suffering caused by oppressive societal strictures), and structures (social and political problems played out at the
individual level).[24] "Melodrama's promise of universally legible meaning
seems to be particularly compelling in the postmodern era, experienced
by many as desperately in need of some kind of grounding," Lynne Joyrich observes.[25] And so, repeatedly, *Brokeback Mountain* was acclaimed
as a universal love story (as well as a Universal love story). According to
Focus Features co-president David Brooks, "We came up with a strategic
line that we all agreed would infuse everything we did, which was: *Brokeback Mountain* is an epic American love story. . . . Ultimately, the movie
is about love – the love between two people – and we knew that would
appeal."[26] Evoking the film's indebtedness to the melodramatic tradition,
Schamus added, "In many ways, it's a truly grand, old-fashioned movie
about two heroes, fighting against all odds to preserve their love."[27] Suf-

ficiently old-fashioned, in fact, not to put off audiences who feel they might not find anything worth identifying with in a story of two men in love. "It affected me as a woman, and I felt it would surely affect anyone else, no matter what their sexual preference," says Ossana. "The feelings are universal – love, loss, pain, regret."[28] Even Proulx eventually got the message; having said at the time of her story's publication that she was initially inspired by seeing a lone older gentleman whom she describes as "country gay" gazing despondently upon some young guys playing pool in a Wyoming bar, Proulx toed the party line when it came time to do publicity for the film.[29] "This is a deep, permanent human condition, this need to be loved and to love," Proulx said in 2005.[30] Yes, but as Proulx's story and the film adaptation make clear, it is a need that is designated a right of only certain members of the population. Reviews of the film further effaced its queer specificity, occasionally going so far as to claim that gender is an incidental quality of the story, as in critic Kenneth Turan's assertion that "the two lovers here just happen to be men. . . . Theirs is a bond unlike anything either man has known before: not because it's a same-sex relationship but because of the strength of the feelings involved."[31] The extent to which Jack and Ennis's desire for one another is predicated on their respective genders is central to my exploration of the film's bisexual spaces. But what all this talk of *Brokeback Mountain* as a universal love story sweeps under the rug is the very real reason why these men could not be together. The tendency to downplay or efface queer specificity proves a tricky foundation for mapping bisexual space. While universalizing queerness may seem to promote empathy and tolerance, it really makes queerness safe only for straights – as an unthreatening, straight-regulated, commercially viable version of queerness that does nothing to displace the social and cultural centrality of straight privilege.

Brokeback Mountain's impulse to sanitize was as strong as its impulse to universalize, evidenced by the privileging of the romantic over the erotic components of Jack and Ennis's attraction in the film's promotional materials and critical reviews. The press kit is full of treacly proclamations such as "Everyone has a right to love," "If you have love, you should hold on to it," and "a pure and beautiful love story." The mainstream press concurred, for the most part: "No American film before has portrayed love between two men as something this pure and sacred," gushed *Newsweek*.[32] Wrote Stephen Holden in the *New York Times*, "Yet *Brokeback Mountain* is ultimately not about sex (there is very little of it in the film) but about love."[33] "Indeed, what will vex some viewers," wrote Anthony Lane (and including himself, presumably) "is not the act of sodomy but the suggestion that Jack and Ennis are possessed of an innocence, a virginity of spirit."[34] The antithesis of New Queer Cinema's flagrant sexual irreverence, *Brokeback Mountain* alternately was praised for or accused of adopting assimilatory rhetoric similar to that used in pro–marriage equality activism: the right to do as heterosexuals do – marry and procreate. "Biases might disappear when you look into the heart of people," Ang Lee stated. "I hope that's the case with our love story."[35]

> "Are you telling me that John Wayne is a fag?!"
>
> JOE BUCK (Jon Voight), *Midnight Cowboy*

"From the opening scene of semiconscious cruising to the final scene of ultimate bereavement," wrote *Village Voice* film critic J. Hoberman, "Lee's accomplishment is to make this saga a universal romance."[36] As with many critics who reviewed the film, Hoberman's praise for *Brokeback Mountain*'s "universal" qualities winds up foregrounding filmic details that seem distinctly queer. Homosexual codes thoroughly saturate this opening scene: Jack using his pickup's rearview mirror to shave his beard calls to mind Andy Warhol and Chuck Wein's *My Hustler* (1965) as clearly as Ennis's laconic pose and roving eyes immediately conjure *Lonesome Cowboys*. Similarly, the very act of Jack's death that makes Ennis's bereavement necessary is anything *but* universal – or rather, these referents are universal in that they are found the world over, but they are definitively and specifically infused with queer allusion and meaning. *Brokeback Mountain* does not merely appropriate these queer codes, but also references familiar cinematic tropes for depicting homosexuality to straight audiences but reinscribed with a gesture of repudiation. At the close of the men's initial summer idyll, when a pained Ennis breaks down dry heaving in an alleyway following Jack's departure, the scene bears not a trace of the homophobic revulsion and self-hatred that pervades screen history – think of *The Crying Game* and its parody in *Ace Ventura: Pet Detective* (Tom Shadyac, 1994), when Jim Carrey vomits at sickening length after discovering his lady love is a man. *Brokeback Mountain* reverts to some level of heavy-handedness with the invention of a scene not found in Proulx's story, in which Ennis returns to the herd after his first night staying with Jack to find an eviscerated carcass, devoured by a wolf, which foreshadows Ennis's imagined vision of Jack's violent death. Shortly before this encounter, Ennis tells Jack that he is content to stick with eating beans rather than risk their boss finding out that they killed a lamb, although after their rations are lost to a marauding grizzly, Ennis becomes willing to partake. Both decisions to follow one's appetites and break the rules result in a bloodied carcass as a reminder to Ennis of the toll for transgression, and as a reminder to viewers that the homophobic brutality that haunts Ennis threatens only those Jack calls "fellas like me and you." Reminders such as these should rupture any complacency audiences are invited to feel over the universality of this coupling, the threat against which is undeniably predicated on their being queer.

Other additions made in adapting Proulx's story work directly to refortify Ennis's and Jack's red-blooded masculinity, as Anthony Lane points out with his characteristic panache: "*Brokeback Mountain,* for all its delicacy, felt obliged to add a couple of clunky scenes, not in Annie Proulx's original tale, in which Jack rebuked his father-in-law, and Ennis chewed out a pair of apelike bikers. As he stood there, with Fourth of July fireworks flaring behind him, I thought, O.K., we get the point – gay men can be strong Americans, too."[37] It came as little surprise when *Brokeback* publicists used the latter image – Ennis against the emblazoned sky, gazing protectively at his wife and children in the distance (and Jack nowhere to be seen) – to proclaim the film's grosses having surpassed the $100 million mark in a centerfold ad placed in industry trade magazines.

More brazenly still, in the lead-up to the Academy Award nominations, voter-targeted ads billing *Brokeback Mountain* "For Your Consideration" began filling trades, using stills not previously in wide release that were clearly intended to underline the film's "universal" appeal. One prominently employed image depicts Ennis and wife Alma (Michelle Williams) cozied up at the drive-in, while another, even more audacious, stages a scene not actually appearing in the film, in which Jack crouches at wife Lureen's (Anne Hathaway) hospital bedside, their new-born cradled between them.[38] Even among Hollywood's "Gay Mafia" it was deemed a more promising strategy to target Academy voters with fabricated images of heterosexual bliss than to commemorate the film's undeniably central couple – one for whom child-rearing and hospital visitation privileges are far from a birthright.

That Jack and Ennis are behaviorally bisexual is obvious. "Maybe it's only when Jack and Ennis are together that they get to truly be them-selves, but the beauty of Lee's evenhanded vantage point is that he lets us see how relative that kind of truth is," observed GQ reviewer Tom Carson. "Their socially acceptable faces as husbands and fathers aren't just hollow roles they're playing; they're emotionally invested in them too."[39] While the film's marketing campaign universalizes the story out of the realm of identity labels altogether, the film itself takes pains to establish that for neither man is sexuality predicated on gendered object-choice. Fleshing out the female characters that appear as mere sketches in the story allows us, as Frank Rich noted, to "see the cost inflicted on entire families, not just on Jack and Ennis, when gay people must live a lie."[40] It also serves to establish clearly that despite Jack's and (especially) Ennis's bowing to the expectation to acquire wife and kids, neither man is com-pletely living a lie in his marriage to a woman. In an unusual instance of actually naming bisexuality, a critic for the London *Observer* read Ennis's fear of being found out as the impetus for "remain[ing] in a state of denial about his bisexuality."[41] Ennis's eldest daughter's speculation about her father, late in the film, that "Maybe he's not the marrying kind," voices the ambivalence evident throughout in Ennis's characterization, where it is never clear whether his trouble is in forging a same-sex relationship or in forging *any* relationship.

Any specification of Ennis's sexual orientation is complicated early by the addition of a line, not found in Proulx's story, that suggests he is a virgin when he first meets Jack. Trying to explain Pentecostal phi-losophy to Ennis, Jack says, "The world ends and fellas like me and you march off to hell." "Speak for yourself," answers Ennis. "You may be a sinner but I've not yet had the opportunity." Ennis's amiable tone of response, at a point in the film when he still reacts skittishly to Jack's

exploratory advances and would most likely not grasp the finer infer-
ences of "fellas like you and me," implies not only that Ennis is a virgin
but that he has been taught that sex of any kind before marriage is sinful.
Once ensconced as newlyweds, Ennis models relations with Alma by
what he knows: romping with Alma in snow banks as he once had with
Jack by the campfire, draping an arm protectively around her shoulders
at a drive-in movie in a pose reminiscent of his last day atop Brokeback
when he comes up behind Jack "sleeping on yer feet like a horse" and
encircles an arm around his neck. Ennis goes by what he knows in the
bedroom, too; as Proulx describes it in the story, Ennis pleasures Alma
then "rolled her over, [and] did quickly what she hated."[42] The film depicts this scene with greater ambiguity – though Ennis flips Alma in
a rough motion similar to the one he used on Jack in the tent, Lee's
delicacy relegates whatever comes next to offscreen space.[43] Apparently
intent on retaining this ambiguity, a later scene in which Alma resists
lovemaking "without taking no precautions" elects *not* to verbalize what
she is thinking in Proulx's story: "What you like to do don't make too
many babies."[44] By keeping this line unspoken, and by highlighting
the tender intimacy Ennis and Alma share in the early part of their
marriage, the film establishes a connection both emotional and erotic
between the heterosexual couple that thwarts any facile assumptions
that Ennis is "truly" gay.

By the same token, Jack is shown eagerly responding to the sexual
advances of wife-to-be Lureen, in an extended sequence for which there
is no basis in Proulx's story. Approaching a tongue-tied Jack in the same
bar where his offer to buy a drink for a rodeo clown had been met with a
rebuff of suspicion the night before, Lureen asks, "What you waitin' for,
cowboy, a matin' call?"[45] Making Lureen the assertive instigator of their
relationship, and establishing that Jack's hesitation as a suitor extends
only to women, implies that his winding up in the backseat of Lureen's
car shortly thereafter is merely the path of least resistance. Yet, as in both
scenes of Ennis and Alma's lovemaking, this episode is rendered so as to
leave no doubt that Jack is readily receptive to, if somewhat astounded
by, Lureen's advances. "Fast or slow, I like the direction you're going,"
Jack tells Lureen when she pauses after disrobing to inquire whether he
thinks she's "too fast."

Ennis: You and Lureen, it's normal and all?

Jack: Sure.

Ennis: She don't never suspect?

Jack: [*Shakes his head "no."*]

While this exchange would seem to indicate Jack's opposite-sex desire, the dialogue is rendered in a way that makes us unsure whether Jack is answering truthfully. A later scene of the men, now a good deal older, implies that Jack may have been lying then as he does now, boasting to Ennis of his affair with a ranch foreman's wife when what we have seen in a previous episode provides every indication that it is not the garrulous Texas belle but her retiring husband (who tentatively suggests a fishing weekend) with whom Jack is involved. These signs of Jack's sexual preference come tangled in the implication that he is simply more cavalier than Ennis, as suggested by the scene of Jack's procuring a male prostitute in Mexico to sate his hunger for Ennis following the rebuff Jack receives when he shows up unannounced during Ennis's custody weekend with his daughters. That Jack seems only passively responsive to the cautious come-ons of these johns and the roving husbands among his Texas social set suggests he is attempting in the only way he can devise (and ultimately in vain) to recreate the bond he shares with Ennis; these substitute encounters appear to be as unfulfilling as Ennis's self-enforced celibacy back in Wyoming.

Early and overt hints show Jack aware of his desire, namely a close-up on his face as he almost imperceptibly battles not to look at Ennis bathing nearby, and the tenderly proffered rag he holds up to Ennis's head wound (the result of being thrown from his horse) before Ennis gruffly snatches it away.[46] That Jack initiates their lovemaking, makes his living through "fancy" rodeo-ing, plays a submissive role as husband to the business-savvy breadwinner Lureen and with his patronizing father-in-law, and his repeated entreaties to Ennis that they settle down in cozy domesticity all cohere to present Jack as the emotional, feminine partner to the more stoic, traditionally masculine Ennis. Yet in evaluating their relationship according to the terms of the romance narrative, as Richard Schickel noted, "Ennis plays the elusive, more feminine role, and Jack is his determined pursuer."[47] In this way, *Brokeback Mountain* adheres to the convention of most "conversion fantasy films," as James R. Keller categorizes gay romances that establish same-sex couples according to a binary categorization of homosexually inclined desiring subject and heterosexually inclined object of desire. This formation constitutes a paradoxically empowering reversal of the traditional gender binary, writes Keller, because

> the characters coded feminine are more courageous in their willingness to face down public scorn by "coming out" than are the masculine characters who find it easier and more expedient to hide their sexuality, perhaps because they invariably blend in better. The feminized protagonists are the more sexually aggressive (at least in their pursuit of their love interests), while the masculine characters are content to remain the passive objects of admiration.[48]

Following his son's death, Jack's father reveals snidely that Jack was verging on replacing Ennis in his longtime aspiration to set up ranching ("This spring, another fella was going to come up here with him"). The question left hanging – had Jack fallen in love with another, or merely settled on a substitute for Ennis – confines what we can know for certain to their love for one another, keeping their sexual preference undefined but more importantly anchored to individual objects of desire constructed as independent of gender.

The film's complication of Jack and Ennis's sexual orientation (and our understanding of it) was curiously at odds with a promotional campaign that undercut this narrative construction of bisexual space. *Brokeback Mountain*'s cast and filmmakers also conveyed mixed signals in interviews and other publicity, but the aim seemed not to complicate monosexuality but to reinforce it – though depending on the audience being addressed at any given time, the "love is universal" rhetoric was abandoned in favor of alternatively claiming Jack and Ennis as fundamentally straight or gay. "I approached the story believing that these are actually two straight guys who fall in love," Gyllenhaal told *Details* magazine, about which Schamus remarked, "Did he really say that? Well, I suppose movies can be Rorschach tests for all of us, but damn if these characters aren't gay to me."[49] Gyllenhaal's replies to journalists' queries about on-set awkwardness were full of similar reversals. While his press kit sound bite says of working with Ledger, "It was wonderful creating an intimacy with him. He made me feel comfortable," elsewhere he admits to "some anxiety while we did the love scenes, the anxiety of hoping we were doing it the right way, the way people who actually do it, do it. But for me, there was no larger anxiety. 'Of course,' he jokes, 'I probably won't go walking into cowboy bars anytime soon.'"[50] Yet on another occasion Gyllenhaal confessed to *Entertainment Weekly* that in filming Jack's advances on Ennis in the tent scene, "I was super uncomfortable, but I was the one who shouldn't have been."[51] Still elsewhere Gyllenhaal suggests the sex scene was more easily simulated with a man: "Maybe just being straight, well, we didn't have the complication that you usually have when you are working with someone who is female."[52]

As the actor who plays the more gay-inclined or bi-curious of the two characters and the one for whom rumors of homosexuality had already surfaced in the media, Gyllenhaal is not surprisingly also the more vocal defender of his offscreen heterosexuality.[53] Ledger, though proving to be the more taciturn partner offscreen as well, spoke up long enough to express first, in the studio press packet, that "I think Ennis punishes himself over an uncontrollable need – love," then to *Time* magazine, "I don't think Ennis could be labeled as gay. Without Jack Twist, I don't know that he ever would have come out. I think the whole point was that it was two souls that fell in love with each other."[54] For the most part, however, Ledger denied having experienced any discomfort with the role's expectations, telling *Variety,* "After the first take it was over. You're kissing another human being. Get over it. Tell the story. What's the next shot?"[55] To *Newsweek,* Ledger scoffed at suggestions that straight men would find the film alarming. "They don't understand that you are not going to become sexually attracted to men by recognizing the beauty of a love story between two men."[56] Added to this mishmash of statements was a noticeable increase in the amount of tabloid space given over to chronicling Gyllenhaal's on-again, off-again relationship with actress Kirsten Dunst – at the time of the film's release, very much on-again – and even more exaggeratedly to the numerous reports proclaiming that Ledger had impregnated girlfriend Michelle Williams on the set of the film. Finally, and although the often uncontrollable factors influencing the timing of theatrical releases defies any suggestion of purposeful design, it seems something more than coincidental that at the time of its release

Brokeback Mountain's stars were concurrently appearing in other film roles showcasing their leading-man credibility: Gyllenhaal as a brawny (first) Gulf War recruit in *Jarhead* (Sam Mendes, 2005), Ledger as that most legendary of heterosexual lovers in *Casanova* (Lasse Hallström, 2005).

These ambiguities at play throughout textual and extratextual materials alike combine to make *Brokeback Mountain* truly a movie for the masses, in the sense of its being moderately progressive, populist, and politically savvy enough to win votes from everyone except at the furthest margins. As *Esquire* critic Mike D'Angelo observed,

> In a strange and troubling way, it's precisely the gay movie America wants right now, tentatively embraceable even by those threatened or disgusted by the idea of two men getting it on. . . . For all its candor and poignancy, it isn't fundamentally about a gay relationship; it's about the absence of one. Their love affair remains tragically unfulfilled, which is precisely what will make it palatable to the masses. It's a subtly malign form of tolerance.[57]

Setting its story at this point in the past justifies *Brokeback Mountain*'s avoidance of a "happily ever after" endorsement for its same-sex couple. By ending its story in 1983 – the year in which AIDS became a full-blown public reality for the American BGLQT community – *Brokeback Mountain* can issue its warning about the violence inflicted on those who came out in a less tolerant time without having to deal with the contemporary danger involved in staying closeted. In this particular way, *Philadelphia* may be the braver film, in actually daring to address (however mawkishly) the damage that HIV inflicted, and continues to inflict, across queer (and other) communities.

Yet despite being set in the pre-AIDS era, and despite registering its culminating incidence of violence as a figment of Ennis's imagination, *Brokeback Mountain* makes homophobia and hate crimes disturbingly and poignantly visible, and on this count deserves recognition for delivering a politically charged polemic. It is far more open-eyed than its contemporaries, fluffy romantic comedies and network shows such as *Will & Grace* (David Kohan and Max Mutchnick, NBC, 1998–2006) and *Queer Eye for the Straight Guy* (David Collins, Bravo, 2003–2007), set in boys' town bubbles such as West Hollywood and Chelsea. *Brokeback Mountain* may seem tastefully tame in comparison to New Queer Cin-

ema, but it breaks substantial ground in normalizing images of gay male
eroticism in the mainstream, where for too long, Keller notes, "only the
verbal declaration of homosexual orientation is permissible, no overt
demonstrations of desire [are allowed]. . . . Gay men can be seen only
so long as they act straight; they can proclaim their sexuality so long as
they do not act it out."[58]

As has been widely noted, Proulx's story appeared in the *New Yorker*
in October 1997, a year earlier almost to the day and in the same vicinity
of Wyoming as the brutal murder of gay teen Matthew Shepard. Lawyers
for Shepard's assailants mounted a defense that claimed justification
for their crime in an inciting incident that provoked temporary insanity: what they perceived to have been Shepard's sexual advances toward
them. However fabricated and obviously void of justification, this claim
suggests how the principal basis for hate crimes and homophobia has
shifted from identity and potential desire to acts and demonstrated desire. From the military to the clergy to "Must See T V," identifying as gay
and having same-sex desires (whether publicly expressed or privately
harbored) is relatively acceptable, in certain circles even trendy. It is in
acting on those desires – in overtly "flaunting" one's queer sexual desire – that one crosses into terrain deemed unacceptable.

The initial excuse that Ennis gives Jack in rejecting his dream to
settle down together on a ranch is indelibly linked to homophobia – Ennis's fears of retribution in a form as vicious as that meted out to an
older cowboy, the sight of whose mutilated body was forcibly engraved
upon a pre-adolescent Ennis's memory. As he recalls to a disbelieving
Jack, "I wasn't nine years old. My daddy, he made sure me and brother
seen it. Hell for all I know, he done the job." But as the years go by and
Jack raises the option once again, Ennis's rationale becomes one of responsibilities – to his wife and children, and his traditional male duty to
support them in the face of the severely limited economic opportunities available to someone of his education and background. While the
threat of social ostracism and hate crimes in the rural West recedes only
marginally as the years pass, in amplifying the importance of personal
responsibility *Brokeback Mountain* again veers away from acknowledging the queer specificity of its male leads' predicament. Had Jack and
Ennis been a heterosexual couple, their respective entanglements would

be simple enough to manage through divorce (Ennis and Alma's own is presented unceremoniously in the space of a single shot) and the subsequent formation of stepfamilies. Specifically because theirs is a same-sex relationship, even having received a divorce does nothing to free Ennis to pursue his deepest experience of love. The film concentrates its third act around two pivotal sequences that taken together constitute *Brokeback Mountain*'s closest approach to explicit comment on contemporary public discourse surrounding marriage equality legislation. In the first, Ennis visits Jack's parents to offer his condolences and to attempt to carry out Jack's wishes to have his ashes scattered on Brokeback Mountain. Though Jack's father refuses to hand over his son's remains, his more sympathetic wife urges Ennis, "You come back and visit us again," as any mother-in-law might. Despite the scene's clear resonance with the ways that current laws deny same-sex couples the rights granted their opposite-sex counterparts, Proulx claims not to have had the contemporary debate in mind:

> The last thing in the world I'd been thinking about when I wrote the story was gay rights. But the film does something I didn't think about. Here is this poor wretched Ennis at the end and he has absolutely zero rights, he has no rights to claim the ashes of Jack Twist. It's the cold wife and the father who hated him who have those rights. Ennis doesn't even have the right to express his sorrow in public, so that he remains smothered and repressed and buried.[59]

The film makes Proulx's unintentional connection clear-cut by following this moment directly with an extended sequence, not found in Proulx's story, in which Ennis's older daughter arrives at his sparsely furnished trailer home, moored on a lonely windswept lot, to announce her upcoming wedding. This sequence is infused with a tone of sentimental melancholia, but a tinge of burning incredulity (of which he may not even be aware) seems to bubble up beneath Ennis's stoic shell at hearing that two teenagers who have known each other "just about a year" can enter a publicly recognized and legally sanctioned union where even after two decades Ennis and Jake could not. After giving his blessing and seeing his daughter off, Ennis goes to stand before the intertwined shirts, his and Jack's, retrieved surreptitiously from the Twist home and now hanging at eye level. Reaching out to grasp the last tangible artifact he has of his beloved, he speaks the film's last line: "Jack, I swear –."[60] It

is an appeal – albeit made in Hollywood's classic emotionally manipulative style – designed to soften the toughest antagonist to gay marriage,
and the film's effectiveness (in theaters if not always at the polls and in
the courts) makes it difficult to argue with its assimilatory centrism. Yet
the more promisingly progressive tactic taken by *Brokeback Mountain*,
to my mind, is its consistent refusal to toe the line of monosexuality.
In yet another self-congratulatory formulation, *Brokeback Mountain's*
official publicity proclaims it "a love story for this generation."[61] In this
assessment, I agree; though set in the past, *Brokeback Mountain* displays
a quite contemporary understanding of the fluidity that characterizes
human sexuality and the inextricable social factors (both then and now)
that determine sexual relationships.

ISN'T IT BROMANTIC?

Brokeback Mountain's skillful manipulation of the melodramatic tradition was a key element in the success with which the film met the challenge of treating non-normative desire in a mainstream text. Melodrama,
with its capacity to elicit woeful recognition of the injustice of whatever
oppressive social conventions or obstacles prevent our heroes' desires
from being realized, presents those obstacles in terms that are simultaneously universal in their "relatability," but individual in their avoidance of
anything but the mildest indictment of systemic factors. The degree to
which *Wedding Crashers* affirms and advances broader understandings
of sexual desire and subjectivity must be appraised with consideration
of its own lighthearted emotional register and broadly comic cadence,
which provokes a different sense of verisimilitude and viewer response
than *Brokeback Mountain* does. Examining *Wedding Crashers'* development out of one tradition of buddy film and into another reveals a path
of genre transformation from the buddy film's 1960s–1970s tragic mode
to its contemporary comic mode: the bromance.

   If the western is, as J. Hoberman describes it, "the most idyllically
homosocial of modes – and often one concerned with the programmatic
exclusion of women," the male buddy film in its postclassical incarnation
during the 1960s–1970s "American New Wave" clearly carried on the
classical Hollywood western's legacy.[62] Often set in the American West

and updated as a road movie on wheels rather than horseback, the buddy film remained a refuge from encroaching threats to white male privilege, heteromasculinity, and the sanctity of the family associated with the social movements of the time. In their homoeroticism and habitual marginalization of women, the films ranged from relatively benign (*Butch Cassidy and the Sundance Kid* [George Roy Hill, 1969], *California Split* [Robert Altman, 1974], *Easy Rider*) to potentially progressive (*Midnight Cowboy, Thunderbolt & Lightfoot* [Michael Cimino, 1974]), to near hysterical (*Freebie and the Bean, Scarecrow* [Jerry Schatzberg, 1973]). While Thomas Elsaesser sees male buddy films as "reviving the ever-present Huck Finn motif in American culture, about the male couple ganging up to escape civilisation and women," Michael Ryan and Douglas Kellner find in this era's buddy films a particularly acute "expression of a natural homoeroticism which a pervasively heterosexual culture does not permit to flourish but which did get articulated in the liberal climate of the time."[63] The contemporary bromance displays the same nostalgia for adolescence and sexual ambiguity that the New Hollywood buddy film did. In surveying the genre's path of transformation from its 1970s tragic mode to its current comic mode, these readings remain telling for the way the buddy film continues to display sexual ambiguity and nostalgia for adolescence. Despite the shift in tone (from tragic to comic) and moniker (from buddy film to bromance), there remains a pressing need to police the borders dividing the acceptably homosocial from the unacceptably homosexual. It is this middle ground of heteroflexible conceptions of millennial masculinity and gender relations that the bromance models so evocatively.

Targeted at a mainstream audience, *Wedding Crashers* like nearly all buddy films refrains from presenting its male duo's rapport as explicitly erotic, and so my reading of the film's bisexual meanings relies on inexplicit "evidence." Such bi-suggestiveness remains ambiguous in order to maintain the film's appeal to a predominantly straight demographic, though as we have seen, contemporary queer visibility *and* queer consumer dollars entice even commercial Hollywood films to entertain readings beyond the straight and narrow. Comedy offers a particularly conducive vehicle for the articulation of bisexuality, in the way that a comic work is theorized as evoking "that space of freedom between the set rules of society . . . [that] automatically predisposes its audience to enter a state of liminality where the everyday is turned upside down."[64] Liberated from the responsibilities of realism, comedy can venture beyond the confines of everyday conventionality, so as to defamiliarize the compulsory monosexuality that governs our logic of desire.

Wedding Crashers' celebrated eight-minute wedding montage in Act One, an orgiastic paean to casual sex that flows from alcohol-fueled revelry to meaningful gazes, flirtatious dancing, the pretense of "getting to know one another" through exchanges selected from the pickup playbook ("Broken man. Hidden past."), and ultimately climaxing in consummation. Cynthia Fuchs notes the profusion of "psychosexual displays" of "explosive discharge" in the buddy action genre: "Again and again, these movies conclude with the partners triumphantly detonating all villains and nearby vehicles."[65] *Wedding Crashers* orchestrates an analogous display of surging champagne bottles and commingling heterosexual bodies (rather than blasting guns and colliding homosocial bodies), filmed with the same quick cuts and slow-motion that Fuchs describes as "penetration and excess at once, an image 'too much' for standard speed, a release 'too much' for the subsequently depleted partners."[66] With seamless continuity, Jeremy and John sweep women from the dance floor to bare-breasted (in the "Uncorked" unrated DVD version) surrender on bedsheets and victoriously mount their prey. But unlike the action film's final shootout, which offers resolution by means of extreme violence, this "psychosexual display" *introduces* the conflict to be resolved.

As a postcoital Jeremy lies chuckling over another successful subterfuge, John finishes on a different note – or doesn't "finish," for a sudden reservation ("I feel like I don't even know you") causes him to pull away from his latest casual conquest. What type of sexual crisis prompts his hesitation: moralistic concern over promiscuity, an ethical dilemma about their deceptive modus operandi, or waning interest in bedding *women*? Confessing his doubts over a champagne toast at sunrise atop the Lincoln Memorial's steps, John asks Jeremy, "Don't you think we're being . . . irresponsible?" Disparaging their behavior as immature, John diagnoses their crasher mentality as stalled (hetero)sexual maturity, imploring Jeremy to "grow up, Peter Pan." As the one more attached to adolescence (he first appears with a sleeping bag tucked under his arm in preparation for a birthday sleepover at John's), Jeremy clearly is distressed by John's admonition but replies defiantly, "I'm a cocksman!" As Act One closes, the monumental Lincoln gazing reprovingly down on the chastened pair might seem an appeal to honesty, a reminder of the Law of the Father, or even a sly reference to historians' indications that Lincoln himself was slow to accept heterosexuality.

Robin Wood interprets Hollywood's buddies of the 1970s as negotiating their era's changing social mores by exhibiting the collapse of "'normality': heterosexual romance, monogamy, the family. . . . [But male buddies] are also the protagonists of films made within an overwhelmingly patriarchal industry: hence they must finally be definitely separated, preferably by death."[67] In *Wedding Crashers*, no longer is it necessary to separate – let alone kill off – the male duo. Instead, at film's end, Jeremy and John are joined in metaphorical matrimony – a crucial departure that works by incorporating elements of the *female* buddy film and the comedy of remarriage in a maneuver that has come to characterize the bromance. *Wedding Crashers* is effectively a gender-inverted update of 1953's *Gentlemen Prefer Blondes* – the only women-centered outing by Howard Hawks, founding father of the male buddy film and great evader of inquiries about his films' homosexual subtexts.[68] Nevertheless, as Alexander Doty argues, *Gentlemen Prefer Blondes* speaks for itself as a bisexual text by giving "roughly equal emphasis to both same-sex and opposite-sex relationships" and by characterizing its female leads as bisexual because "Lorelei [Marilyn Monroe] and, especially, Dorothy [Jane Russell] aren't like most straight women as they make their relationship with each other the defining center of their lives, but they also aren't like most lesbians as they allow men into their lives as romantic/sexual partners."[69] As Doty goes on to show, dialogue, framing, and performance create and sustain the impression (watched over by a vigilant Production Code) of an erotic/romantic bond between the women that "fosters bisexual spaces and spectator positions."[70]

No more explicit despite the intervening years, *Wedding Crashers* also places equal or greater emphasis on the central same-sex relationship as on the more conventional opposite-sex relationships. Its promotional campaign milked the chemistry between Vaughn and Wilson, downplaying the female love interests, with co-star Rachel McAdams (who plays John's object of affection, Claire) shouldered out of print advertisements. The film's opening sequence, in which Jeremy and John sit cozily framed as a couple, juxtaposes their finish-each-other's-sentences intimacy against the opposite-sex couple bickering through divorce proceedings across a boardroom table's expanse. Within minutes, Jeremy and John effortlessly harmonize a duet of the wedding reception standard "Shout" – like Lorelei and Dorothy, these two make beautiful music together – and *Wedding Crashers* continually highlights Vaughn and Wilson's improvisatory verbal pas de deux. Rather than repeatedly disavowing any hint of "gayness," Jeremy and John eat off one another's plate and link arms to dance the Hora, exhibiting the same "comfort with each other's bodies" that Lucie Arbuthnot and Gail Seneca notice of Lorelei and Dorothy.[71]

Wedding Crashers' potential to critique heteronormativity is again relatable to its roots in the 1970s male buddy film, for what Wood notes the genre's customary absence or insignificance of women implies: "If women can be dispensed with so easily, a great deal else goes with them, including the central supports of and justification for the dominant ideology: marriage, family, home."[72] Whereas twenty-first-century male buddies venture out of the "man cave" long enough to exhibit substantial skirt-chasing stamina, as in the case of ladykillers John and Jeremy, their 1960s–1970s brethren are more skittish when it comes to the female of the species – to a degree that resulted in Hollywood comedy's turn thereafter to the highly libidinal, raunchy "animal comedies" that William Paul charges with perpetrating "the impossibility of [heterosexual] romance" in Hollywood films of the period.[73] In the contemporary bromance, adolescent awkwardness such as that keeping *Superbad*'s pubescent duo from scoring chicks is still seen regularly, and women are just as often relegated to the sidelines, but much to the indignation of bromance critics and some viewers even the slacker-losers end up with the hot girls.[74] *Wedding Crashers* hardly dispenses with women altogether but, like the buddy films Wood observes, it is a male love story at heart: "In all these films the emotional center, the emotional charge, is in the male/male relationship, which is patently what the films are *about*."[75]

Though *Wedding Crashers* revises male buddy film tradition by making its heterosexual romances significant, it does not exhibit from the outset *Gentlemen Prefer Blondes'* bi-philia, of which, Doty notes, "It's never a matter of the woman choosing either men or each other, but of having both women and men available to them."[76] That Jeremy and John face considerable difficulty in maintaining their same-sex bond suggests society's greater acceptance of close relationships between women. Jeremy and John start off as a couple, but (unlike Lorelei and Dorothy) a flawed one – the foundation of their bond and its fulfilling potential is thrown into question by John's crisis of faith in crashing. As their fractiousness escalates, they spend less time together and their once-enlivening riffs give way to a prolonged rift. And so *Wedding Crashers* hybridizes the buddy film with the comedy of remarriage, in which, Stanley Cavell writes, "the drive of its plot is not to get the central pair together, but to get them *back* together, together *again*."[77]

Yet the fictional duo's ease with one another contrasts with the actors' discomfort, on the DVD's audio commentary track, over certain suggestive scenes – most blatantly when John tenderly asks Jeremy, "Can I just say one thing without your getting mad? I love you," and is answered with a sheepish "I love you too."

> Vaughn: [*high-pitched laugh*] Kind of like ruining a nice moment.
>
> Wilson: We were just kind of b.s.'ing. . . . These guys really
> do have this like kinda crazy like friendship.
>
> Vaughn: It really solidifies their friendship but not in a way that's overly sincere.
> You jeopardize what you want – which is [Claire] – to check in and say I appre-
> ciate your staying. It shows that the friendship really is kind of important. . . .
> I think because my mouth is so filled with food, I say "I love you too," it's not
> over the top, it does a lot to go, "Okay, this is a really good friendship."
>
> Wilson: 'Cause you can imagine if you read in the script they argue and then I
> say I love you, I love you too, it'd be like, that stinks, it's not going in, but then
> right just the way you've described it it does work in a kinda funny way where
> you still get the emotion of it.

Their overcompensation continues into the next scene, set aboard a sailboat so "coincidentally" prompting their commentary to turn to discussion about the allure of a *Playboy* cruise ("Deal me in on that," Wilson tells Vaughn). Scrambling to brush away the implications of homosexual desire, these comments relocate to an extratextual space that crucial giveaway found in what Wood calls "surreptitious gay texts," and which is identifiable "not from anything shown to be happening between the men, but, paradoxically, from the insistence of the disclaimers: by finding it necessary to deny the homosexual nature of the central relationship so strenuously, the films actually succeed in drawing attention to its possibility."[78]

Wood further notes the standard presence in male buddy films of "the overt homosexual (invariably either clown or villain) [who] has the function of a[nother] disclaimer – our boys are not like *that*."[79] Enter Todd Cleary (Keir O'Donnell), the gay son tormented by and considered threatening to his prominent political family. Despite relying on stereotypes – Todd is maladjusted and hypersensitive, paints instead of playing football, and makes a predatory pass at Jeremy – *Wedding Crashers* exhibits a measure of queer sensitivity unusual for a mainstream American comedy. Discussing his son's artistic ambitions, Secretary of the Treasury William Cleary (Christopher Walken) derides Todd's conceptual work as "crap," recalling conservative rhetoric condemning queer or otherwise "offensive" art deemed undeserving of public funding and First Amendment protection. Deferential up to now, John politely but firmly reminds the secretary that "some people consider that art." When Jeremy displays similar generosity in noticing Todd's lack of appetite, Todd's explanation ("I don't eat meat or fish") prompts his grandmother to interject "He's a homo" – a non sequitur that mocks the facile maneuver that lumps non-normative identities together. That this and other homophobic outbursts (calling Eleanor Roosevelt a "rug muncher") come from an elderly, loopy character who also verbally abuses the family's Afro-Caribbean servant indicates that such a perspective is archaic and indefensible. Yet whereas Granny openly acknowledges Todd's sexual identity, Secretary Cleary refers to it with euphemistic selfishness ("Polling shows a majority of the American people would ultimately empathize with our situation") or, when confronted with clear evidence of his son's sexual preference, feigns obliviousness. The Cleary clan's public veneer of respectability conceals a decidedly "un-American" family – philandering parents, kinky but straight daughter, gay son, and bigoted grandma – wherein, predictably, only Todd is considered a political threat. Reading Jeremy's friendliness as having "had a moment," Todd pays him a midnight visit and urges him to give in to his desire: "It's okay – I was where you are a year ago." Panicked at hearing someone approaching, Jeremy urges Todd *into the closet,* yet later insists upon commemorating the episode with a fig-leafed portrait by his suitor. Though it may seem merely perfunctory, even cheeky, in its shows of support to gay identity, *Wedding Crashers* stands noticeably apart from its buddy film precursors and mainstream comedy contemporaries in the sympathy it extends Todd, even if he is still relegated to an abject position.

To offer a comparative case, 2005's other R-rated comedy blockbuster, *The 40 Year Old Virgin,* far more luridly portrays the tensions between tolerance and homophobia, in a number of exchanges that call on protagonist Andy (Steve Carrell) to defend his heteromasculinity. Assuming nonchalance, co-worker Jay (Romany Malco) reassures him, "Dude, it's not a big deal. You like to fuck guys. It's cool. I got friends who fuck guys . . . in jail." This pretense of gay acceptance comes couched in an ironic, "not that there's anything wrong with that" register that is ultimately undercut by a series of punchlines that return homosexual behavior to the realm of the desperate and deviant. Unlike the sympathetic Pakistani co-workers who react angrily to their exclusion from a staff party ("What are we, al-Qaeda?"), never does a queer character materialize to confront and undermine the leads' homophobia. Indeed, the film goes out of its way to avoid having even a stereotypical gay character when the domineering female boss (played by out lesbian Jane Lynch) aggressively proposes being Andy's "fuck buddy."

Paranoia over male sexuality continues in the extended "You know how I know that you're gay?" riff between Cal (Seth Rogen) and David (Paul Rudd), whose rejoinders range from the mild "because you like Coldplay" to the unabashed "because your dick tastes like shit," and are amplified by the videogame violence they are inflicting on each other ("I'm ripping your head off. . . . Fuck you!"). That the exchange is voiced by a couple of underachieving slackers, albeit likeably amusing ones, indicates how adroitly the film steers between purporting to be queer-tolerant while still giving homophobia the last laugh. Notably, the gag commences because a recently cuckolded David has sworn off women, to Cal a clear indication that he must be "turning gay" (much like the cliché that women hurt by men turn to lesbianism). That David eventually gets the last word *and* a new girlfriend offers reassurance that celibacy is neither unmanly nor "gay," thereby supporting the film's entreaty to delay sex (preferably until marriage); like Andy, he will find the love of "a good woman" his reward. Likewise, from the opening shot of his considerable morning erection, the film repeatedly emphasizes that although a virgin, Andy has no problems with potency – rather, his delayed deflowering is attributed via flashbacks to adolescent traumas inflicted by a series of callous females.

Returning to *Wedding Crashers,* just as Todd reassures mainstream audience members that "our boys are not like *that,*" *Wedding Crashers* offers a converse figure of excessive heteromasculinity in two-timing misogynist Zach (Bradley Cooper), whose sadistic competitive streak Secretary Cleary fondly excuses as "five generations of Lodge family breeding." A reference at once eugenic and animalistic, this suggestion that Zach's cutthroat brutality could be an inborn rather than an acquired trait – in the secretary's words, "Nature versus nurture, nature always wins" – seems inane next to John's simpler explanation: "I think he's on steroids!" Rather than making "our boys" look comparatively wimpy or effeminate, Zach's testosterone-fueled ferocity reassures viewers that being manly doesn't require sadistic measures, joining with Todd's homosexuality to position John and Jeremy between "pathological" extremes. No unmanly lack of footballing prowess leads to Jeremy's thumping on the field, but rather it is caused by Zach's unbridled aggression in this and another Cleary family tradition: quail-hunting. Jeremy snarkily assesses the "sport" and its rabid practitioners as hypocritical ("Mr. Environmental is also a hunter?" he challenges Zach) and ludicrous ("Why do I have to be in camouflage – so the big bad quail doesn't see me?"). John's game attempt at enthusiasm ("Why can't we hunt something cool like a hawk or an eagle, something with some talons?") is met by Jeremy's sarcastic contempt: "That'd be awesome. Even like a gorilla or a rhinoceros . . . or a fucking human being? That'll get you jacked up!" This mockery of the rugged pursuits associated with Hemingway-esque masculinity is rare in a mainstream American film, especially in being voiced by a straight-

identifying male. "There's something not right about these guys . . . ,"
Zach says, and in what seems like punishment for Jeremy's dismissive
attitude toward homosocial ritual, "accidentally" causes Jeremy to be
shot, in the rear and at close range.

Yet Zach and the crashers employ similar strategies in their pursuit
of women: deception, surveillance, and a bogus "sensitive guy" routine
– Mr. Environmental's stories of rescued sea otters; Jeremy and John's
choked-up remembrances of tragic feats of courage ("We lost a lot of
good men out there"). Jeremy and John's growth relies on their gaining empathy by experiencing sexism from the woman's perspective – for
John, through appreciation of Claire's integrity; for Jeremy, by undergo-
ing the figurative transvestism that Wood finds a necessary component
in evening the inequality of the sexes, which

> can only be resolved when the boundaries of gender construction become so
> blurred that men can move with ease, and without inhibition, into identifica-
> tion with a female position . . . [as] our culture's inherent sexism has always
> encouraged women to understand and accept the "superior" male position, while
> making it unnecessary and even demeaning for men to lower themselves to
> identifying with the female.[80]

Jeremy, the more remorseless crasher, meets his worthy adversary in
the perpetually randy Gloria (Isla Fisher), who administers an overdose
of his own medicine: a torturous stream of sex ("Why don't you go enjoy yourself while I go ice my balls and spit up blood?"). Recounting to
an oblivious John how he was forcibly bound and gagged by Gloria in
preparation for "making all his fantasies come true," Jeremy refers to this
episode as *rape* – striking terminology for a male character describing
a heterosexual encounter (no matter how violent or nonconsensual).
Forced to experience rape as a victim – complete with intimations of
having asked for it and of finding it enjoyable, and with his next-day trau-
matized account falling on deaf ears – Jeremy says, "I felt like Jodie Foster in *The Accused* [Jonathan Kaplan, 1988] last night," a comment that
initially maligns Gloria as a sexual "freak" and does so with *Disclosure*-
style backlash of the "women can be rapists too" variety. But that Jeremy
becomes smitten suggests his pleasure in submission and his respect for
an assertive woman. Initially depicted as a psychotic nymphomaniac
("Never leave me," she warns Jeremy, "because I'll find you"), Gloria

ultimately resists vilification/punishment *and* redemption/domestica-
tion. Ultimately, the man changes to suit *her*, as Jeremy comes to "dig"
her kinky proclivities. "That ain't normal," he confesses to Father O'Neil
(Henry Gibson), "but maybe that's what it takes to make you feel like
you're connected to somebody."

Though they arrive with their own ulterior motives, openly scoping
out contenders, the other female wedding guests who fall for Jeremy and
John's charms are implied dupes rather than partners in a consensual
transaction – easily taken in by tall tales, unwilling to go through with
sex if called by the wrong name. Yet these women also defy the chastity
and sanctity of the marriage myth by asserting their desire – not to be domesticated but to enjoy virtually anonymous sex. When Jeremy proposes
marriage, Gloria interjects with a proposal for group sex, reversing the
typical gender dynamic even if it is still the man who pops the question,
and even if marriage to some degree legitimates their queer desire. Gloria's proposition undercuts the common perception that commitment inevitably leads to vanilla sex, celibacy, and/or adultery, and suggests that
queer desires of some kind may be expressed even within the context
of heterosexual coupling. While she never quite shakes off her reverse-
stereotypical characterization as a straight male's nightmare-turned-
fantasy, Gloria's casual encounter with Jeremy blossoms into a loving
relationship without losing its sexually subversive edge, and therein the
conventional good/bad woman dichotomy is undermined.

In evaluating *Wedding Crashers'* discourse on women, it again proves
illuminating to draw comparison to *The 40 Year Old Virgin* and its own
representation of the "sex-crazed" second sex. Having established that
abstinence *is* safely hetero, sufficiently manly, and to be rewarded in
time, *The 40 Year Old Virgin* goes on to stigmatize casual (read: premarital) sex and to denigrate single women who pursue sexual fulfillment. Whereas Jeremy and Gloria's emotional commitment accommodates their transgressive sexual desires, *The 40 Year Old Virgin* retraces
the same old lines between good women (those fit for marriage) and
the disposable "bitches" and "sluts" targeted for Andy to practice his
flailing moves. After contending with his predatory boss, a bachelorette who drives drunk and vomits on him, and a butch lesbian named
"Gina" (pronounced like the female genitalia), Andy meets an enticing

bookstore employee named Beth (Elizabeth Banks). Accompanying her home, Andy is shocked when Beth "warms up" by masturbating with a shower nozzle. Dismayed, he slinks away and admits to Cal, "That woman scares the shit out of me." The remainder of the film chronicles Andy's lengthy, "pure" courtship with Trish (Catherine Keener), single mom and youthful grandmother (the result of a teenage pregnancy), who finds redemption by waiting, this time, until marriage.

In contrast, *Wedding Crashers* negotiates between the men's emotional allegiance and their respective heterosexual couplings without sacrificing sexual adventure *or* female independence and agency. Noting their historical linkage to the generation following the suffragettes' movement that resulted in women winning the vote in 1920, Cavell finds that classic comedies of remarriage offer "parables of a phase of the development of consciousness at which the struggle is for the reciprocity or equality of consciousness between a woman and a man."[81] *Wedding Crashers* stems from a similarly (third wave) feminist moment when struggles for gender equality have waned in the wake of women's stronger presence in the workforce and greater access (for now anyway) to reproductive freedoms, even as persistent glass ceilings and inequitable salaries send women scrambling for marriage as a way out of professional disappointment. The result is the reinforcement of gender binaries as a generation of American women assured they could "have it all" find themselves stymied by occupational discrimination and an inadequate child care system, yet goaded into marriage and motherhood by domestic benefits and alarmist admonitions that "the clock is ticking."

With the first Cleary wedding off to a predicable start, with John guessing accurately that the reading will come from 1 Corinthians, the bride and groom's having written their own vows to draw on their shared devotion to sailing ("Sailing is like sex to these people," Jeremy tells John) suggests a more progressive pledge to come. The groom's "I, Craig, take you, Christina, to be my wife, my best friend, and my first mate," implies a union based on equality. Yet the bride's reply ("I, Christina, take you, Craig, to be my best friend and my captain") just as quickly restores her to the traditionally inferior role in conjugal duties (of all sorts, given the sailing-sex association). But unlike the similarly themed *My Best Friend's Wedding* (1997), in which Cameron Diaz's character, a budding architect, drops out of the University of Chicago to accompany her sportswriter husband on business trips, *Wedding Crashers* does not endorse the bride's subordination of her professional ambitions but encourages instead our identification with Claire, who audibly conveys disdain by tittering at every sailing metaphor and consequently endears herself to (as cutaway shots reveal) a mesmerized John.

Their ensuing flirtation continues this cynicism, with John exposing the crass commercialism of wedding gift-giving (no less predictable and depersonalized than the Bible readings) by correctly guessing the "useless consumer products" encased within fussy wrapping. Claire disparages the wedding guests as attending only for the privilege of "suckling at the power teat" of her father. John, having just engaged in such toadying himself, offers another rationale, redolent of religious conviction and a far cry from his known motives: "People come to weddings because they want to believe in true love." Claire pushes John to define true love. The definition he provides ("True love is your soul's recognition of its counterpart in another") succeeds in overcoming her skepticism. "Well, it's a little cheesy, but I like it," she concedes. "I saw it on a bumper sticker," he admits. Delivering her bridesmaid's toast a while later, Claire's honest poke at the newlyweds' superficiality receives silent stares until she draws on John's homily in a last ditch rescue that finally earns an approving response – demonstrating just how profoundly the sentimental concept "soul mates" is lodged in our collective consciousness.

Defending her long engagement to Zach on grounds that "We still have a lot that we want to accomplish," Claire's choice of pronoun belies the reality that marriage is predominantly a hindrance on *women's* goals. As the enduring tradition of wives taking their husbands' surnames makes clear, marriage marks a woman's handover from being her father's property to her husband's. Confirming Gayle Rubin's observation that marriage functions as a patriarchal traffic in women, Claire is relegated to an object of political leverage with her father's remark, "Once Claire and Zach tie the knot, two of the great American families, the Clearys and the Lodges, will finally unite."[82] John's sardonic response – "And then you can challenge the Klingons for interstellar domination" – undercuts this upper-crust amassing of influence; that only Claire laughs demonstrates that the power elite's devotion to dominance is no joke. When Zach announces their engagement without ever having proposed, Claire's disempowerment is made shockingly clear. Despite qualms, Claire resolves to marry Zach. "I figure everyone feels that way before they get married," she says. "That's my rationalization and I'm sticking to it." That Claire ultimately breaks tradition by opting out of the arranged marriage designed around the consolidation of power makes for another transgression of heteropatriarchy.

Wedding Crashers takes place in a fantasy version of our nation's capital and its neighboring enclaves of the elite, a milieu that underlines how privilege and power – political, ecclesiastical, patriarchal, socioeconomic, heteronormative – are connected and handed down through generations. The recurring low-angle shots of church steeples, looming alongside the Washington Monument, repeatedly emphasize the twin towers of church and state – presided over by the legacy of two "founding fathers" – in contemporary American ideology. Forgoing the bootstraps defense which typically creates sympathy for characters empowered by wealth and status, Secretary Cleary laments his son's lack of gumption: "Twenty-two years old, the whole world in front of him. Every advantage in life, advantages I never had. Ah, that's not exactly true – he has the same advantages I had, which is a hell of a lot of advantages." Looking the part of all-American WASPs, Jeremy and John assimilate into this world far more smoothly than does Ben Stiller's character in *Meet the Parents* (2000), who endures endless humiliation in pining after his blonde shiksa fiancée before eventually proving worthy of marrying into her tony family. Unlike Stiller's visible ethnic otherness, Jeremy and John's bisexual otherness can be hidden. The crashing metaphor analogizes their talent for blending into so-called "bisexual privilege" even as it allows them to penetrate this privileged sphere, showing how permeable are its barriers to those with the appropriate look and deportment. Moreover, that this wedding is interchangeable with the previous Jewish, Italian, Indian, and Chinese ceremonies (the same church standing in for synagogue, cathedral, and Hindu and Buddhist temples) suggests the diluted cultural specificity that Western cultural imperialism has wrought and reveals the marriage myth's universal sway as an ideological tool of heteronormativity. What cultural markers are on display are superficial, stereotypical trappings such as

costumes, songs, and cuisine. "They'll have great tempura!" John predicts of a Japanese wedding.

In joining contentious couples together in amicable divorce, Jeremy
and John reverse the priest's role and debunk the marriage myth as a
reversible, property-based legal contract. "The real enemy here is the
institution of marriage," Jeremy proclaims. "It's not realistic, it's crazy!"
Divorce is the common-sense solution, and their greatest selling point is
the freedom it offers for sexual adventure ("Get out there and get some
strange ass!"). Their mediation tactic succeeds by reminding estranged
couples of the "good times," namely the wedding, in such a way that returns marriage to the realm of romance even while crashing all it holds
sacred by boiling it down to pop standards (the aforementioned "Shout")
and crab cakes. As the life of the party, Jeremy and John are indefati-
gable envoys for these ritualized nuptials, but their desanctification of
holy matrimony through deceitful procurement of casual sex and by
professionally greasing the wheels of divorce proceedings unleashes a
disruptive force onto compulsory monogamy just as bisexuality does. To
"mediate," according to the *Oxford English Dictionary,* is to "try to settle
a dispute between two other parties."[83] Bisexuality works as a negotiator
between (or beyond) heterosexuality and homosexuality, acknowledging the fluidity and complexity of desire and so destabilizing the rigid
binary that polices it. As metaphorical mediators, Jeremy and John practice the same sexual realism that they, as literal mediators, persuade their
clients to embrace.

Zach's "outing" Jeremy and John as wedding crashers falsely mas-
querading as brothers, followed by Todd's accusation that "Jeremy made
a pass at me," analogizes their ruse to gay partners passing as straight.
Questioning John's culpability, Claire demands, "Is it true? It's a yes or
no question." John's equivocal reply, "Yes – with shades of gray," alludes
to his crisis of conscience and sincere feelings for her, but also to his
refusal to concede that his "behavior" with Jeremy is worthy of guilt, or
that sexuality is reducible to an either/or response. Nonetheless the boys
are expelled from the Cleary compound, with Jeremy hauling Todd's
portrait along as if burdened with a brand of their (sexual) dishonor.
With opposite-sex and same-sex couplings continuing to mirror one
another, Claire's banishment of John is followed by his breaking off his

relationship with Jeremy upon discovering his friend in flagrante delicto with Gloria – another in Jeremy's ongoing efforts to hide his heterosexual activities from view. (Jeremy previously struggled to remain inconspicuous while receiving a hand job under the dinner table, endured a fatherly chat while naked and tied to bedposts, and similar sticky situations.) He "didn't know how to tell" John, Jeremy apologizes. "I'm sorry you had to find out that way." The analogy in this scene to the discovery of adultery again sexualizes the men's relationship, as does the subsequent heartbreak montage with its melancholy ballad and scenes of romantic loss (watching the same televised ball game across the divider of their respective apartments).[84]

Rebuffing Jeremy's attempts at reconciliation, John hunts up a new male companion to make Jeremy jealous ("He's a great guy. We've been having a ball together"). Like "flaming" Todd and meathead Zach, the eleventh-hour appearance of witless womanizer Chazz (Will Ferrell) offers one last reassurance that "our boys are not like *that*." This middle-aged man-child embodies all the elements of the Peter Pan syndrome: he still lives with his mother, watches cartoons, and jeers at the news of Jeremy's engagement ("What an idiot, what a loser! Good – more for me and you"). On cue, a gorgeous woman descends from an upstairs bedroom and bids Chazz a sensuous farewell. "I'm just living the dream," Chazz preens. So implausible is it that Chazz's charmlessness gets results that he remains as pathetic as he initially appears. *Wedding Crashers'* penultimate scene shows Chazz with a woman improbably draped on each arm, purposefully catching Todd's eye to gesture lewdly. Needing to prove his straightness in the eyes of other men by objectifying women, he instead provokes the exact thing the gesture was designed to prevent: a homosexual come-on by Todd. Though this last sight of Todd keeps him pitiable and alone in a manner that is hardly queer-affirming, the moment seems designed primarily to render Chazz the more abject, with the suggestion that his macho swagger is but the overcompensation of a closet case.

Jeremy and John's reconciliation amid the merriment of their double wedding to the Cleary sisters again recalls *Gentlemen Prefer Blondes,* in which Lorelei and Dorothy marry their rich man and poor man respectively and also, symbolically, each other – undermining church-and-state

consecration of heteronormativity, as Doty observes: "The double-dou-
ble nature of the wedding (men marrying women, women "marrying"
women) makes it no 'normal' ceremony."[85] *Wedding Crashers* concludes
similarly, with men marrying women and men "marrying" men. John arrives in medias res at Jeremy and Gloria's wedding just as Father O'Neil
intones, "While each man thinks he knows love, love we have learned is
a mystery." First glimpsed peering through a chapel window in homage
to *The Graduate* (Mike Nichols, 1967), John arrives not to prevent but to
join the proceedings as Jeremy's best man – in both senses. John (rather
than the bride) is seen advancing down the aisle to come face-to-face
with Jeremy, take his hand, and speak lines of devotion. Predictably,
Vince Vaughn, on the actors' DVD commentary, goes into overdrive to
justify this reaffirmation of vows: "It's a real guy thing too where it's like,
that's enough, you don't have to talk about it a lot. You don't want to." As
if to signify this overcoming of religious opposition to same-sex unions,
John takes up a position at the altar that obscures a crucifix previously
visible. As the scene progresses, its shot–reverse-shot construction keeps
Jeremy and John tightly framed and without any reassuring female presence. Instead it is Todd who is positioned between the men as they recite
their "vows."

Once reconciled and metaphorically remarried, John moves to Jeremy's side in support of the conventional nuptials taking place and, facing
Claire, declares his love in a stage whisper that disrupts the solemnity of
the proceedings by refusing to yield the floor to the priest – never heard
to utter the all-important "I now pronounce you man and wife." Neither
do we see Secretary Cleary engage in the traditional giving of the bride.
When commanded by Zach to intervene, Cleary refuses to exert patriarchal authority, telling Claire, "It's up to you." Whereas earlier John issued
his own command ("You can't marry [Zach]!"), now he acknowledges
Claire's agency and professional ambition: "I'm not asking you to marry
me; I'm just asking you not to marry him." Doty notices that *Gentlemen
Prefer Blondes'* wedding scene "connects male-female and female-female
couples to each other rather than separating them into two opposite sex
couples," and *Wedding Crashers* employs similarly inclusive framing at
this moment.[86] Over John's right shoulder, Jeremy holds Gloria's hand;
over his left stands Todd. Having embraced his bisexual desire and now

offering a nontraditional proposal, John is not just in between the (queer) heterosexual couple and the gay character, but joins the two together.

The four newlyweds speeding into the sunset may appear to capitulate to conventional marriage rhetoric as well as Hollywood formula, but this queer wedding affirms female independence and partnerships between same- and differently gendered individuals. John and Jeremy continue crashing (with a man still at the wheel), but now Claire sets the agenda, consenting to crash a wedding-in-progress and even concocting their sham identities. No longer an exclusively male domain, the previous driving forces of female objectification and sexual conquest take a back seat to the subversive – if celebratory – transgression of wedding ritual by this newly formed nontraditional household. Modernizing the comedy of remarriage by refusing to curb liberated women's (professional and sexual) independence, *Wedding Crashers'* genre revisionism moreover undermines the male buddy film's work to reaffirm heteromasculinity; these male buddies work out their attraction neither by retreating into overdetermined heterosexual couplings nor with explosive "psychosexual displays." Jeremy coaxes John into reaffirming their relationship and accepting his crasher identity, metaphorically translated as affirmation of bisexuality. John convinces Jeremy to convert bisexual desire into something less irresponsible and concealed. They each find love with an unconventional "good woman," but not at the cost of their own relationship – they'll even be honeymooning together. Borderline assimilatory in its utopian "marriage for everyone!" plea, *Wedding Crashers* revises rather than rejects overall the marriage institution, yet dares to visualize a bisexual, feminist, sex-positive, nontraditional household version of "happily ever after."

Again comparison can be made to *The 40 Year Old Virgin*, which ends with the eponymous hero and his "good woman," blessed by state and church decree, finally free to go forth and (presumably) procreate. In the absurd end credits sequence that follows, Andy's orgasmic nirvana is conveyed via the classical Hollywood device of a musical number, with the cast appearing in 1960s regalia to perform "The Age of Aquarius" from the musical *Hair*. This use of the familiar hippie anthem to free love strikes a thoroughly dissonant note, ridiculing a bygone era that challenged (and came closest to casting off) restrictive sexual mores yet exploiting its allure in promising sexual paradise to those who wait for marriage. Though *Wedding Crashers'* reverential final shot of the Washington Monument is not so obviously suffused with phallic connotation as was Alfred Hitchcock's choice to send a train hurtling through a tunnel in the last shot of *North by Northwest* (1959), it remains unclear whether the monument's looming large is intended ironically. It may well constitute *Wedding Crashers'* unconscious impulse to reassure itself and its target mainstream audience of heteropatriarchy's enduring potency; then again, sometimes a cigar is just a cigar.

FROM THE "PATHOS OF FAILURE" TO "JUST FOR LAUGHS"

In what we might regard as a foreshadowing of the bromance, a 1978 *National Lampoon* parody ad sent up then-current football-themed buddy movie *Semi-Tough* (Michael Ritchie, 1977) by depicting its stars Burt Reynolds and Kris Kristofferson holding hands in promotion for a film titled *Semi-Sweet*. A quarter-century on, the term and the phenomenon of the "bromance" has gained popular cachet with audiences (my students unfailingly register my meaning when I refer to it), even as it remains virtually unaddressed by media scholars despite its visibility and clear investment in mediating among contemporary masculinities and male same-sex relationships. *Wedding Crashers* still serves as the genre's stud horse, though three figures not involved directly in that film have emerged as most (ir)responsible for its contemporary brethren of relatively low-cost, high-earning (albeit not particularly merchandisable) bromances. Director Todd Phillips directed *The Hangover* and its sequel, *Old School, Road Trip* (2000), and *Starsky & Hutch* (2004), which also starred Vince Vaughn and Owen Wilson. Adam McKay, along with his creative partner the comedian Will Ferrell, is responsible for *Anchorman, Step Brothers* (2008), and *Talladega Nights: The Ballad of Ricky Bobby* (2006). Easily the best known of the bromance auteurs is Judd Apatow, the much-feted director of *The 40 Year Old Virgin* and *Knocked Up* (2007), and producer of *Forgetting Sarah Marshall* (Nicholas Stoller, 2008) and *Superbad*.[87]

When a full-on Hollywood parody of NASCAR racing and Southern manhood ends, as *Talladega Nights* does, with two men (Will Ferrell and

3.2. Will Ferrell and Sacha Baron Cohen's climactic embrace on a NASCAR finish line in *Talladega Nights*.

Sacha Baron Cohen at that) locking lips for an extended amount of time in front of a stadium of cheering fans (with an encore performance at the MTV Movie Awards, after winning the award for Best Kiss), it might appear that contemporary Hollywood filmmakers and their audience have grown more comfortable with the sight of homoeroticism. Or is it simply comfort with the *sight gag* of homoeroticism? After all, Baron Cohen's character is a walking stereotype of the effeminate French fop, and the clinch between the men, while certainly played as celebratory rather than predatory (Ferrell's good-ol'-boy character initiates), could never be mistaken for trying to convince us that these men are actually falling for one another. The performances, framing, and general tone all work against its being taken as a truly romantic (or even erotic) moment, and toward its serving as an instance of conspiratorial irony between text and viewer.

A similar bait-and-switch of tease and disavowal is used to romanticize the relationship between the cop duo in *Starsky & Hutch*. As Hutch (Owen Wilson) croons "Don't Give Up On Us, Baby" while strumming his guitar, a shot–reverse-shot structure has him serenading a coked-up Starsky (Ben Stiller) as the two stare soulfully into one another's eyes, while the two women they are ostensibly double-dating are cut out of frame (and mind) completely. Neither subconscious nor subtextual, the homoeroticism of this scene is meant to be noticeable and is even endorsed, albeit within a fantasy context that, in order to include Hutch, demands that Starsky's admission that "I've always had a thing for blondes" predilection be drug-induced.

Here and in *Dude, Where's My Car?* (Danny Leiner, 2000), *In & Out* (Frank Oz, 1997), and *Pineapple Express* (David Gordon Green, 2008), leading men kissing and groping one another seems merely one more way to top all of the outrageous transgressions and gross-out moments that have come before – the latest provocation in a trend that started fifteen years ago with Ben Stiller getting his penis caught in a zipper and his bodily fluids used for hair gel in *There's Something About Mary* (Bobby and Peter Farrelly, 1998). By 2012, it's a phenomenon viewable on American screens almost weekly courtesy of *Saturday Night Live,* which in 2009 aired a parody trailer for a movie called *The Fast and the Bi-Curious* ("Just like the Vin Diesel version, but slightly gayer"). The bromance recasts the American male as more heteroflexible, yet employs a strategy of containment designed to defuse any threat to heteromasculinity by presenting it as intended just for laughs, in fulfillment of what Dennis Bingham observes is "the gentling of white masculinity [as] an apparent strategy for holding on to power during shifting times."[88] But granting that comically de-eroticizing male same-sex desire defuses its threat, it must also act to familiarize "man love," as the politics of homonormativity demonstrate.

Foregrounding the unspoken, unacted-upon homoerotic (or homosocial) desire between certain couples pushes one to consider how these relationships would work differently if not governed by a monosexual logic of desire. The recent romantic comedy and girl buddy film *Bride Wars* (Gary Winick, 2009) gives us some idea of how deeply loving female friendship can be, even as the film itself models heterosexual ritual – the very thing that leads best pals Liv (Kate Hudson) and Emma (Anne Hathaway), first seen as young girls dressed up in gown and tux, respectively, to rehearse their future weddings, to devolve first into "frenemies" then into something far less impassioned: the "(just) good friends" they become after their marriages to men. Only barely and not nearly as seriously interested in considering how heterosexual marriage breaks apart female friendships as are the women-scripted and/or -directed films *Bridesmaids* (Paul Feig, 2011), *Girlfriends* (Claudia Weill, 1978), *Romy and Michele's High School Reunion* (David Mirkin, 1997), and *Walking and Talking* (Nicole Holofcener, 1996), *Bride Wars* pits women against one another as an effect of feeding the chick-flick quota and the wedding industrial complex. Yet there is quite clearly something queer here, in the way these women participate in a shared lifelong fantasy in which the role of male love interests is beside the point as far as the brides, the movie, and we the viewers are concerned. This is not to devalue friendship or to insist that all emotionally intimate relationships do or should contain an erotic element, but rather to point out that another missed moment lies in presumptively dividing the heterosexual from the homosexual, and the homosexual from the homosocial.

For the real trauma being dramatized here is the rift caused to female relationships by heteronormative conformity, and the real drama hinges not on getting the women down the aisle but rather on getting them "back together, together again," even if this happy ending has a bittersweet tinge of defeat.[89] As in *Superbad*'s conclusion, in which following a night-long demonstration of their love and commitment with heroic feats and tender confessions (including an unprecedentedly unironic exchange of "I love yous"), teenage best friends Evan (Michael Cera) and Seth (Jonah Hill) part ways, we are left with a melancholy certainty that both couples' intimacy will fade away in the transition to marriage and what is dubiously deemed sexual "maturity." Much more typical of the recent resurgence in buddy comedy, the male-male configuration noticeably remains safely rooted in the comic vein, even if it occasionally slides toward the tragicomic in these wistful realizations that heterosexual coupling necessitates same-sex uncoupling. In *I Love You, Man,* the crucial issue is not that newly engaged Peter (Paul Rudd) needs a guy friend to serve as best man at his wedding ceremony, but that marriage is an emasculating institution and that he needs a male friend to survive it without becoming feminized. Whereas in *Wedding Crashers* marriage harmoniously coexists with rather than displacing male friendship, in *I Love You, Man* male friendship is a necessary defense against the feminization connected to marriage. But quite unlike the melodramatic tone that typifies female-friendship films such as *Fried Green Tomatoes*, *Heavenly Creatures* (Peter Jackson, 1994), and most of those discussed in chapter 2, male friendship (on- and offscreen) resists emotive excess in favor of the safe distancing that comedy allows. Despite its enforced lightheartedness and irony, the bromance's happy ending is often a conflicted one even when the friendship vows are renewed. What I have been calling an updated comedy of remarriage may also be viewed as an uncoupling comedy, in the sense that the uncoupling happens between two men forced to adapt their relationship with one another in the face of encroaching compulsory monosexuality and compulsory monogamy. Theirs is the central emotional bond of their lives, one that must be negotiated, fought over, fought for, saved, but there is at best the possibility of a compromise: saving *friend*ship.

To conclude, I will explore an outgrowth of the bromance that offers the potential for enunciating male same-sex desire in a way both comic and dramatic, while also (crucially) realistic. "Mumblecore" is the name coined for and applied half-sarcastically to a highly naturalistic, DIY style of millennial filmmaking that occupies an industry niche several commercial notches below the relatively big-budget brigade of Hollywood bromances discussed here, even as it shares a similar structure of improvisational comedy crafted by coteries of performers and (mostly) male "auteurs." Two such films that appeared at the start and end of the twenty-first century's first decade have special resonance for my discussion of the bromance. *Chuck & Buck* (Miguel Arteta, 2000) and *Humpday* (Lynn Shelton, 2009) both tell bittersweet but unsentimental stories of male same-sex relationships that first impinge on then ultimately adapt to heterosexual couplings. Both films are about once-inseparable male friends who are reunited after a significant period of time, during which one of the men has formed a committed relationship with a woman.

In a portrayal that provoked allegations of offensive gay stereotyping, the unmarried Buck (Mike White) of *Chuck & Buck* has become an emotionally stunted man-child, linked in oblique terms to his curtailed youthful sexual experimentations with the soon-to-be-married Chuck (Chris Weitz). Although *Chuck & Buck* was released a half-decade before mumblecore was named and so serves more as a prototype of the genre, it presaged mumblecore's aim to represent sexuality authentically, provocatively, and (for many) cringingly, in "dar[ing] to suggest that many 'straight' men have had same-sex relationships in their past."[90] For *Humpday*'s less abject but comparably thwarted man-child Andrew (Joshua Leonard) and his childhood buddy Ben (Mark Duplass), no such past intimacy is revealed. But in twin acts of desperation and defiance, the two concoct a way to justify their respective self-identities, both of which are thrown into crisis when adventurous Andrew suddenly reappears seeking respite from his nomadic existence amid Ben's buttoned-down life and comfortable marriage. One needing to justify his unbridled existence and the other chafing at the responsibilities and monotony of his own, the guys get inebriated at a bohemian artists' party and challenge each other to collaborate on a surefire competition winner for a local amateur porn festival. Having sworn to have sex on camera, as the day of the shoot approaches they act increasingly anxious yet resolutely determined not to back down.

Humpday takes the bromantic theme of dude-on-dude love and soberly sizes it up to consider what gets lost when heteronormativity (not women, as is often and unfairly perceived in cultural discourse) divides friendships between men. The impetus for *Humpday* was "simply a curiosity about why so many straight men fear gay sex," explains writer-director Shelton, who is married to a man but describes herself as having "definite bisexual leanings." "Even if they think of themselves as really progressive and open-minded, and they don't care if the rest of the world is gay," she says, "it's very important that everybody knows that they are straight and that they themselves can be assured that they are straight."[91] As sex advice columnist Dan Savage remarked of Shelton, "She's really calling the bluff of the Apatows of the world. How far can you go with the 'I love you, man' stuff and still be straight guys? And Lynn is saying you can go all the way."[92] *Humpday*'s sexual politics inspired vigorous debate among critics, some of who praised the film as "widen[ing] the definition of straightness" while still "challeng[ing] homophobic fears that somehow people can be converted into becoming gay."[93] Others felt it avoided any genuine exploration of homosexuality by depicting Ben and Andrew "as blobs of flesh with hairy parts but without the tiniest suggestion of latent heat," and by being "less about the blurring boundaries of male friendship than an examination of a classic alpha-male power struggle."[94]

In the two scenes from *Humpday* that rattle heteronormativity's cage most vigorously, Andrew's broad-minded pose is shaken during a threesome with a lesbian couple who insist on using a dildo, while Ben confesses to having had a crush on a male video store employee. That neither scene is played for laughs constitutes *Humpday*'s clearest departure from the bromance. What happens when Ben and Andrew finally face one another, camera running, belongs among the most serious treatment given to "straight" men exploring their sexuality that I can recall seeing in American film (*Chuck & Buck* and *The Daytrippers* [Greg Mottola, 1996] are others), even if the men (and the film) ultimately decide to go no further than do Holden and Banky in *Chasing Amy*. Two straight-identified men kissing one another on the lips without its being staged as simply a comic moment is a rare sight; while a far greater degree of sexual intimacy is implied between the questioning male couples of *Chuck & Buck* and *The Daytrippers*, it is kept offscreen. Ever the sexual iconoclast, Bernardo Bertolucci dares to display two bisexual men's sexual explorations with one another in *The Dreamers* (2003), but that film's overblown tone and rehashing of crude tropes relating bisexuality to incest and decadence make it difficult to consider as a mature, nonjudgmental representation.

Returning to *Humpday*, what occasionally gets lost in the debate over its same-sex grappling is the importance of the heterosexuality on display as well, namely in its honest depiction of longtime couples' struggle to maintain an active, passionate sex life in balance with everyday obligations and desires. Perhaps not so surprising given Shelton's authorship, the generous treatment given the role of Ben's wife Anna (Alycia Delmore) sharply departs from the bromance's handling of womenfolk, who exist nearly exclusively as hindrances to males' bonding and fun. Anna is hardly supportive of the guys' scheme to shoot a porno, but she is neither pushover nor shrew. As the most grounded and self-knowing of the trio, she is realistically perturbed but at the same time committed to (understanding, supporting, and loving) Ben as well as respectful and encouraging of his and Andrew's friendship. Anna offers Ben the steadiness and patience that gives him ballast without being his savior or safe haven, and Anna's own growth is privileged as well as predicated on enabling the men to take responsibility for themselves. Moreover, when Anna confesses to her own momentary dalliance, she uses gender-

3.3. *Humpday*'s Ben (Mark Duplass) and Andrew (Joshua Leonard) debate becoming something more than buddies.

unspecific terms that leave it unclear – and irrelevant – whether it was with a man or woman.

Both *Chuck & Buck* and *Humpday* end according to the conventional bromance formula, with male friendship refortified but reassuringly subordinated to heterosexual marriage. While there is no suggestion that the just-married Chuck or *Humpday*'s best dudes will alter their sexual orientations or behaviors, the "queer threat" has been neither violently contained, nor cathartically released, nor laughed off. Moreover, both films' figurative remarriages between male friends are accomplished not by closing women out, but by each man's opening up to a woman about his relationships with men and accepting women's support in facing up to and ultimately embracing those relationships. Having the premise if not the tone to justify its marketing misfire as an Apatow-style bromance, the woman-directed *Humpday* attracted only a modest audience.[95] As much as the Hollywood bromance is still kicking girls out of the clubhouse and snickering over gay jokes, if *Humpday* is any indication, at heart it may sincerely wish to grow up.

Alice (Leisha Hailey): I'm looking for the same qualities in a man as I am in a woman.

Dana (Erin Daniels): Big tits!

THE L WORD ("Pilot," 1/18/2004)

FOUR

Bisexuality on the Boob Tube

AS THE FLIPPANCY OF THIS CHAPTER'S NAMING AND EPIGRAPH
suggest, the vast majority of representations of bisexuality in television
involve femme women, with the bi-suggestive character or narrative
inevitably reconsigned to monosexual logic – if not immediately (as
with Dana's retort above) then soon thereafter. As a number of lucid if
lesbian-centric readings have pointed out, televisual representations of
non-monosexuality historically have featured sensationalized forays
into "lady love" sparked by the short-term appearance of an alluring
temptress timed to coincide with network sweeps periods or as a last-
ditch effort to revive flagging ratings. These "very special episodes" (as
networks are known to bill them) feature visits by characters established
to be "real" lesbians, thus serving, as Sasha Torres argues about their
frequency in the single-woman sitcom, to "ease the ideological threat of
such 'feminist' programs by localizing the homosexuality which might
otherwise pervade these homosocial spaces."[1] But rather than fully re-
surveying that history here, I wish to consider the rich (though rarely
realized) potential of serial television's extended narrative format to
create spaces for representing sexual fluidity, and to consider what's
happening lately – by asking how and to what degree representations of
alternative sexualities escape the constraints of bisexual disavowal and
compulsory monosexuality in contemporary English-language serial
television.

Where the default-to-status-quo structure of episodic television
and the contained temporality of feature films create a pressure to resolve questions of sexuality, the narrative open-endedness and expanded

time-frame that characterize serial television drama offer a particularly promising site for mounting long-range and multifaceted explorations into bisexual characters' identities and experiences. Television narrative encourages bisexual representation by permitting it to unfold over time, necessary for the accumulation of experiences that renders bisexuality not practically *viable* – for any individual is potentially bisexual, no matter his or her behaviors to date – but rather representationally *legible*. But while it has become commonplace for television relationship dramas to introduce female same-sex couples, this potential for bisexual story arcs and character development has in practice been stymied by the predilection of TV characters to undergo radical personality tranformations from one season to the next – or even one episode to the next, as in the case of nighttime teen soap *The O.C.* (Josh Schwartz, Fox, 2003–2007), in which the second-season romance between two femme young women, reportedly an attempt to boost ratings, lasted a mere four episodes and, once concluded, appears not to have caused series regular Marissa (Mischa Barton) another thought.[2] Olivia Wilde, who played Alex, object of Marissa's momentary affections, went on to play secretive bisexual Dr. Remy "Thirteen" Hadley on *House M.D.* (David Shore, Fox, 2004–2012), though seemingly with the stipulation that she not act on her same-sex desire except in her occasional self-destructive, drug-fueled one-night stands prompted by her difficulty accepting that she has a fatal disease. When Wilde leaves the show at the end of season eight, it is in the arms of her character's girlfriend, only recently revealed onscreen though still not warranting a name or a single line of dialogue despite her role in whisking Thirteen away from her doctor duties to a new life in Mykonos.

This type of character noncontinuity is not uncommon in televisual attempts to explore female same-sex relationships, with notable exceptions such as the three-season-long coupling between Wiccan coeds Willow (Alyson Hannigan) and Tara (Amber Benson) on *Buffy the Vampire Slayer* (Joss Whedon, WB/UPN, 1997–2003), and between high schoolers Spencer (Gabrielle Christian) and Ashley (Mandy Musgrave) on *South of Nowhere* (Tommy Lynch, The N, 2005–2008).[3] Though *The O.C.*'s Marissa and Alex are presented as being at the end of their teens and early twenties, respectively, and with considerable previous sexual experience, one might apply a different set of criteria when looking at young adult characters such as those in *South of Nowhere* as well as two U.K. shows featuring young queer teens, *Skins* (Brian Eisley and Jamie Brittain, Channel 4, 2007–present) and *Sugar Rush* (Katie Baxendale, Channel 4, 2005–2006).[4] As with the female institution films featured in chapter 2, owing to content regulations and cultural concerns about adolescent sexuality, younger-aged characters may be less readable as bisexual in some ways (limited sexual experience, pressure to conform socially) and more bi-suggestive in other ways. In *Sugar Rush*, for instance, the crush that protagonist Kim (Olivia Hallinan) develops on enthralling bad girl Sugar (Lenora Crichlow) is torturous precisely because Sugar's adolescent impetuousness and exhibitionism send such mixed signals, while the slow-build relationship between teens Naomi (Lily Loveless) and Emily (Kathryn Prescott) – or "Naomily," as their fans christened them – in season three of *Skins* proved enormously satisfying to viewers for its explicitness and poignancy on sexual and emotional fronts. The American remake aired on M T V to lukewarm ratings in 2011 and was canceled after a single season, though its debut ensemble included a lesbian-identified cheerleader (thought to be more audience-friendly than the gay male character in the U.K. version whom she was based on) who questions her sexuality after sleeping with a male friend, and ends up coupled with a girl at season's end.

In the United States, *The L Word* (Ilene Chiaken, Showtime, 2004–2009) was widely recognized for being a game-changing instance of queer women gaining media visibility and voice, created as it was primarily by, for, and about queer women. Before long, the series was criticized for constructing a narrow range of representations focused predominantly on white, economically unchallenged, gender-conforming, mostly femme lesbian-identified women. While these criticisms focused on what the show left out, even more egregious (to this viewer) was the initial inclusion and endorsement, followed sharply by the vehement disavowal, of bisexual lead Alice Pieszecki (Leisha Hailey), who goes from proudly proclaiming her bisexuality in the pilot episode and throughout season one, to admitting that "bisexuality *is* gross" in season three, to dating women exclusively and not once uttering the B word for the next three seasons.[5] As evidenced by the sarcastic response to Alice's bi pride quoted in this chapter's epigraph along with another season-one comment that referred to bisexuals not having "their own team" (quoted in my introduction), *The L Word* seemed to harbor its own reservations about Alice's bisexuality from the start. But that the show ultimately chose to project its own monosexism through the voice of the one character who initially defied such limitations set a new record for implausible character noncontinuity, at the same time as it closed down one of American television's most prominent discourses on bisexuality.[6] As creator Ilene Chaiken defended the show's choice not to pursue Alice's previous openness to relationships with men past the first season, "We just haven't been interested in exploring those stories with Alice. We really like this character and we like stories of her with women."[7] The cost of this preference put into action, of course, is that American television's most visible, affirmative, and appealing representative of female bisexuality to date – Karen Walker (Megan Mullally) of *Will & Grace* might have been a contender if she were allowed to explicitly self-identify – was summarily effaced and her character shamed.[8]

As bi-shy as *Sex and the City* (Darren Star, HBO, 1998–2004) was heterocentric, *The L Word* ultimately lived up to its season one tagline ("Same Sex. Different City") by proving a lesbocentric correlative to the Showtime megahit melodrama that only once in six seasons of sexual explorations broached the B word, during a third-season episode that finds Carrie (Sarah Jessica Parker) discomfited by finding out that the younger man she is seeing dates both men and women.

> Samantha (Kim Cattrall): You know, that generation is all about experimentation. All the kids are going bi.
>
> Carrie: You know, I did the 'date a bisexual guy' thing in college, but in the end they all ended up with men.
>
> Miranda (Cynthia Nixon): So did the bisexual women.
>
> Carrie: I'm not even sure bisexuality exists. I think it's just a layover on the way to Gaytown.
>
> Samantha: I think it's great. He's open to all sexual experiences, he's evolved – it's hot.
>
> Miranda: It's not hot! It's greedy. He's double dipping.

Samantha: You're not marrying the guy, you're making out with him. Enjoy it, don't worry about the labels.

Charlotte (Kristin Davis): I'm very into labels: gay, straight, pick a side and stay there.[9]

Only one season later, *Sex and the City*'s bi-phobia encompasses even sexually adventurous Samantha, who describes herself as a "try-sexual – I'll try anything once." After finding herself irresistibly attracted to Brazilian painter Maria (Sonia Braga), the emotional oversharing and lesbian bed death sets her straight again after only two episodes. While BBC series *Lip Service* (Harriet Braun, 2010–2012) could hardly deny its debt to *The L Word*, which is particularly evident in the visual and narrative mirroring between the two shows' ladykillers Shane (Katherine Moenning) and Frankie (Ruta Gedmintas), the British show's first season exhibits as much potential willingness to go beyond monosexuality as did the initial season of *The L Word*. When an intoxicated Frankie spontaneously sleeps with a male mate, neither she nor the show's other lesbian-identified leads respond as if there's been a lesbian security breach. That Frankie, figured as the longest-term lesbian and certainly the least gender-conforming among the show's leads, occasionally exhibits bisexual behavior suggests a fluidity and lack of judgment about identity far from the policing that characterized later seasons of *The L Word*. The difference between Frankie's one-off sexual experience with a man and that of the various female characters who temporarily "turn gay" for sweeps week hinges on the former show's willingness to integrate what Anna McCarthy calls "everyday queerness," embedding queer characters and noninterruptive storylines within the textual fabric but without necessarily applying identity labels or normalizing queerness into apolitical nonspecificity.[10]

My study of the queer representational politics and queer counterpublic potential of these and other postmillennial television series – network and cable, and alternately centered on straight or queer characters – registers growing tolerance for the presence of "gay TV" within the living rooms of "straight" America, at the same time that those representations and audiences' acceptance of them remain overwhelmingly couched within homonormative values and monosexist logic.[11]

Nevertheless, the expanding capacity of twenty-first-century television to encourage narrative complexity, mature content, niche viewership, and fan communities engenders ways of seeing beyond compulsory monosexuality and counters bisexuality's elision in our cultural logic of desire and its representations. Largely confined to sweeps week on network television and condemned by a lesbian-helmed and -targeted show on premium cable in the early years of the new millennium, bisexuality seemed more (in)visible than ever on the small screen – with the prominent exception of a reality-style dating series that debuted to record ratings on z in October 2007.[12] Where *Chasing Amy* let the B word go unspoken and where *The L Word* rejects it entirely, *A Shot at Love* (Riley McCormick, MTV, 2007–2008) renders it hypervisible in the persona of self-proclaimed bisexual bachelorette Tila Tequila (née Nguyen).[13] Although the token gay or lesbian character – usually paired with a homophobe to generate the kind of conflict on which the genre thrives – has been a staple of reality television since MTV's *The Real World* (Mary-Ellis Bunim and Jonathan Murray, 1992–present), Tila is television's first openly bisexual personality or character to headline a reality *or* dramatic series, and one of very few to occupy a central, ongoing role. When compared to lesbian exclusivity on *The L Word* or the sweeps-week syndrome of shutting down a bi-suggestive relationship just as it gets started, *A Shot at Love*'s explicit, consistent affirmation of the B word offers a unique opportunity to examine how bisexuality gets constructed in contemporary popular media discourse, specifically that disseminated to cable-subscribing or computer-owning (i.e., mostly middle class) American youth, a generation generally perceived to be more sexually fluid and less attached to identity-based labels and causes than their uptight elders.[14]

MISSED MOMENT: WILL THE REAL BISEXUAL
PLEASE STAND UP? THE "REALITY" OF
ROMANCE ON *A SHOT AT LOVE*

Prior to its MTV debut, *A Shot at Love* was touted with this titillating premise: bisexual Tila, still searching for "the one," takes charge by "inviting 16 luscious lesbians and 16 sexy straight guys over to her place" (a four-story rental mansion in the Hollywood Hills) and subjecting them to an escalating series of challenges and eliminations culminating in a final winner of Tila's love at season's end.[15] The complex, interstitial understanding of *queer* bisexuality that informs my approach to analyzing the B word and its representations shares the aim of "Third Way postfeminism" as articulated by Stéphanie Genz: to "engender a destabilization of and movement *across* binaries and establish a contested in-betweenness."[16] The question of whether *A Shot at Love* makes available a politicized postfeminism rooted in Third Way thinking is as fraught as the show's attempt to negotiate queer bisexuality. The polysemic nature of postfeminist culture, Yvonne Tasker and Diane Negra warn, prevents us from making "straightforward distinctions between progressive and regressive texts."[17] While I am not interested in pronouncing either *A Shot at Love* or Tila herself a step forward or back for bisexuality and feminism, I wish to queer and query the postfeminist discourse circulating within this text, star persona, and audience response. My aim, then, is to discern in what measure *A Shot at Love* as media spectacle and cultural phenomenon recasts bisexuality as complex and queer rather than reductive and heteronormative, and to what degree it reinforces or undermines restrictive gender roles and compulsory monosexuality.

Given its youthful target audience, it was tempting to hope that *A Shot at Love* might proceed from a perspective of everyday queer bisexuality rather than by rehashing simplistic, stereotypical representations of bisexuality. Any optimism in this regard was dulled from the get-go, by what was either a lost irony or a deliberate exclusion on the creators' part: where, pray tell, were the *bisexual* contestants? The question goes unaddressed throughout the first season, in which Tila alone claims a bisexual identity. For all of Tila's proclamations that "it's not about the gender of the person," the premise itself – pitting men versus women (or "lesbians," as they were termed in official MTV materials), then eliminating male and female competitors in equal numbers – relies on a reductive understanding of bisexual desire as still fundamentally determined by gender. Alas, here again bisexual nameability and even visibility do not themselves constitute a move beyond compulsory monosexuality. Season two's Kristy, the show's only bisexual-identified contestant under Tila's reign, manages to live up to every bisexual stereotype and is, by the end of her run, literally labeled a "heartbreaker." To be fair, *all* the contestants vying for *A Shot at Love* are notably opportunistic and materialistic, motivated less by love than by an opportunity for fame (or notoriety) that might be monetized. The show stages the "reality" of romance as a twisted version of bisexuality's laws of desire – as much about profit as pleasure, and still entirely dependent on gendered rules of attraction. Aside from the token soft butch per season, the women are gender conforming, and "girl on girl" action remains the show's chief source of erotic titillation. Finally, as in *Chasing Amy* and so many romantic comedies, coupled monogamy remains the hallmark of a happy ending. But coupledom turns out to be as elusive for Tila as for Holden and Alyssa. After two romantically rocky seasons, a still-single Tila ceded hostessing duties to the bisexual, identical Ikki twins, Rikki and Vikki, who at last literalize the bisexuality-as-twinning metaphor.

Though contestants are not asked explicitly to self-identify in their casting applications, initially it seemed to be unofficial policy that female contestants represent exclusively as lesbians. Early into the first season, one of Tila's female suitors is discovered making out with one of her fellow contestants, a man, prompting Tila to demand, "Are you a lesbian or not?" What Tila perceives as her unsatisfactory response and disrespectful promiscuity gets the female philanderer booted soon thereafter. This early indicator of the show's self-reflexive preoccupation with authenticity and its promotion of monogamy also foreshadows *A Shot at Love*'s assimilatory politics. Here and elsewhere, Tila and her suitors construe sexual orientation as an involuntary, inborn trait. As I argued in chapter 3's discussion of marriage equality discourse, this "no-fault queerness," which regards nonheterosexuals as a small, fixed minority, makes for smart strategy when claiming civil rights yet tends to reinforce the lines between "normal" and "different," ignores the malleability and contingency of desire as actually experienced, and further entrenches restrictive definitions of sexuality.

This discursive agenda becomes especially problematic when it represents bisexuality as a temporary phase en route to a "mature" identity as heterosexual or homosexual. Tila claims to be coming out publicly as bisexual for the first time in the pilot episode, and it seems she views *A Shot at Love*'s pleasure dome as something of a halfway house when she states her intention for the challenge underway: "I'm trying to figure out whether I want to be with a guy or a girl." While defying the stereotype that bisexuals are capricious and chronically non-monogamous, Tila's aim as she articulates it here constitutes a retreat to a decidedly un-queer understanding of bisexuality as an impermanent, undeveloped state, an understanding which confirms the primacy of the gender binary in individuating people and defines sexuality by gendered object choice. That *A Shot at Love* follows a pattern of elimination in which the number of male and female contestants remains equal reinforces this binary logic. Although Tila ejects the male contestant who states, "I don't think there's any such thing as a lesbian. It's a phase," she continues to voice sentiments suggesting she regards bisexuality as temporary. Instead of concurring with the account of bisexual desire that Jane Litwoman describes as a rejection of the gender fetishism that structures monosexual desire, gender conformity is Tila's turn-on – or turn off.[18] Self-reflections on her prospects abound with gender clichés along the lines of "Chicks can be a bit overemotional . . . they keep talking and talking," and, after a fight breaks out between two male contestants, "Girls would never do something like this" (they will soon prove her wrong). While Tila laments this overheated exchange as "typical guy stuff . . . that's not what *real* men are like," she excuses their machismo as instinctual (letting their "testosterone get in the way"), but meanwhile threatens "mama's boy" Michael with elimination unless he manages, in a constant refrain of the show, to "man up."

The *real* "real man" here is, despite her diminutive stature, Tila herself – insofar as she is the head of house, invested with unquestioned authority that veers between dictatorial benevolence and aggression. The challenges Tila sets in the contest for her heart both reinforce and reverse traditional gender roles, such as the season-one opener that has girls parade down a red carpet dressed in scanty costumes while guys must maneuver down the same walkway in high heels – and, in a challenge more figuratively predicated on getting guys to walk a mile in women's shoes, having their nether-regions waxed ("It's time to see what a woman really goes through in order to look good"). Gradually, though, the potential for lesbian-feminist coalition formation made available by *A Shot at Love*'s "guys vs. girls" devolves into a case of every person for him- or herself, with Tila purposely provoking jealousies and introducing challenges that encourage contestants to take sides against one another. Unlike the B word, the F word (feminist) goes unspoken, making *A Shot at Love* exemplary of what Tasker and Negra describe as postfeminism's "peculiarly silent visibility."[19] Assertive, confident, and (apparently) financially independent, Tila herself is an exemplar of post-feminist sexual and romantic agency and empowerment, for whom love is business and the business of love is self-promotion. Even as she views coupling as a natural, enticing goal, she makes clear that she will not sac-rifice career-wise in order to achieve it; indeed, she brings her final can-didates along to her recording studio for a day as a test of whether they are supportive of her ambitions and can conform to her professional lifestyle. Only then does she select her suitor and pop the question, an event staged to highlight its gender-role reversal by positioning Tila at the end of an aisle, poised to proclaim her vows to the approaching "bride."

Though at the start of season one Tila announces to her admiring ensemble that "I'm attracted to each of you for entirely different reasons," she still articulates these laws of attraction in strictly gendered terms. She describes male sexual magnetism as stemming from "his suit, his strong hands, the roughness of his face," whereas what she likes about women is "the way they smell, they're so soft, it's a sensual experience that's different from with guys." Describing her emotions for her two final suitors at season one's end, Tila describes Dani as having the "soft touch of a woman but yet [she] can be tough like a man. It's the best of both worlds," while to Bobby she says, "You may have the hard exterior of a man on the outside, but I know you're a softie on the inside." But in the voiceover that accompanies this scene suggests, Tila has evolved to a more complex wisdom regarding sexual desire: "Now it's about people. Love has no gender. As time passes, I no longer see boy and girl, I see [first season finalists] Bobby and Dani. I've realized it's not about being a boy or a girl, but about who's the best for me." While these statements suggest Tila's evolution toward a queerer bisexuality, in her commentary up to this point she consistently reverts to a binary understanding of gender as an oppositional structure that allows for roles to be exchanged and even conflated, but that remains polarized and natural rather than fluid and learned.

Following her breakup with season-one winner Bobby Banhart during the show's hiatus, season two begins with the single-again Tila announcing "I'm still bisexual," almost as if her bisexual status were a symptom of her singleness. Retitled *A Shot at Love 2*, season two ushers in another bisexually identified woman: statuesque blonde model Kristy Morgan, who admits to no more than having "messed around with girls" but pronounces herself "really bisexual. I'm really ready for a relationship." Initially worried that female co-contestants do not find her "worthy" because she is not a lesbian, she goes on to win the key to Tila's heart but ultimately declines her shot at love, stating that she does not feel ready for a relationship with a woman after all. Whereas Tila progresses in articulating – if not always enacting – a queerer conceptualization of bisexuality, Kristy's performance of bisexual subjectivity amounts to a confirmation of bisexual stereotypes, realized in the opportunism and capriciousness emphasized throughout her time onscreen. By refusing to see past the gender of her object choice – her explanation implies she would not be fearful about embarking on a relationship with a man – Kristy fails to overcome the gender fetishism with which Litwoman charges monosexism. In keeping with reality television's conflict-baiting penchant for pitting victim against villain, this showdown between "good bisexual" Tila and "bad bisexual" Kristy acts simultaneously if paradoxically to authenticate bisexual possibility (embodied by self-assured, open-minded Tila) and enforce bisexual impossibility (embodied by indecisive, repressive Kristy).

A Shot at Love's ritualization of brutally competitive sexual politics encourages experimentation with multiple partners en route to the heteronormative – and perhaps homonormative – twin goals of coupled monogamy and monosexuality within the teleology of its premise: the promised creation of the couple. Tila holds firm to her pronouncement early in season one that "in the end I want to be with one person," even as her situation grows more complicated by season's end. "Never in my wildest dreams did I think I would fall in love with more than one person simultaneously," she gushed. "I feel like the luckiest girl on the planet." The house is a harem over which Tila presides, but it is also an experiment in nontraditional communal living, complete with a massive bed in which all sixteen contestants sleep. Yet Tila sleeps apart, and one of the surest ways of earning an early dismissal is to come on too strong. While the house rule against "hooking up" with anyone besides Tila seems to have less to do with morality than egomania, there is a puritanical strain running through the show that mirrors that of contemporary America overall, in which hypersexualized media images of women flourish even as sex negativity grows ever more repressive. Any possibility of poly-amory or unconstrained monogamy goes unmentioned; Tila believes she must limit herself to being with only one person, with her suitors voicing mounting jealousy as they are forced to share Tila's affections. Not until she has narrowed her cadre of admirers to the final three does she treat each to a sleepover date, but in a rare gesture of modesty prevents us from glimpsing behind her closed bedroom door, leaving us uncertain whether the implied consummation has actually taken place. These encounters occur only after Tila travels to meet her final four contestants' families, whose welcome and acceptance of Tila is second in importance only to each suitor's willingness to utter on-camera the all-important "I love Tila." With the power-conferring status of a speech act, this utterance makes its speaker worthy of winning Tila's heart; the suitor who shies from saying it does not remain around for long. For all the hedonistic foreplay, that for Tila to sexually consummate a relationship and form a couple requires a declaration of love associates her and the show with chastity and constrained monogamy.

As the other anchoring element in Duggan's conception of homo-normative culture, conspicuous consumption abounds in *A Shot at Love* – from Tila's McMansion and never-ending costume changes to the limo rides, lavish meals, and exotic getaways showered on contestants. One challenge has rivals compete to "bring home the bacon" by devising get-rich-quick schemes that pay out play money, giving Tila the opportunity to shame one male of whose scanty offering she protests, "I can't go shopping on that!" The luxury spa treatments and shopping excursions along with the gym-toned, surgically enhanced bodies that sustain America's beauty-industrial complex factor equally substantially in *A Shot at Love*'s product placement and general show of conspicuous consumption. As Tasker and Negra suggest, in returning women to pin-up status, discourses of postfeminism promote guilt-free consumerism, just as "stripped of its original confrontational political agenda, queerness can be effectively co-opted through a rhetoric of choice such that sexual identity is primarily expressed through consumption practices."[20] Through the vehicle of the show, Tila and her lovelorn "lesbians" epito- mize what Genz describes as postfeminist women in that they "become the 'entrepreneurs of their own image . . . stag[ing] a sexualization of the feminist body in order to construct a new femininity (or, new feminini- ties) around the notions of autonomy and agency." This "shift from sexual objectification to sexual subjectification," as Rosalind Gill puts it more sternly, uses a rhetoric of choice to endorse and encourage women's ac- tive, intentional service to commodity culture.[21]

No matter how legitimate the lesbian and bisexual identifiers that *A Shot at Love*'s roster of female contestants uses, they display a lack of rep- resentational diversity comparable to that of *The L Word*. Apart from the token soft butch – firefighter Dani in season one and softball coach Lisa in season two – female contestants have been uniformly femme, con- veniently justified by Tila's oft-repeated assertion that she is usually at- tracted to "lipstick lesbians." Though sticking out in a sea of cleavage and exposed midriffs, Dani's and Lisa's non-normative gender presentations are relatively tame – Dani being, as Tila calls her, "sort of a tomboy" and Lisa a long-haired "sports dyke." As the enthusiastic fan appreciation ex- pressed on sites such as Remote Control and AfterEllen indicates, Dani was far and away the popular choice for Tila's love in season one. Yet ultimately audience desire is thwarted when Tila announces jubilantly, "In the end I chose a man!," explaining she loves but is not in love with Dani, so does not wish to disrupt Dani's life as a Florida firefighter. Still barred from this inner sanctum, the queer woman's rejection is staged as public shaming, as she is forced to endure the camera's persistent gaze as she walks dejectedly and abjectly away, this footage later cross-cut with that of the ecstatic straight couple's amorous embrace.

As Kathleen LeBesco writes about reality television's BGLQT- identified individuals, "Because these characters are framed as honest- to-goodness people and not merely the figments of wild Hollywood imagination, their representation and reception carry significant weight in terms of reaffirming or altering ideas about sexual difference."[22] Yet much as bisexuality and feminism bear shared accusations of obsoles- cence, bisexuality and reality television are both subject to allegations of inauthenticity. The question raised in this section's title ("Will the real bisexual please stand up?") relates not only to the elusive queer bisexuality that goes missing in simplistic representations such as *A Shot at Love*'s, but also to the complicated play between performance and authenticity engendered by the reality dating series as genre. When a first-season contestant known as the "Southern gentleman" is eliminated and proceeds to verbally eviscerate every remaining contestant before making his exit, we are reminded of how romantic suitors turn on the charm even as we are no closer to knowing which is "the real Ashley." Tila's suitors' frequently remark on her own endless reserves of charm ("You make it so hard not to fall in love with you"), but the second-season reunion special introduces an unfamiliar, trash-talking Tila, who bitterly confronts the wanton woman who left her at the altar. Although Tila swears "[her] intentions are pure" and that "these are my real feelings we're talking about," whether the offscreen Nguyen is actually bisexual and single is a matter of some speculation.[23] No accusations of fakery arise until late in the first season, when testy rivals Vanessa and Brandi break into a catfight when the former charges the latter with having disguised her attraction to men so as to take advantage of the publicity gained by appearing on the show. The only thing viewers can know for sure is that the explicit enticement of romantic partnership dangled before the show's contestants (and viewers) is inevitably bound up with its attendant celebrity exposure and potential financial rewards.

The showrunners doubtless felt it necessary to address *A Shot at Love*'s skeptics, because such allegations become standard practice in season two, with Tila herself regularly insisting on the show's authenticity as a strategy for refuting charges of fakery. One of the first contestants to be cut is an aspiring performer expectantly named Fame, about whom Tila says early on, "I need to watch out for her motives in being here," then quickly dismisses with an arch "This isn't *American Idol*. Your shot at love has ended." Eventually Tila's skepticism about her suitors' motives is directed back at her: in a show of insubordination occurring shortly before her dismissal, a disgusted Lisa tells Tila she is "fake as hell." At the same time, instances of unabashed exhibitionism proliferate ever more outrageously in *A Shot at Love 2*, in which the flashing and brawling make it seem increasingly improbable that any of the contestants are competing strictly for the prize of Tila's hand.

The presence of onscreen lesbian eroticism is tied up with this question of "how much is real." Despite the rebuke voiced by a female contestant in response to a male contestant's request to see two girls kiss – "We're not your entertainment!" – MTV ogles every same-sex clinch as avidly as it zooms in fetishistically on curves and musculature. Tila's embraces with her male suitors, while not shied away from, are noticeably fewer in number, more physically restrained, and with the emphasis on romance. In the show's most spectacular moment of lesbo-erotic display, an all-girl make-out session in the hot tub unfolds for the delectation of voyeurs on- and offscreen, evidenced by multiple cutaways to the transfixed male contestants. Given this penchant for sapphic staging, it seems reasonable to speculate that season one's voluptuous blonde Amanda, whose onscreen charisma made her an otherwise improbable contestant for Tila's affections, was kept around until the next-to-final round in order to maximize the opportunity for femme-on-femme action. This strategy is sustained by the subsequent season's victor Kristy, who observes blithely, "Tila and I standing next to each other is every guy's fantasy. If it's not, you're gay." At least, that is, until Kristy veers radically off-script (or does she?) and turns Tila down flat. In a reunion special titled "One Shot Too Many" that aired two months after season two's conclusion, Kristy attempts an explanation: "I didn't want [us] to be another phony reality [television] couple." Echoing Lisa's allegation about the show's inauthenticity, Kristy too refuses to play along in the performance of romance. Not one to be outmaneuvered, Tila fires back, "I think you are so fake," and, turning to the studio audience, "This bitch was just trying to be on TV." With that Tila stalks offstage, but it is Kristy who has the last word: "You want the truth? *She's* a bitch."

That a queer coupling orchestrated by a bisexual woman constitutes the romantic centerpiece of a popular dating show seems able to achieve representation on contemporary American television only because both women are gender conforming, and because monogamy is the aim and re-enacting conventional gender roles the means. Any implication that the producers dictated Tila's curious first-season preference for Bobby over Dani as well as her second-season dismissal of Lisa is unverifiable, given that there's no accounting for taste and that confidentiality waivers are signed. Perhaps Tila simply has a thing for statuesque, hypercompetitive, full-on femmes who, as she says excitedly about Kristy, remind her of Barbie dolls. We can only speculate that those unsuccessful female contestants who dominated the challenges and demonstrated charisma and unmistakable chemistry with Tila lost out because producers were fearful of pairing her with a (however soft) butch lesbian. Yet narrowing the field to a final four that together comprise a spectrum of gender presentation suggests that producers were trying to cultivate audiences by maximizing the diversity of contestants' appeal up to the last hour. To whatever degree Tila's preference was decided for her, that the butch/femme couple fails where the femme/femme succeeds – if briefly – aligns with Tasker and Negra's assessment that "postfeminism absolutely rejects lesbianism in all but its most guy-friendly forms, that is, divested of potentially feminist associations and invested with sexualized glamour."[24]

The question of whether Tila will find "true love," in both senses, is therefore superseded by the question of whether Tila will find love *with a woman,* a challenge particularly resonant for many female bisexuals. Yet, in both the first and second seasons, the creation of the couple – opposite-sex *and* same-sex – fails. This repeated unhappy ending for lovelorn Tila is doubly attributable to a shopworn cynicism about bisexuals' incapacity for romantic fulfillment and to the simple pragmatics of serial television drama: if Tila finds lasting love, the show's over . . . or is it? Having announced that Tila would relinquish hostessing duties following *A Shot at Love 2,* the show unveiled a third season with a revamped premise and new name. *A Double Shot at Love* stars bisexual co-hostesses and identical twins Rikki and Vikki Ikki (Erica and Victoria Mongeon), former Hooters waitresses and Playboy models billed by MTV as "small town girls [who] have had their hearts broken by both men and women" and are now promising "twice the jealousy and twice the drama."[25] The other guarantee – though not, presumably, one to which MTV would admit – is that this set-up would allow a man *and* a woman to be chosen . . . and so it was that *A Shot at Love* finally got to have it both ways. Predictably, the last two contestants left standing in the season finale are a man and a woman. The surprise comes when both women reject Rebekah, a single mother and bartender, in favor of blond boat captain Trevor, with whom both twins attest to being in love. When the choice passes to him, Trevor hesitates momentarily, then chooses Vikki, swearing, "I'm definitely in love with you, and I promise to be faithful to you. . . . You're the one that I want to spend the rest of my life with." A distraught Rikki, looking on, remembers that (as we are reminded in flashback) Trevor professed to loving her too. "I hope you can be more real with her than you were with me," Rikki tells Trevor disgustedly before stalking off. Her sister watches sadly as she goes, but does not break from Trevor's embrace and proceeds to gush in her wrap-up interview, "I'm so happy that he's all mine, and I'm all his." But a seed of doubt has been planted, in Vikki as well as in viewers; when it is revealed shortly after the season's wrap that Vikki and Trevor have broken up, the "realness" of their love is indeed called into question. What is certain, however, is that *A Shot at Love* bypassed not one but two chances to create same-sex pairings, even if the twins' apologetic rejections of Rebekah make no claim to gender being a motivating factor. Ultimately the B word goes unspoken entirely, in favor of a final endorsement for the heterosexual monogamous couple whose creation necessitates rejecting one queer woman (Rebekah) and devaluing the importance of the relationship between two others, the twins whose primal bond the show finally succeeds (however temporarily) in severing.

> Lesbians are big business right now. If we teach her to golf,
> we're way ahead of the game.
>
> TOMMY GAVIN (Denis Leary) to his wife, upon hearing
> that their daughter is dating a woman, on *Rescue Me*
> ("Inches," 9/8/04)

While the long-format arc of serial television drama offers the potential for characters to "prove" their bisexuality over time and through character development and multiple relationships, bisexual characters in situation comedies, though fewer in number, can brave a greater degree of explicitness with the freedom of episodic structure (in which consequences need be faced for only half an hour) and an emotional register of lighthearted nonchalance. While the aforementioned Karen Walker from *Will & Grace* gives perhaps the mouthiest performance of bisexual subjectivity without ever actually uttering the B word, hit sitcom *Rose-*

anne (Matt Williams, ABC, 1988–1997) led the charge with the casting of real-life bisexual Sandra Bernhard as out bisexual Nancy Bartlett, who had multiple male and female partners during her six seasons on the show and, although safely gender conforming and frequently on the belittling end of Roseanne's sarcastic barbs, nonetheless offered a highly appealing embodiment of bisexuality.[26] Though allowed relatively free rein within the "just for laughs" logic of comedy as opposed to in more serious dramatic treatment, bisexuality, when delivered in this unthreatening, outrageous vein goes down as easily as bromantic bonding – even if characters such as Karen Walker and Nancy Bartlett constitute a more transgressive, and longer-running, challenge to monosexuality. Though confined to only a single episode, far more typical is the comic treatment given bisexuality in an episode of *Curb Your Enthusiasm* (Larry David, HBO, 2000–present) titled "The Bi-Sexual" (8/21/2011), in which the primary plotline is mirrored in theme and outrageousness by the subplot's preoccupation with the unfathomable rituals of another "exotic species," the Japanese, whose traditional bowing customs are subjected to as much skeptical interrogation as is the authenticity of the wily bisexual. After lead Larry David and guest star Rosie O'Donnell, playing themselves, strike a spark with the same woman at an art opening, they commiserate over their mutual indignation:

> Larry: Obviously she's bisexual. Fuckin' hate that.
>
> Rosie: What is that? Pick a side already.
>
> Larry: Can't you make up your mind? Half the population isn't enough for them? Why do they have to do everything they want? So selfish!

Though it hardly casts bisexuality in a flattering light, this "non-denial denial" of bisexuality as a real if censurable identity demonstrates the B word's continuing cultural valence, especially for the Generation X and Y audiences that *Curb Your Enthusiasm* primarily targets. As their competition over the obscure object of their mutual desire gains force, Rosie elaborates on bisexuality and its vicissitudes, warning Larry that "most of these women who say they're bi, they're really gay and they just can't say it. She's a dyke – deal with it." Despite reassurance from a male buddy that "having the penis" gives him the edge, Larry becomes so concerned that "lesbians have an advantage [with women, because guys] don't know what they're doing down there" that he resorts to juicing with Viagra to contend with "the lesbian advantage," anticipating (rightly) that to outdo his competition sexually will require performance-enhancing drugs. Though every bit as tongue-in-cheek as *Rescue Me*'s romp through its bisexual plotline, discussed below, "The Bi-Sexual" refreshingly undermines the presumed phallic preference on the part of women and offers the bisexually identified character a final affirmative acknowledgement when Larry, overjoyed that his date likes baseball, exclaims that dating a bisexual is "like being with a great guy that happens to have a vagina." Yet as the sitcom's episodic structure permits, she like so many of television's bisexual characters is never to reappear (Leary and Peter Tolan, FX, 2004–2011).

One final missed moment offers a similar case of treating bisexuality ironically and irreverently; only marginally less notorious than Tila's "bi-athlon," and with sarcasm as sharp as Larry David's, FX series *Rescue Me* was a pioneer of what the *New York Times* heralded in 2005 as the triumph of "What Men Want: Neanderthal TV."[27] Given its penchant for expressing reactionary politics, around gender particularly, *Rescue Me*'s representation of bisexuality seems all the more momentous for having extended over an entire season, involving a lead character, and (singularly and most significantly) making that bisexual character male. As it became increasingly evident that Hollywood films could deliver product and pleasures to satisfy long-denied queer spectators without forsaking mainstream palatability, American television adopted similar strategies for addressing queer audiences, eventually striking gold in the 1990s with hit programming such as *Ellen* (Ellen DeGeneres, ABC, 1994–1998), *Will & Grace,* and *Queer Eye for the Straight Guy.* Yet these crossover successes raised the hackles of some queer audiences and media scholars every bit as much as the earnest, politically correct pioneering works of gay and lesbian cinema like *Making Love, Desert Hearts* (Donna Deitch, 1985), and *Philadelphia* did in decades past. In his 2006 book *Gay TV and Straight America,* Ron Becker documents how recent American television manufactures and mobilizes images of affluent, assimilatory gays and lesbians (notably *not* bisexuals and transgenders) to cash in on an increasingly visible market share of hip queer consumers.[28] The effects of this decade-long injection of homonormative representational content into American television are ultimately underwhelming: squeaky-clean saints, fey comic relief, and lipstick lesbians shift from supporting characters to center stage, yet remain firmly positioned in relation (and deference) to straights, with their primary purpose still to educate – and titillate – heteroflexible viewers. Reversing Becker's formulation to consider instead the relationship between straight TV and gay America, I propose that edgier images of nonconformity and more innovative discourses of queerness may be located in the unlikeliest of places: among the ostensibly reactionary programming sprung from post-9/11 television drama's concerted re-heteromasculinization of American manhood, as represented in the case of the FX network and its hit show *Rescue Me*.

MISSED MOMENT: HOMELAND INSECURITIES –
RESCUE ME AND TELEVISION'S POST-9/11
RESURRECTION OF AMERICAN HETEROMASCULINITY

Launched as a basic cable network in 1994 by News Corporation subsidiary Fox and known for its male-targeted, edgy programming, FX established itself through its prime time triumvirate *The Shield* (Shawn Ryan, 2002–2008), *Nip/Tuck* (Ryan Murphy, 2003–2010), and *Rescue Me*, which collectively constituted an exceptional instance of straight male-targeted narrowcasting.[29] At first glance, *Rescue Me* seems solidly to subscribe to the cockswinging, ballbusting ethos embodied by its straight male leads, yet nearly every episodic subplot and several seasonal arcs grapple provocatively with current sex and gender politics – coming out, workplace discrimination, domestic abuse, rape, hate crimes, same-sex marriage, sex work, transgenderism, sadomasochism, polyamory, and bisexuality. Yet these spaces of interstitial queerness arise alongside conventional narratives of patriotic and patriarchal heroism by white male subjects, allowing *Rescue Me* to accommodate alternatives – sexual and otherwise – even while refortifying traditional American heteromasculinity. Is FX merely co-opting "commodity queerness" to attract a diverse viewership, or does the irreverent FX sensibility deserve credit for prioritizing verisimilitude and complexity over political correctness and identity politicking? Acknowledging that the day-to-day infrastructure of these shows' production is distant from the purview of Rupert Murdoch–controlled News Corp.'s conservative agenda, FX's bad boys remain effective agents for manufacturing heteronormative consent while simultaneously encouraging the push-pull relationships through which queer spectator-fans engage with ostensibly hostile media texts.

FX recently concluded its Emmy- and Golden Globe–nominated series *Rescue Me* at the end of its seventh season, timed to coincide with the tenth anniversary of 9/11. Created by Peter Tolan and actor-comedian Denis Leary, who also stars, *Rescue Me* chronicles the exploits of firemen behaving badly within a post-9/11 New York City that flagrantly defies assignations of the city as an irony-free zone (as numerous commentators proclaimed it in the wake of the attacks). But *Rescue Me*'s irreverence is decidedly *not* directed at the catastrophic events of 9/11 and their traumatic aftermath – these are given the sort of earnest genuflection that befits a show inspired by and dedicated to the heroic efforts of the New York City Fire Department. Rather, the show takes tongue-in-cheek aim at the contemporary American cultural mores deemed to have left the nation vulnerable and the apex of its high-finance sector castrated. Parsing the ways in which *Rescue Me*'s men struggle to reassert American heteromasculinity in the wake of threatening social and sexual differences, I focus on two male leads in particular: Leary's character Tommy Gavin, who struggles with literal and figurative emasculation (bouts of impotence, depression, and addiction brought on by the twin traumas of first 9/11 and then his young son's sudden death), and Mike Silletti (Michael Lombardi), the "probie" (or probationary fireman) whose explorations of his sexual orientation in *Rescue Me*'s third season, which ran from May to August 2006, make him one of only a handful of recurring male bisexual characters in television history.

In each episode of *Rescue Me*, a requisite firefighting scene ritually restages the 9/11 tragedy, but this time as success, thus reassuring Americans of our impregnability. In her 2007 book *The Terror Dream: Fear and Fantasy in Post-9/11 America*, cultural critic Susan Faludi argues that state-sponsored rhetoric and popular media discourse resuscitated traditional gender narratives as a way to manage homeland insecurities in the wake of 9/11.[30] Faludi's observations on the United States' post-9/11 climate echo American cultural historian Elaine Tyler May's assessment of similar rhetoric promulgated in the 1950s nuclear era, as Cold War discourse charged female professional and sexual independence with being a critical threat to national security, when it was – and is – more accurately a threat to U.S. political strategy, the military-industrial complex, and consumerism. The U.S. government, military, psychiatric profession, popular authors, and Madison Avenue, says Tyler May, acted in unison to prescribe chastity, early marriage, and family stability, extolling so-called "republican mothering" as a patriotic act of "domesticity in service to the nation, [with] marriage itself as a refuge against danger."[31] In the post-9/11 context, Faludi suggests, an effort equal to putting women "in their place" was simultaneously enacted to put men back in *their* place – one which, both Tyler May and Faludi asserted with regard to their respective eras, was seen as threatened by the "soft life" and flaccid masculinity wrought by America's becoming either a postindustrial nation of managerial-class men in gray flannel suits (then) or feminized metrosexuals (now). In *Rescue Me,* this neo-heroic rhetoric privileges such socially upstanding yet ruggedly physical pursuits as firefighting above cushy desk jobs and other "soft" white-collar professions; the symbolic protectors of national security and American values are depicted as blue-collar and white, and above all heterosexual and male.

Rescue Me's most insistent endorsement of the notion that crafting good citizens requires adherence to conventional gender roles comes with the season-two decision to abruptly write off the show's sole female firefighter, Laura (Diane Farr), despite her having finally received the grudging acceptance of her male cohort after two seasons' worth of job discrimination and sexual harassment. "I came all this way to learn my father was right," she says before bowing out – not in frustration over the persistent hazing she's been forced to endure, but in humiliation over her exposed romance with a co-worker. "I'm just a girl," Laura says more matter-of-factly than bitterly. "I don't have anyone to blame but myself." Not until season four is another recurring female character who works outside the home introduced: volunteer firefighter Nona (Jennifer Esposito), whose physical brawn and sexual bravado renders Tommy literally impotent. *Rescue Me* invites us into a male point of view, preventing easy identification with female characters, who are onscreen less and rarely likeable enough to warrant sympathy comparable to that

engaged by the men. Despite these female characters' strong personali-
ties – and those of the actresses playing them, including Gina Gershon,
Tatum O'Neal, Susan Sarandon, and Marisa Tomei – it is hard to ignore
that nearly every woman on *Rescue Me* is represented as either sexually
demanding and emotionally unstable, or, alternatively, as sexually and
emotionally withholding. Frequently, these women's quests for personal
and sexual self-fulfillment endanger their children's well-being or even
their lives, and never – not even in the case of the female firefighters – are
we invited to see the women as heroes too (an erasure similar to that of
the women on duty during the 9/11 rescue effort). Together, *Rescue Me*'s
women exhibit the same "power to control men's actions" and "figura-
tion of female treachery" that television scholar Ina Rae Hark notices
uniformly characterize female roles in another post-9/11 fable, the Fox
series 24.[32]

Yet, testifying to its success in having it both ways, *Rescue Me* has
proven startlingly successful with female viewers – as have fellow "men
behaving badly" series of late such as *Californication* (Tom Kapinos,
Showtime, 2007–present), *Hung* (Colette Burson and Dmitry Lipkin,
HBO, 2009–2011), and *Mad Men* (Matthew Weiner, AMC, 2007–present). To understand what motivates women's embrace of the bad-boy
trope – which is, after all, nothing new, stretching as it does from *Jane
Eyre* to the Harlequin romance to Bridget Jones to *Sex and the City* – it
begs investigating to what degree female discourses of disavowal (wom-
en know such men are bad for them, yet want them just the same) are
voiced in *Rescue Me*'s active online fan community, and those of similar
series. For whereas today's cinematic male buddies seem increasingly
converted into family men, television's male ensembles defy the sensitivity training foisted upon their big-screen buddies in the Will Ferrell,
Judd Apatow–led brigade of twenty-first-century sex comedies. Finding
humor in men behaving badly is nothing new, nor is its political inflection – from Ralph Kramden and Archie Bunker to *Animal House* (John
Landis, 1978) and *Old School*, politically incorrect male comics stage
anarchic alternatives to the status quo, depicted as having been rendered
ineffectual by old-fashioned class privilege or by newfangled notions
such as women's equality and affirmative action. The aggressively mas-
culinist quality that characterizes this "buddy politic" in male-centric

sex comedies strikes me as indicative of an ongoing need to buttress het-eromasculinity by rejecting the feminine and, even more, the bisexual.

Although its premise serves as a reminder of post-9/11 America's perceived need for heteromasculine valor and vigor, *Rescue Me*'s fire-fighting heroics take a backseat to sexual shenanigans in what could often pass as *Sex in the City* on testosterone, except that the city in which Carrie Bradshaw and her liberated gal pals frolicked appears, from the vantage point of *Rescue Me*'s equivalent sextet of mostly Irish-Catholic firefighters, as a "freak show" (as one character remarks) of sexually in-satiable, emotionally unstable women alongside queer men overwhelm-ingly portrayed as predatory and perverse – ranging from a violent stalker to a pedophilic priest to a firefighter who temporarily charms the crew with home-cooked meals and backrubs before it's discovered he moon-lights as a transvestite at a S & M dungeon. As if this warning of the queer threat lurking within "sensitive" men were not enough, later episodes find Tommy emasculated by antidepressants, which inspire in him such out-of-character impulses as writing poetry and dancing. When he goes so far as to bring caramel macchiati to hockey practice, Tommy gets thrown off the team for having gone soft and is subjected to a co-fire-fighter's lament:

> The Tommy Gavin I used to know was a lying, cheating, scheming, brawling, skirt-chasing son of a bitch. I looked up to him. You always knew where you stood. But this new Tommy – fancy coffee-drinking, pastry-eating, kind, sweet, sincere Tommy Gavin – I don't trust him as far as I can throw him.[33]

Tommy kicks the happy pills soon thereafter, wrenching himself back into respect on and off the rink by beating an opposing team member into unconsciousness.

The revolving cast of queer one-off characters provides constant reassurance that, to again borrow Robin Wood's phrase, "our boys are not like *that*."[34] *Rescue Me* devotes a considerable chunk of screen time to scenes of the firemen sitting around the firehouse kitchen (a traditionally female space) comparing sexual exploits and penis size, a means to de-fuse latent tension but simultaneously a forum in which, gender theorist Kathryn Ann Farr suggests, men "learn and celebrate the masculinity of camaraderie, competition, aggressiveness and independence."[35] Yet despite strangely frequent remarks about how nice gay relationships must be – "all blowjobs and ballgames" – to actually hang out with guys who are not unimpeachably straight is inevitably risky, even when engaging in traditional masculine pursuits such as watching sports – as happens with self-proclaimed (albeit briefly) bisexual Mike, whose status as firehouse "probie" suggests a not-yet-assured heteromasculinity that corresponds to simplistic understandings of bisexuality as a temporary, unformed state. As the "borderline homosexual" who makes the other men seem less so, Mike provides an ever-ready target for the homophobia that queer theorist Eve Kosofsky Sedgwick suggests regularly infuses male homosocial bonding.[36] Mike increasingly displays what his fellow crewmembers believe are homosexual tendencies – for example, remarking in reference to his latest girlfriend, a doctor of Amazonian proportions, "It's nice not to have to be the man all the time." "Only you could turn a relationship with a woman into a gay experience," his buddy responds ("Sensitivity," 7/19/2005). That shortly thereafter Mike becomes sexually involved with his male roommate is hardly startling given the show's foreshadowing, but no less notable given *Rescue Me*'s exclusion of consensual male homosexuality from the inner sanctum of the firehouse and lead character ensemble up to this point, *and* given that male bisexuality is so rarely broached on gay *or* straight television. Moreover, as demonstrated by the following confrontation, *Rescue Me* encourages us to see through the roommates' fervent attempts to contain the nature of their homosexual experimentation and the labels put to it.

[*Sitting on their couch, drinking beer and watching a ball game.*]

Mike: I'm not gay.

Chris (Timothy Adams): Neither am I.

Mike: We live together and everything, but it's not like we *live* together or sleep together or any of that shit.

Chris: It's just blowjobs. They don't even count as sex anymore so it's not like we're doing anything sexual . . .

Mike: . . . and definitely not anything *gay.*

Chris: Exactly.

Mike: I'm getting the blowjobs, so I'm *really* not gay.

Chris: Are you saying I'm gayer than you? [*Mike shrugs*] Don't piss me off, Michael. I'll beat your face in, asshole.

Mike: Dude, if I'm not gay at all, how can you be gayer than me? Use your logic, dude.

Chris: Oh yeah . . . sorry. [*Both laugh.*] So . . . you think you'll ever want to try it?

Mike: What?

Chris: Going down on me.

Mike: Uh, no dude. Never.

Chris: That's cool. Don't forget the old expression, though: "Never say never."

Mike: No. I'm saying never, loud and clear.

Chris: Why do you have to be a dick?

Mike: Shut up.

Chris: You shut up.

Mike: You shut up!

Chris: You shut up! [*He punches Mike in the jaw and begins wailing on him. The two fall to the floor fighting.*]

While we may be invited to view Mike's behavior as the ashamed, homophobic protestations of a closet queer, we are nevertheless prodded to view this and similar exchanges with a degree of disgust and suspicion around roommate Chris, who soon proves to be both jealous and two-timing, making him another in the show's long line of vilified queer supporting characters. When he subsequently shows up at the firehouse and rats Mike out as "playing for the other team," Mike's crew subjects him to an intervention in which Mike vows he is not gay, offering proof of having just bedded a woman. Nevertheless his disbelieving buddies appeal to the chief, demanding that he be prevented from showering alongside them or from discussing distasteful "gay topics" such as "Liza Minnelli or ass toys" ("Pieces," 8/1/2006). Even as this reference presumes knowledge of queer culture on the parts of both characters and viewers, it also serves to signal heteromasculinity's dependence on homophobia; the slurs and provocations that pepper *Rescue Me*'s dialogue and plot turns both flatter the knowing liberal spectator and please the homophobic, while encouraging everyone to laugh it off. This ironic syntax, present throughout *Rescue Me*, enables the show's teasing evasion of attempts to pin it down as certifiably sexist, homophobic, or ideologically skewed in any clear unilateral direction. It also operates, as Sasha Torres observes of the ironic postmodern television text with which audiences have a love-hate (or love to hate) relationship, as a "structure of disavowal, in which the acknowledgment of critiques somehow renders them unimportant."[37] Certainly the serialized television format itself encourages and even necessitates these mixed meanings, in that writers leave open possible avenues of future plot development while courting an ideologically diverse viewership. Ultimately *Rescue Me* reverses the classical Hollywood mantra "please everyone, offend no one" with its politically incorrect jabs and provocations all backed by its claim to be an equal opportunity offender, defiantly unwilling to censor the so-called "authentic" bigotry expressed by its central characters. Not to say that the show's politics or pleasures would be enhanced if its bad-boy firemen were suddenly to say only positive things about women, homosexuality, and racial others – for it is not the terms being used and the opinions expressed which betray the show's stance, but rather the invitation being extended to admire, desire, identify, and empathize with these men, to approve of their political incorrectness and "old school" defiance no matter how reactionary or vitriolic, and above all to commend the show for its ostensible authenticity in representing what *real* men are *really* like.

Yet even as it idealizes – and rationalizes – these men behaving badly, the show constantly takes them down a notch. In so doggedly articulating and enacting a traditional male code alternately disparaged and legitimized, *Rescue Me*'s bad boys compel viewers to question heteromasculine values even as the series' plotlines coalesce around combating heteromasculinity's dissolution under fire from sexually and professionally liberated women and the alternative sexualities of contemporary urban Americans. Ultimately, *Rescue Me* seems less like the simplistic reactionary gender-policing that Faludi tracks in post-9/11 media, and more an instance of the anxiety and fear that Faludi claims were airbrushed out of media reports on actual 9/11 firemen. Again, this ambivalence is not without its commercial advantages. By encouraging multiple read-

ings, both across diverse audiences and on the part of individual spectators, *Rescue Me* serves as a prime example of contemporary television's
multivalent text: one that facilitates, invites, and benefits from multiple
interpretations and is thus widely dispersible and more likely popular
and profitable. In the case of *Rescue Me*, this polyvalence aims to partially
concede, as a means to ultimately sustain, heteromasculine privilege
post-9/11. By humanizing – even at times humbling – its images of heroic
masculinity, *Rescue Me*'s male buddies refortify an idealized (or idol-
ized) image of American manhood accommodating of – but not limited
to – FX's target straight male audience. When an outed Mike threatens
to transfer to another firehouse, Tommy paternally comes to his defense,
reminding the crew of the valiant rescue Mike recently performed – one
which seemed directly precipitated by his successful conversion back
into the heterosexual fold with his recent one-night stand. In the world
of *Rescue Me*, questionable life phases are forgivable if you can pull your
weight as a hero; a willingness to run into burning buildings is proof
enough of the show's much-repeated maxim: "It's all about balls." But
habitual transgressions are strictly discouraged by Mike's crew and the
series alike, evident in the ultimate choice by both not to endorse Mike's
bisexuality. As chance would have it, a threesome with a brother-sister
team causes Mike to rethink whether bisexuality is so desirable after all,
as he forlornly concedes to his buddies back at the firehouse in season
three's finale.

> Mike: Go ahead, bust my balls.
>
> Tommy: I'd love to, I just don't know where they've been . . .
>
> Lou (John Scurti): I'd like to say something in the lad's defense.
>
> Mike [*getting up*]: Goodbye.
>
> Lou [*stopping him*]: No, Mike, stay. I want to defend your right to bang
> Hansel and Gretel and not be judged too harshly by your peers.
>
> Mike [*correcting him*]: Sarah and Gregg.
>
> Lou: Press on. . . . What's with the double standard, gentlemen? A chick
> who bangs guys all of a sudden decides she wants a lesbian experience,
> should she be pissed on for that?

Sean (Steven Pasquale): Wait a second, it's a lesbian thing, when she gets pissed on? That's hot.

Lou: Yeah, that's not what I'm talking about, dipshit.

Sean: Think about it.

Lou [*thinking*]: Actually it is a little hot.

Sean: Yeah . . .

Tommy [*irritated*]: I don't think it's hot at all. But we don't judge women when they experiment sexually.

Franco (Daniel Sunjata): No, we encourage it.

Tommy: Sure we do!

Lou: But a guy decides he wants to change it up a little bit, change his stripes a little bit, suddenly he becomes an object of ridicule . . . which, you know, you do really well, Mike.

Mike [*grudgingly*]: Thanks.

Lou: And in conclusion, gentlemen, I say we should not *bust* Michael's balls, we should *applaud* Michael's balls, for having the courage to lead the charge against this terrible injustice.

Sean: Wait, by that logic, we should all be able to bang guys?

Lou: Yeah, that's right.

Sean: Hello? Who's actually going to want to do that?

Lou [*motioning to Mike*]: Oh, probably just this little queer.[38]

In lobbing this last insult, the older, wiser Lou reasserts the hetero-masculinity which he and Mike's other superiors embody as the last word on the matter. Having ever only received (never given) oral sex, Mike remains "virginal" and thus eligible for heteromasculine redemption – even as he ruefully reclaims his status as both probie and "queer." And so, although he will spend it literally and figuratively incapacitated – on crutches and off duty following an accident on the job – unlike all the other queer characters who precede and follow him on *Rescue Me*, Mike lives to see another season . . . and remains a series lead, his sexuality always subject to speculation if not affirmation, through to *Rescue Me*'s conclusion.

Moreover, the bromantic strain of bisexual suggestiveness in recent Hollywood cinema covered in chapter 3, and that *Rescue Me* continues, can be seen across contemporary television, from MTV's 2008 reality-style series *Bromance* (Ryan Seacrest et al., MTV, 2008), a spin-off of its more popular *The Hills* (Adam DiVello, MTV, 2006–2010), to the much-noted affection evident between colleagues Gregory House (Hugh Laurie) and James Wilson (Robert Sean Leonard) on *House* M.D. and between Alan Shore (James Spader) and Denny Crane (William Shatner) on *Boston Legal* (David E. Kelley, ABC, 2004–2008).[39] Another questionably platonic love affair (quite clearly intended by its creators) has been read into the steadfast partnership between Lucy Lawless's title character on *Xena: Warrior Princess* (John Schulian and Robert G. Tapert, USA, 1995–2001) and her "traveling companion" Gabrielle (Renée O'Connor) by the legion of fans who turned a camp fantasy from Down Under into a cult series. Prone to suggestively soap one another in the bath ("A Day in the Life," 2/17/1997) among other affectionate gestures, Xena and Gabrielle's alliance to one another and their missions was the show's bedrock, neither threatened nor precluded by their respective relationships with men.

But perhaps an even grander bisexual fantasy involves television's most distinctive male character readable as bisexual, who also is supernatural: Captain Jack Harkness (John Barrowman) as the sexually fluid time-traveler on *Doctor Who*–spinoff *Torchwood* (Russell T. Davies, BBC, 2006–present), in which temporal transportation and character metamorphosis liberate the sexual subject to a superhuman degree, even if it remains the stuff of science fiction. Though American television continues to be far more bi-shy when it comes to male sexuality, the recent coming-out of an ensemble lead character on friends sitcom *Whitney* (Whitney Cummings, NBC, 2011–present) constitutes another line crossed. Having recently broken off his engagement to a woman, Neal (Maulik Pancholy) finds himself attracted to a male colleague ("G-Word," 3/14/2012). Interrupting a romantic dinner between the two, his friends react with shock at discovering that Neal has – as they put it – gone gay, but his ex-fiancée reassures him that she too experiences sexuality as fluid and encourages him to explore. As a finicky, submissive Indian American, Neal predictably fills the stereotype of the queer male as effiminate and exotic, yet he also stands out by virtue of being a queer man of color in a leading role on a network sitcom. Nonetheless, as was the case across the five decades of art cinema, sexploitation, and mainstream Hollywood we have considered, bisexual representation continues largely to be the province of women, both on- and offscreen. Witness the reaction to actress Anna Paquin's announcement that she was bisexual, in a taping of a public service announcement for BGLQT advocacy group the True Colors Fund in 2010, on an episode of late night comedy show *Chelsea Lately* (Chelsea Handler, E! Entertainment Television, 2007–present).

> Chelsea: She says, "I'm Anna Paquin, I'm bisexual, and I give a damn." . . . Well, who isn't? We've all slipped up a couple of times.
>
> Male Guest: If I were her fiancé [actor Stephen Moyer] – and clearly she picked a side, she's engaged to a man . . . I'm actually a little scared – because now there's a whole other pool of people she can cheat with.
>
> Chelsea: If you're gay, I get that – if you're lesbian, you're gay, whatever. That's fine. But if you're bisexual, penis always wins.
>
> Female Guest: I feel like only girls can be bisexual. Men, once you're bisexual – no you're not, you're gay.
>
> Chelsea: If you have sex with a man once, you're an artist. Twice, you're a bisexual.
>
> Male Guest: I think saying you're a bisexual is like saying you're a vegetarian who eats meat. It's a little selfish, you know what I'm saying? You're trying to take from both sides of the table.[40]

On *True Blood* (Alan Ball, HBO, 2008–present), the show over which Paquin prevails as a sort of bayou ambassador to the undead, her vampire co-stars clearly invoke sexploitation's linking of vampirism and bisexual fluidity, though it is the tough, working class woman of color Tara (Rutina Westley) whose bisexuality is revealed shortly before she is shot in the head and her girlfriend killed. In the show's fifth and latest season, in which out lesbian Angela Robinson (*D.E.B.S., The L Word*) joined the writing team, the newly undead Tara is romantically paired with Pam (Kristin Bauer van Straten), the aristocratic white vampire who resuscitated her. Vampire lore dictates that this enslaves Tara to Pam, who in rich bitch fashion wastes no time restyling her protégée as a femme. More troubling still, Tara's friends as well as the show's fans quickly revert to the term "lesbian" in reference to both women, despite their previous behaviors and self-identifications suggesting their more fluid logic of desire. On the more recent and reality-based addition to the premium cable roster, *Nurse Jackie* (Evan Dunsky et al., Showtime, 2009–present), recurring character Dr. Eleanor O'Hara (Eve Best) reveals herself to be bisexual in a far less extreme manner, neither with the suggestion that this is a newly formulated identity nor with any dire consequences; so far, the show's fans have followed Dr. O'Hara's lead in adopting the B word to describe her.

But it is not only premium cable shows that have ventured into multiple-episode bisexual storylines. The romance subplot between two women, one a single stripper and the other a middle-aged divorcée, on *Desperate Housewives* (Marc Cherry, ABC, 2004–2012), might at first glance seem a typical instance of short-term, sensationalized sweeps bisexuality: it appears in the series' lagging sixth season, features a lusciously styled femme (Julie Benz) in the role of sexually ambiguous temptress Robin Gallagher, and lasts only five episodes. Thus it is a surprise when the relationship between Robin and the newly single Katherine Mayfair (Dana Delany) is treated with a maturity and sincerity that runs counter to the show's trademark campiness, even if Katherine's full disclosure to her girlfriends on Wisteria Lane results immediately in the storyline's ending – Katherine and Robin ostensibly off to enjoy a new life elsewhere, and Delany and Benz summarily gone from the cast roster (admittedly, both were slated to star in new shows). Also on ABC, though it resuscitated the fleeting bisexual temptress character as late as 2009 in the person of Dr. Sadie Harris (Melissa George), *Grey's Anatomy* (Shonda Rhimes, ABC, 2005–present) has gone on to maintain the bisexual identity of lead Dr. Callie Torres (Sara Ramirez), who has multiple relationships with men and women before marrying her female partner Dr. Arizona Robbins (Jessica Capshaw) and co-parenting the child she conceived with her long-term nonplatonic male friend Dr. Mark Sloan (Eric Dane).[41] Though the homonormative slant of this segue into married monogamy should not theoretically delimit Callie's bisexual identity, it seems doubtful that there will be much occasion for development now that she is effectively de-eroticized, given the show's conservatively rendered depiction of Callie and Arizona's relationship as monogamous and sexually chaste.

> Dana (Monica Raymund): I have never said this before, but I am now going to say it to you: I am not a lesbian.
>
> Cary (Matt Czuchry): I know a lot of people who weren't anything until they met Kalinda.
>
> *The Good Wife* ("Death Row Tip," 11/11/2011)

As a recent *Slate.com* piece titled "Why Bisexual Women are T V's Hot New Thing" points out, "a bisexual character does seem to double a show's chances of building a fan base."[42] The sexually ambiguous woman constitutes a new form of having it both ways, in being a recurring character whose sexuality remains perennially unresolved while providing an exotic thrill and erotic titillation in every episode. Kalinda Sharma (Archie Panjabi), the Indian American investigator on *The Good Wife* (Michelle King and Robert King, CBS, 2009–present), is just such a bi-sexually-behaving femme, and as Cary's above assessment reveals, her powers of seduction are potent.[43] While *The Good Wife* balances scenes of Kalinda in (mutually or individually) desiring circumstances with men and women, she remains serially single and, it is always implied, devoted to her work. While her single status paradoxically allows for greater bisexual explicitness in giving her multiple opportunities for sexual partners, it also frames her every erotic encounter as a transactional exchange for information – making Kalinda a bisexual mercenary of the sort discussed in chapter 2, for whom power and pleasure are conflated within a covetous logic of desire. A similar, if substantially more sensationalized, version of mercenary bisexuality comes over Nancy Botwin (Mary-Louise Parker), the pot-dealing protagonist of *Weeds* (Jenji Kohan, Showtime, 2005–2012), when she lands in the slammer and must negotiate her way into an advantageous alliance – the same-sex institution still providing a rich setting for bisexual representation here and, even more pronouncedly, in British prison drama *Bad Girls* (Maureen Chadwick et al., I T V, 1999–2006).

The Good Wife's third season, however, suggests that Kalinda finds her new colleague Dana, and sex with women generally, appealing in a way that is not reducible to fruitful disclosure. After Dana's baiting between tequila shots that "without a penis involved, it's like baseball without a bat," Kalinda responds, "It's different; a woman's lips. And you get a woman excited – it's not like a man . . . it's aggressive, slow, suspenseful." Though leaning on a predictably binary ordering of sexual experience on the basis of gendered object choice, Kalinda's musings implies her rules of attraction (to women, at least) are predicated on more than just professional considerations. Nonetheless Kalinda continues to be kept at arm's distance by fickle Dana, who recounts their cocktail chat in postcoital pillow talk with the male colleague and Kalinda competitor she falls in bed with; it's a cliffhanger typical of network drama, leaving us suspended as to whether Dana's denial of her lesbianism voiced above are famous last words. Perhaps not; as AfterEllen recently reported, much to the indignation of its readers, *The Good Wife*'s showrunner predicts Kalinda will be getting a male partner in the near future.[44]

> Whoever thought that being fluid meant that you could be so stuck?
>
> SANTANA (Naya Rivera), *Glee* ("Sexy," 3/8/2011)

While this line invites us to regard non-monosexual identities with the skeptical stigmatization that we have seen time and again, Santana's dismissal of her BFF-with-benefits Brittany (Heather Morris) is noteworthy both for sounding the (other) F word – suggesting it to be a term in common usage among the teens that *Glee* (Ryan Murphy, Fox, 2009–present) primarily depicts and targets – and for the behavior it criticizes. But it is also a line that suggests there to be a certain breaking point when it comes to bisexual representability – whatever the medium, and whoever the target audience. Through the long gestation of this project I have seen bisexuality's screen visibility refined and its nameability increased – though its discursive depth remains boundaried. As a fluid identity position identifiable across an expanse of shows and films, the B word is still deployed, as my conclusion relates, for better and for worse.

AND BISEXUAL/Get Used To It

slogan on a Queer Nation sticker

Welcome to bisexuality, Captain Kirk, where gender
has nothing to do with who you want.

KIRK/SPOCK slash fanfiction

The queerest irony of all would be a queer
world that had no place for queers.

MARK SIMPSON,
It's a Queer World

Queer/ing Bisexuality

AS I AM WRITING THESE FINAL PAGES, SEARCH ENGINE extraordinaire Google, at the lobbying of bisexual advocacy group Bi-Net, consented to allow "bisexual" to be algorithmically prioritized as a search term and thereby no longer ghettoized as a presumed route to accessing pornography. That a global information provider of this magnitude persisted in effacing bisexual organizations and resources until now reveals how marginalized sexualities remain systematically suppressed despite the ostensibly more open sphere of web-based information conveyance. Bisexual (in)visibility clearly remains as entrenched a cultural contradiction despite bisexuality's heightened visibility on screens big and small. This past holiday season saw David Fincher's English-language adaptation of *The Girl with the Dragon Tattoo* (2011), based on the first installment in Stieg Larsson's best-selling Millennial Trilogy, opening in wide-release in mainstream theaters across the United States, further disseminating the riveting image of bisexual Goth-punk hacker Lisbeth Salander (played, in the American version, by Rooney Mara) already made nearly ubiquitous by Larsson's books (which promptly returned to the top of the *New York Times'* Best Seller list) and the Swedish-language film adaptations (among 2011's most popular streaming selections by Netflix customers). The matter-of-factness with which Lisbeth's bisexuality has been received – by readers, viewers, critics, cultural commentators, and others – strikes me as, in a word, thrilling. Yet Lisbeth is acceptable to her fans precisely because she is exceptional – exotic, unrepressed, fearless. Lisbeth has been embraced by the mainstream, but she herself is not mainstream; her bisexuality is tolerated and even celebrated precisely because she is so "other." Though it seems an odd aim, more banal, bisexual-every-week representations (such as those created by Tsai Mingliang, mumblecore, and *The Good Wife*) to go along with the exceptional and one-off (female vampires and sweeps bisexuals) are needed to break down prescriptive definitions of sexuality. But Lisbeth strikes me as both exceptional and of the everyday – she is brazenly provocative yet flesh-and-blood, a complexly rendered character whose bisexuality is but one of her nonconformist traits. Yet to once again raise a question that this book's prologue posed about *Chasing Amy*, what does it mean, and to what extent does it matter, if the B word goes unwritten (in Larsson's books) and unspoken (in the adapted films)? What I hope to have demonstrated through my analyses is that the explicit articulation of the B word itself matters less than its enunciation in practice – in depictions of desire that go beyond gender determinism. What has made this book feasible and (I hope) worthwhile is the rich array of such screen depictions; but what makes this book *necessary* is the contrary void when it comes to discourses of desire around sexuality as experienced offscreen. Bisexuality remains the blind spot of queer formations and queer studies. We may be beyond the B word, but we are not yet beyond compulsory monosexuality.

As the Queer Nation proclamation that commences this conclusion indicates, it is an ongoing source of frustration and disappointment that bisexuality still frequently goes unacknowledged and uninvited. Certainly I did not anticipate the degree to which I would be forced on the defensive by my choice to work within a specifically bisexual (rather than queer) framework. Indeed at times, when discussing or presenting my work, it seems my role has been less that of a media scholar and more that of a spokesperson for bisexuality studies, and that my project was becoming something of an apologia. While I receive a good many affirmations for my use of bisexuality to "unthink" compulsory monosexuality, I have also come to appreciate just how problematic the B word itself is for certain people, provoking reactions that range from the dismissive to the contentious, and therefore inspiring my book's euphemistic title. It is an unsettling realization for a nascent scholar to learn that the core premise of her project – that bisexuality has a distinct representational history and epistemological value – is, for some, unacceptable.

As a case in point, in the course of my research I came across a film that initially promised to offer direct insights into bisexuality's function in contemporary Hollywood filmmaking. This film, a recent American independent feature titled *The Dying Gaul* (Craig Lucas, 2005), based on the stage play of the same name, takes as its highly self-reflexive premise the trials endured by a gay screenwriter (played by Peter Sarsgaard) whose autobiographical account of his lover's death from AIDS-related illness is transformed by the male studio executive who green-lights it (and with whom he enters into an affair) into a conventional heterosexual romance. The studio executive (Campbell Scott) delivers a speech intended to persuade the screenwriter that making his story palatable to the audiences who *should* and *need* to see it ought to be their primary objective; insisting on creative and personal integrity will result only in an empty theater. "Most Americans hate gay people," the executive states. "If they hear it's about gay people, they won't go." Ultimately it is not this speech but something more basic – money – that convinces the screenwriter to sell out (his lover's medical expenses put him severely in debt). Thus *The Dying Gaul* directly dramatizes the movie biz ploy of having it both ways, and moreover aligns – indeed personifies – this strategy with a closeted bisexual studio executive who maintains a heteronormative front with his wife and children while clandestinely exploiting the male screenwriter both professionally and sexually.

As *The Dying Gaul* was written and directed by prominent gay playwright and screenwriter Craig Lucas, whose 1990 film *Longtime Companion* (directed by Norman René) was one of the first to address the AIDS epidemic, we might assume he drew on his own experiences of "getting in bed" with Hollywood executives. But what starts off as a mature, measured deliberation on the compromises necessary to achieve representational and personal visibility escalates into a bizarre and near-hysterical denouement that has the studio executive forcefully exclaiming to the screenwriter, "I'm bisexual – I *need both*." The instant the words have left his mouth, the phone rings. Taking the call, he learns that his wife and children have been killed in a head-on collision. The film ends there, with the studio executive felled, slumped on the floor in a re-creation of the Roman sculpture that inspires the film's title.

Encountering this type of hostile paranoia about bisexuality in the ostensibly enlightened realm of contemporary queer independent film is gravely disappointing, and almost enough to send one scurrying back to the multiplex – where, granted, expectations for finding queer-positive representations are lower and so perhaps that much more rewarding when they do emerge. Consider a mainstream Hollywood case from the same historical moment as *The Dying Gaul*, which also explicitly voices the B word in its final sequence. In the bromance comedy *Dodgeball: A True Underdog Story* (Rawson Marshall Thurber, 2004), our underdog hero Peter (Vince Vaughn) is shocked when his love interest, Kate (Christine Taylor), falls into a passionate embrace with Joyce, an old flame who shows up for the big game. That Kate wasn't straight seems not to have occurred to him – though it occurred to his (gay-coded) teammate, who, gawking alongside, chides Peter, "I *told* you she was a lesbian." Kate interrupts her reunion kiss with the lithe redhead to say, "Hey, I'm not a lesbian. I'm a *bisexual*." With that, she grabs Peter's shirt and pulls him, dumbfounded, into her embrace as the credits roll. Again the B word's utterance ends the film, though with none of *The Dying Gaul*'s bloodshed or hysteria. Kate, speaking in the present tense, gives no sign of abandoning her bisexual identity or her relationship with Joyce in her move toward Peter. Yet as quickly as Joyce appears, she is swept offscreen to make room for the final heterosexual clinch. Whether the intention was to leave open the possibility of a non-monogamous arrangement or just a titillating three-way in the (not yet realized) sequel, we cannot be sure – because the B word is the last word both of the film and on the matter. *Dodgeball* doesn't vilify or sensationalize the bisexual, does not closet her or set her straight. But it does treat her and Joyce as an unthreatening spectacle for men to ogle, and with bisexuality conveyed comically and fleetingly, and as such its threat easily deflected.

Ultimately it seems *Dodgeball*'s treatment of bisexuality embodies the kind of compromise urged in *The Dying Gaul* but not achieved by that film or in other recent dramatic treatments of male bisexual characters. In the latest remake of John le Carré's espionage thriller *Tailor Tinker Soldier Spy* (Tomas Alfredson, 2011), bisexual Bill Haydon (Colin Firth) is the cocky, debonair bisexual and KGB double agent who makes a cuckold of our hero George Smiley (Gary Oldman), then is killed by his male lover with a shot through the heart. In the not always subtly moralistic *Shame* (Steve McQueen, 2011), Michael Fassbender plays a sex addict whose "hitting bottom" moment comes when he is driven to enter a sleazy gay club for a backroom tryst with a male stranger. That explicit representations such as these are still configured in such alarmist extremes suggests that male bisexuality still provokes deep anxiety even within films that otherwise offer affirmative or at least sympathetic portraits of queer characters.[1]

The resistance I encounter in writing about bisexuality is often challenging to navigate, both rhetorically and personally, and I must at times concede a point. I have, for example, gradually embraced the term *queer bisexuality*, which seems redundant (the queerness of bisexuality being, to me, implicit) yet effectively conveys my understanding that bisexuality and queerness are not mutually exclusive – rather, bisexuality constitutes one realm of queerness, though with a specificity and idiom that deserves its own mode of inquiry. In this and other ways, being impelled to clarify my terms and defend my position has been enormously constructive for both my project and my development as a scholar (and I hope my book will have similar import for bisexuality studies). As Barbara Johnson writes, "Any discourse that is based on the questioning of boundary lines must never stop questioning its own."[2] The conceptual model of bi-epistemology I have laid out here would be enhanced by encompassing more fully theories of political economy, transnational feminisms and queerness, and spatiality, to include a fuller assessment of global capitalism's impact on sexual identity and the economy of desire. I wish also to continue exploring bisexuality's intersections with feminist and critical race theories, and with alternative identity formations including trans-, intersex, BDSM, and non-monogamy/polyamory/unconstrained commitment that also operate both through and in excess of gender orthodoxies and so insist on conceptual complexity. Furthermore, this book's claims about bisexuality's ubiquity are exemplified by our identifications and interactions in electronic culture, where gender-swapping and sexual fantasy practices proliferate in cyber-identities, game play, and web-based fan cultures; the possibilities for bisexual readings of and for seeing bisexually in the cyber-realm are rich indeed.

Above all, I hope to have made visible the bisexual sites and sights proliferating in the unlikeliest of places: at a theater near you and, increasingly, in your home theater. In seeking to account for bisexual (in) visibility, I have suggested that it is not the quantity or even the quality of bisexual images that are lacking but rather that it is our perception of bisexuality – challenged by the temporal and behavioral components allegedly required to "prove" bisexual imagery, itself further complicated by our culture's ideological, institutionalized privileging of monsexuality and monogamy – that requires refinement. In parsing the bisexual screen corpus, I have proposed that these films' and shows' resistance to monosexual readings is an effect of structures and practices of narration, production, promotion, and reception. Encompassing a flexible range of erotic subjectivities and sensibilities, bisexuality as a discursive mode is ideally situated to fulfill the contemporary media industry's need to accommodate diverse and dispersed audiences. The complexity of this commodified bisexuality, with its effect of commercializing and sanitizing, at once suggests non-normative desire and undermines it as a genuine alternative. Yet at this point of conclusion I find myself feeling optimistic, for the presence of these already-apparent alternative spaces – whether they are called bisexual, queer, fluid, or "ambiguous in-between stigmatized identities" – indicates that we currently have one foot planted outside not just the monosexual paradigm but outside all binary systems, thus constituting an initial step toward a world without fences.[3]

Notes

PROLOGUE

1. I am referencing George Chauncey's seminal work, *Gay New York: Gender, Urban Culture, and the Makings of the Gay Male World, 1890–1940.*

2. Henderson (2008), 137.

3. See Rich (1993), 227–254.

4. My sense of contemporary American youths' embrace of the term *bisexual* over *queer* is informed by popular press accounts. See, for example, Denizet-Lewis (2009).

5. Wood (2003), 65.

6. Duggan (2002), 179.

7. Quoted in Michel (1996), 65.

INTRODUCTION

1. James (1996), 228–229.

2. Butler (1999), 94.

3. Doty (2000), 132.

4. Hemmings (2002), 2.

5. See Laplanche and Pontalis (1986), 5–34.

6. See Hansen (1994); Stacey (1994); Stamp (2000); and Weiss (1994), 330–342. See also Clover (1992).

7. Dyer makes this comment in an on-screen interview in the documentary *The Celluloid Closet* (Rob Epstein and Jeffrey Friedman, 1995), based on Vito Russo's 1981 book of the same name.

8. Doty (2000a), 132.

9. The Production Code Administration (PCA) was the chief regulating body for the censorial code put into strict effect in 1934 by the Motion Pictures Producers and Distributors of America (MPPDA), in an attempt to ward off regulation of motion picture content by federal and state governments, which were under persistent pressure from religious and moral groups to "clean up" the movies. Believing that self-regulation would be the more satisfactory option, the PCA took as its guiding principle that "no picture shall be produced which will lower the standards of those who see it," and regularly demanded of filmmakers that modifications be made or denied them outright its seal of approval, considered a necessity for a film's chance at financial success. With the influx of foreign films (not as strictly subject to Code regulation) into American theaters starting in the 1950s, and defiance by a few U.S. directors who chose to release their films *sans* seal, the PCA's authority was gradually dispelled. In 1968, the Code was replaced with the ratings system that remains in place today, overseen by a contemporary version of the MPPDA now known as the Motion Picture Association of America (MPAA).

10. Weiss (1994), 331.

11. DeAngelis (2001), 180–237.

12. Barry King (2003), 45.

13. King (2002), 42–43.

246

NOTES TO PAGES 21–36

14. Gledhill's feminist analysis focuses on female spectators' negotiations of films produced within a patriarchal industry, but her claims can be applied to the bisexual spectatorial pleasure negotiated in response to conventionally monosexual narratives and audience responses. See Gledhill (1999), 166–179.

15. Bright's remark also comes from *The Celluloid Closet* documentary. I intentionally refer to female same-sex eroticism only, as queer viewers have received even less than crumbs in the way of male-on-male erotic imagery, which is almost nonexistent outside of gay pornography and a smattering of art films. Of course, *Brokeback Mountain* attempted to overturn this legacy; the question of how successful it is in doing so will be taken up in chapter 3.

16. Quoted in Kristal and Szymanski (2006), 100.

17. Clark (1993), 195.

18. LaPlanche and Pontalis (1973), 52.

19. Freud (1962), 86.

20. *Trans* refers to the various identities and discourses of gender variance, including transgender, transsexual, post-transsexual, drag, butch, femme, and genderqueer.

21. Freud (1962), 2; Freud (1953–1974), 227–228.

22. Freud (1962), 14–15.

23. See Fink (1995).

24. Cagle (1996), 240. Kinsey's corollary study of women, published in 1953, revealed that "by age forty, 19 per cent of the females in the total sample had had some physical contact with other females which was deliberately and consciously, at least on the part of one of the partners, intended to be sexual," though only a small proportion (about 3 percent) of his admittedly homogeneous sample had been exclusively homosexual up to that point.

25. The most surprising instance of controversy occurred when a National Public Radio affiliate in upstate New York caved

to pressure groups intent on mounting a boycott. The federally funded network ceased running advertisements for the film and censored all promotional spots then running in syndication.

26. Quoted in Angelides (2001), 1. Sedgwick is recorded as having made this statement in a February 6, 1991, interview with *Outweek* magazine.

27. See Carey (2005). Not surprisingly, a new Northwestern study and another in the *Archives of Sexual Behavior,* both released in 2011, largely discredit Bailey's findings. See Tuller (2011).

28. Bennett (1992), 207.

29. Litwoman (1991), 4.

30. See Doty (2000a); Garber (2000); and Hall and Prammaggiore (1996).

31. Hemmings (1997), 16.

32. Garber (2000), 473.

33. Rust (1995), 49.

34. Erickson-Schroth and Mitchell (2009), 298.

35. Däumer (1992), 97.

36. BDSM (sometimes called *kink*) is an umbrella term referencing the diverse desires and practices associated with bondage and discipline, dominance and submission, and sadism and masochism.

37. Butler (1991), 14; Traub (1995), 131.

38. Pramaggiore (1996a), 2–4.

39. Hemmings (1993), 129.

40. Doty (2000b), 148–149.

41. Martin (1996), 86.

42. Cohen (1988), 174.

43. du Plessis (1996), 20–21.

44. Yescavage and Alexander (2003), 125.

45. White (1990), 1. See Castle (1993).

46. Knopf (1996), 157.

47. Doty (2000a), 132.

48. Burston (1995), 120.

49. Doty (2000), 2.

50. Hemmings (1997), 14.

51. See Doty (2000a).

52. In *The Apparitional Lesbian,* Castle defends her choice to "refer to Greta

Garbo as a lesbian, despite the fact, as some readers will know, she occasionally had affairs with men as well as women. Why not refer to her, more properly, as a bisexual? Because I think it more *meaningful* [Castle's italics] to refer to her as a lesbian." Castle (1993), 46.

53. Richard Maltby discusses the now-famous *Casablanca* (Michael Curtiz, 1942) dissolve, in which it could be interpreted that Rick (Humphrey Bogart) and Ilsa (Ingrid Bergman) sleep together, merely one instance of Code-era Hollywood's ambiguity in depicting what goes on in the bedroom. Maltby, (1996), 434–459.

54. Pramaggiore (1996b), 275.

55. Industry rumor has long held that Hughes was forced to change the ending of *Pretty in Pink* after test audiences responded negatively to his intention to have Andie (Molly Ringwald) end up with Duckie rather than with the more conventional – and colorless – Blane (Andrew McCarthy).

56. See Girard (1990).

57. Maria Pramaggiore considers three such contemporary triangle films: *The Crying Game* (Neil Jordan, 1992), *The Hunger* (Tony Scott, 1983), and *Three of Hearts* (Yurek Bogayevicz, 1993). See Pramaggiore (1996b).

58. Karen Hollinger proposes approaching the "ambiguous lesbian film" with a similar understanding: in "refusing to identify itself unequivocally as a portrayal of female friendship or of lesbian romance," such a film ascribes to a continuum model of female-female relationships and leaves viewers to read the text largely as they wish. Hollinger (1998), 6. See also Holmlund (1991).

59. Empson (1972), 30, 33.

60. Ibid., 34.

61. My coinage of the term *bi-textuality* was done independently from that of Robert Samuels, who uses the same term to describe a related but distinct mode of

connoting bisexuality through representational uses of dreams, jokes, wordplay, and symbolism. See Samuels (1998).

1. UNTHINKING MONOSEXUALITY

1. Self (2002), 61, 173.

2. *Boys Don't Cry* director Kimberly Peirce and producer Christine Vachon have both reported on the trials endured to secure the film an R rating, with the chief hindrance being a scene in which Chloë Sevigny's character is shown receiving oral sex from Hilary Swank's character.

3. See Bordwell (2002) and Galt and Schoonover (2010).

4. Pramaggiore (1996b), 277.

5. Neale (2002), 116–117.

6. Betz (2003), 202–222.

7. d'Hauteserre (2004), 243.

8. Ibid., 237.

9. Michel (1996), 61.

10. Fraser (1996), 261.

11. Alex Doty gives an insightful, persuasive reading of Charles Foster Kane as a bisexual character. See Doty (2000a), 17–20. *Velvet Goldmine* (Todd Haynes, 1998) is another queer rewriting of *Citizen Kane* that features a bisexual quadrangle.

12. The eponymous anti-heroine of *Sweetie* (1989), an early film by Campion, also resembles Mona in that both women refuse to subordinate themselves to others' desires and expectations for so-called ladylike appearance and behavior.

13. Strain (2003), 17.

14. d'Hauteserre (2004), 241.

15. Crouch (2004), 92.

16. Winokur (2001), 241.

17. In her compelling reading, Hilary Neroni argues that *Holy Smoke*'s narrative is driven by tension between Ruth's pursuit of and others' resistance to feminist jouissance. See Neroni (2004), 209–232.

18. Crouch (2004), 92.

19. Ruth's occupation as a social worker does recall the missionary, a troubling

emblem of colonialism. Moreover, *Holy Smoke* avoids giving any indigenous person – either Indian (though Baba briefly holds sway visually and narratively, he remains depersonalized or even dehumanized) or Aboriginal (none of whom are in sight) – access to narrative voice, which as Kathleen McHugh has demonstrated is substantially tied up with power and agency in Campion's films. The voice of the subaltern, then, remains silenced. See McHugh (2001), 193–228.

20. See Žižek (2000).

21. Perlmutter (2005), 125.

22. See Gabbard (1980), 258.

23. Perlmutter points out the additional narrative parallel whereby "as in *Persona,* a crisis is reached in *Three* [sic] *Women* when one character reads incriminating remarks about the other and changes personality." Perlmutter (2005), 129.

24. For all Diane's revealed infatuation with Camilla, the loaded moment in which her dream-self Betty meets eyes with film director Adam Kesher (Justin Theroux) on the movie set recalls other intensely locked gazes in the Lynch canon – *Blue Velvet* (1986), *Lost Highway* (1997), *Wild at Heart* (1990) – always indicative of a romantic couple's erotically charged, soulful connection, yet one that also signifies a dangerous, potentially self-destructive desire. Also, though it may be merely the fabrication of desire by a sublimely gifted actress, Betty gives a persuasive simulation of passion for the sleazy Woody Katz during her transformative audition.

25. Appearing twenty-five years before Bram Stoker's *Dracula,* this Gothic tale provides the inspiration for many of the female vampire films discussed in chapter 2. It begins much as *Mulholland Drive* does, when a mysterious woman injured in a carriage accident wanders into another young woman's home in search of help, and the two remember each other from

a dream they shared in the past. See Le Fanu (1999), 243–319.

26. Strangely, Andrews uses bisexuality in reference to Diane rather than Camilla (the more obvious choice). In describing *Mulholland Drive,* Andrews writes, "Think of *Sunset Boulevard* [1950] as narrated from Norma's perspective. Better yet, think of a paranoid Poe narrator, updated as a bisexual female, imagining yet another revenant woman." Andrews (2004), 25–40.

27. Sontag (1967), 124, 142. Sontag's statement mistakenly reverses the characters' actions; it is actually Elisabeth who sucks Alma's blood.

28. Perlmutter (2005), 126.

29. Andrews (2004).

30. Toles (2004), 8.

31. Love (2004), 127.

32. Ibid., 128.

33. Ibid., 123.

34. Ibid., 122–124, 126.

35. Cagle (1996), 239.

36. Hayworth, *née* Margarita Carmen Cansino, was of Spanish extraction on her paternal side, a feature that was highly manipulated – though not altogether elided, as is often assumed – in the construction of Hayworth's star persona. McLean uses archival material to document how Hayworth's allegedly erased half-Spanish identity "was always present in Rita Hayworth as a star text." Hayworth was not overwhelmingly viewed as a fantasy woman but rather, according to McLean, "was *always* a 'flesh-and-blood woman'³ with whom her fans identified and . . . was accessible as such through widely available promotional and publicity materials." McLean (2004), 1, 11, 207.

Harring is a Latina born in Mexico, naturalized as a U.S. citizen when she was fourteen years old. A former Miss El Paso, Miss Texas, and Miss USA (the only Latina ever to be awarded the latter), she retains her title as Countess after a brief marriage to Count Carl-Eduard von

Bismarck of Germany, a descendent of the nineteenth-century chancellor Otto von Bismarck.

37. Rita's disguise again evokes Hayworth, who cut and bleached her famous red hair (allegedly at Orson Welles's request and to Harry Cohn's dismay) for her role in Welles's 1947 noir *The Lady from Shanghai.*

38. The mention of La Llorona is also an allusion to *Vertigo* (Alfred Hitchcock, 1958); for a riveting analysis of the relationship between these two films, see Shetley (2006), 112–128.

39. McLean (2004), 1.

40. Hudson (2004), 17–24.

41. Pramaggiore (1996a), 6.

42. *Mulholland Drive* was initially to have been an ABC television drama series, but after executives rejected Lynch's pilot, he used French financing to reshape it as a feature film – thus providing rather damning evidence of the allegation set forth by Paul Schrader at chapter's start.

43. Taubin (2001), 53.

44. McGowan (2004), 74.

45. Hudson (2004).

46. Ibid.

47. Ibid.

48. McGowan (2004), 70–71.

49. Several scenes later, another Freudian symbol for female genitalia – the jewelry box – will be despoiled with pink paint when Adam Kesher discovers its owner and his wife, Lorraine (Lori Heuring), in bed with another man. That Adam becomes the humiliated cuckold in Diane's fantasy is fitting, though punishment is also directed at Camilla in this symbolic representation of what Diane perceives as her lover's sullied loins.

50. Nochimson (2004), 173.

51. Perlmutter (2005), 126.

52. The "salacious" still was published in reviews in *The Times* (London), *Film-Dienst* (Germany), and *Film Ireland,* among others, but the only instance of it that I came across in an admittedly limited search of the U.S. press was accompanying Manohla Dargis's review in alternative paper *LA Weekly* and on the cover of *Film Comment. Mulholland Drive* press packet courtesy of Universal Focus Features, Margaret Herrick Library, Academy of Motion Picture Arts & Sciences.

53. Hain (2007), 278.

54. Bordwell (2002), 9.

2. POWER PLAY/S

1. See Hart (1994) and Holmlund (1994), 31–51.

2. *Basic Instinct 2* (Michael Caton-Jones, 2006) is an exception in this regard for receiving an (albeit brief) theatrical release and with Sharon Stone reprising her role from the original. Co-star Michael Douglas and director Paul Verhoeven declined to participate in the sequel. For a thorough and illuminating discussion of contemporary sexploitation, see Andrews (2006).

3. See Gledhill (1999), 166–179.

4. Paulin (1996), 58.

5. Ibid., 63.

6. Hennessey (2000), 4.

7. See Rubin (1997), 27–62.

8. Traub (1995), 123.

9. Deleyto (1997).

10. Ibid., 261.

11. Quoted in Wood and Walker (1970), 108. Traub (1995), 123.

12. Cairns (2006), 66.

13. Paulin (1996), 42.

14. Cohan (1998), 272, 276.

15. Commenting on the direct role that wealth and whiteness play in determining Catherine's bisexual privilege, Donald Morton notes that "for Catherine, wealth sustains pleasure-seeking adventures (with drugs, sex, etc.) and produces a state of consciousness in which desire seems to have escaped mere need" wherein "the regulation of desire-resisting temptation" is "irrelevant." Morton (1995), 378.

16. See Austin (1999), 4–21.

17. Stacey (1994), 29, 174–75.

18. Gledhill (1999), 166–179.

19. See especially Mulvey (1989), 29–37.

20. Paulin (1996), 44. Though Hedy is the most interesting and, in many ways, sympathetic of the film's characters, *Single White Female* has been much maligned for its paranoid portrayal of the queer female as obsessive psychotic. It is interesting to note, then, that the film's first-time screenwriter, Don Roos, would go on to write and direct such subversive, queer-friendly films as *The Opposite of Sex* (1998) and *Happy Endings* (2005).

21. Brinks (1995), 5.

22. Irigaray (1985), 76.

23. See Butler (1993).

24. Brinks (1995), 10.

25. Ibid., 5.

26. Marina Heung finds *Black Widow* to be problematic for feminist recuperation because of the film's alleged indictment of Alex as professionally ambitious to a fault and consequently asexual and self-devaluing. See Heung (1987), 54–58. To challenge Heung's assessment, I would point to Alex's indignant response to her boss's condescension at her lack of a personal life. "It's like shit from my mother," Alex explodes. "Make me happy – give me an assignment." Alex also deflects her male assistant's sexual come-on by telling him that he is too valuable an employee to lose to an interoffice romance. While I concede to Heung that *Black Widow*'s male writer-director team of Bob Rafelson and Ronald Bass seems for the most part oblivious to their own depiction here of sexual harassment in the workplace, the character of Alex is written and performed in such a way that manages to transcend these limitations, and it seems to have been Winger's hand both on- and offscreen that inspires queer women's embrace of the film. In particular, Winger seems to have worked to keep the heat on the homoeroti-

cism; at the time of the film's release, *Vanity Fair* reported that she ate pizza with garlic before filming her heterosexual love scene, sabotaging it so as to make only the lesbian chemistry convincing. Quoted in Smyth (1995), 139.

27. Wood and Walker (1970), 110.

28. Chabrol quoted in Guy Austin (1999), 45, 47–48, 49. As Austin notes, *Les Biches* makes "a very astute prediction about the outcomes of the social unrest which swept France a few weeks later."

29. Quoted in Ibid., 48–49.

30. Coffman (2006), 207.

31. Wood (2003), 71.

32. Wood (2003), 74.

33. Cairns (2006), 69.

34. By referencing Tamsin Wilton's seminal collection *Immortal, Invisible: Lesbians and the Moving Image*, I encourage an accounting for bisexuality within its purview. I have inserted *insatiable* to reference how the female vampire figure seems especially readable as bisexual for reflecting cultural associations of bisexuality with a voracious and undiscerning sexual appetite. See Wilton (1995).

35. Pramaggiore (1996b), 292.

36. Case (1991), 3.

37. Weiss contends that while "it would be reductive to explain the former as solely the product of the latter, the emergence of the lesbian vampire in this period does, in some measure, symbolize this threat" from contemporaneous second-wave feminist and gay liberation movements. Weiss (1993), 84, 90.

38. All three screenplays are credited to Tudor Gates (likely a pseudonym) and are loosely based on Le Fanu's 1871 story "Carmilla."

39. See Williams (1989).

40. Creed (1993), 61.

41. Garber (2000), 97.

42. Ibid., 97. A reading of the contemporary vampire narrative as AIDS metaphor is ably performed by Ellis Hanson in his

1991 essay "Undead," though it concerns itself more explicitly with discussions of the male vampire. See Hanson (1991).

43. An early 1990s survey of lesbian-identified women found concern about HIV infection relatively low among lesbian respondents compared to the population at large, but notes that they looked upon bisexual women as a significant AIDS risk group. See Rust (1995), 78.

44. In a defiant nod to this association of bisexuality with an unbridled, indiscriminate sexual appetite, this was adopted as the title of a leading bisexual publication.

45. Hanson (1999), 216.

46. Garber (2000), 100.

47. Case (1991), 9.

48. See Gomez (1991); Hanson (1999), 188.

49. Empson (1972), 66.

50. Deneuve's status as a queer icon is most vividly signaled by her having inspired the naming of U.S. lesbian culture magazine *Deneuve* before it was renamed, after a trademark dispute, *Curve.*

51. Graham (1995), 170.

52. Hanson (1999), 195.

53. Graham (1995), 174.

54. See Freud, "Fragment of an Analysis of a Case of Hysteria" (1905) and "Hysterical Phantasies and Their Relation to Bisexuality" (1908) in Freud (1953–1974). See also Yukman (1996), 124–141.

55. Coffman (2006), 11–12.

56. See Lacan (1977).

57. Rubin (1993), 12, 15.

58. Cairns (2006), 52.

59. See Faderman (1981).

60. Dyer (2002), 74.

61. Doty (2000a), 132.

62. See van Gennep (1977). See also van Gennep's follower Turner (1977). In adapting van Gennep's concept "to cover a range of circumstances not confined to ritual in the strict sense," Turner's insight, according to media scholar Nick Couldry, "was to see that van Gennep's model of

ritual passage could explain the form which transitional social crises, even in more complex societies, regularly take." Couldry (2003), 32.

63. Turner (1977), 91.

64. Ibid., 33.

65. Drew Barrymore is another actress who (like Jolie) made proclamations of bisexuality to the press early in her career and even played a bisexual in the sexploitation feature *Poison Ivy,* but gradually downplayed such admissions and veered toward "straight" roles in direct correlation to her ascent to stardom. In a June 2002 interview in *Rolling Stone,* actress Natalie Portman made comments suggesting that she too identified as bisexual: "I think it's much more the person you fall in love with," she remarked, "and why would you close yourself off to fifty percent of the people?" Quoted in Kristal and Szymanski (2006), 207. Most recently, Anna Paquin announced, "I'm bisexual, and I give a damn," in a public service announcement for BGLQT rights organization the True Colors Fund, shortly before marrying her male *True Blood* co-star Stephen Moyer.

66. Stasia (2003), 181–201.

67. Haywood-Carter, a veteran script supervisor, received her first directing job after *Foxfire*'s initial director, Mike Figgis, transitioned into an executive producer.

68. Graham (1995), 163–181.

69. See Kaysen (1993). Kaysen's title is taken from the Vermeer painting *Girl Interrupted at Her Music.* Ryder reportedly became interested in the project after spending time in a mental institution and brought those experiences to bear in her performance.

70. Claymoore is the fictional stand-in for McLean Hospital in Belmont, Massachusetts, where the teenage Kaysen was briefly a patient.

71. Doty reads the film as a tale of a young girl's sexual development in which

the lesbian temptress (the Wicked Witch of the West) and the heteronormative guide (Glinda the Good Witch) duke it out for possession of Dorothy. See Doty (2000a), 49–78.

72. See Hollinger (1998).

3. OF COWBOYS AND COCKSMEN

1. Theatrical gross reported by boxofficemojo.com. The term "comedy of re-marriage" was coined by Stanley Cavell to refer to a subgenre of American romantic comedy made between 1934 and 1949. See Cavell (1981). I thank Vernon Shetley for the initial insight into regarding *Wedding Crashers* as a comedy of remarriage, and for the many other insightful observations he has shared. The term *bromance* reportedly was coined in the late 1990s by writer-editor Dave Carnie in the American skateboarding magazine *Big Brother,* to refer to the close relationships between skate-buddies. It is not clear when or by whom the term was first applied to film.

2. Rubin (1997), 28.

3. The term *blockbuster* is applied rather loosely in film industry parlance (and still more loosely in the popular idiom) but generally refers to a film that grosses over $100 million at the box office.

4. *Brokeback Mountain* made $178 million in global theatrical release, edging just past *The 40 Year Old Virgin*'s $177 million worldwide gross.

5. Aired March 25, 2004, accessed June 9, 2011, http://www.charlierose.com/guest/view/1558.

6. Same-sex marriage has been kept at bay through the implementation of the Defense of Marriage Act (DOMA), a Congressional bill signed into law on May 7, 1996, by President Bill Clinton, which specifies that "the word 'marriage' means only a legal union between one man and one woman as husband and wife, [while] the word 'spouse' refers only to a person of the opposite sex who is a husband or a

wife." At this writing, an effort to repeal DOMA is underway, with the Obama Administration pledging its refusal to defend in court the constitutionality of the section of the bill quoted above and a revised Respect for Marriage Act recently introduced to Congress. States that currently allow marriage between individuals of the same sex are Vermont, Connecticut, Iowa, Maryland, Massachusetts, New Hampshire, New York, Washington, as well as the District of Columbia. Alternative forms of same-sex union, including civil union, give full or partial rights and responsibilities of marriage (without calling it marriage) to same-sex couples in California, Hawaii, Illinois, Nevada, and New Jersey. A majority of states have prohibited same-sex marriage by adopting amendments to their state constitutions that restrict marriage to two people of the opposite sex, or by refusing to acknowledge same-sex marriages performed in any other state or country, which DOMA's statutes allow.

7. Duggan and Kim (2005).

8. Willis (2007).

9. See Clark-Flory (2012).

10. Benefits granted to opposite-sex married couples but denied to same-sex couples include bereavement and sick leave, pension or social security continuation, the right to keep a jointly owned home, joint tax returns or exemptions for primary relationships on estate taxes, veteran's discounts, and immigration and residency for partners from other countries.

11. Minkowitz (2004), 36.

12. D'Emilio argues that the transition from family-based subsistence to a wage-labor system in nineteenth- and twentieth-century Western industrialization and capitalist expansion made possible the emergence of a gay identity even as it cast gays and lesbians as scapegoats for social ills perpetuated by a capitalist society – namely the ideological instabil-

ity and material dissolution of the nuclear family. See D'Emilio (1996), 39–47.

13. Schamus quoted in Higgins (2005). In addition to being *Brokeback Mountain* director Ang Lee's longtime producer, Schamus is known as a steadfast patron of such resolutely anti-mainstream American independent films with distinctly queer visions as *Auto Focus* (Paul Schrader, 2002), *Happiness* (Todd Solondz, 1998), *Poison* (Todd Haynes, 1991), and *Swoon* (Tom Kalin, 1992).

14. Rich (2005).

15. See Chauncey (1985). John D'Emilio cites Alfred Kinsey's evidence that in isolated regions of the United States this mentality lasted into later decades: "Among men in the rural West in the 1940s, Kinsey found extensive incidence of homosexual behavior, but, in contrast with the men in large cities, little consciousness of gay identity." D'Emilio (1996), 43.

16. Diana Ossana quoted in *Brokeback Mountain* press kit, Focus Features (a division of Universal Pictures). Courtesy of Margaret Herrick Library, Academy of Motion Picture Arts and Sciences.

17. Quoted in Durbin (2005). In a rare moment of uncharacteristic gall for which he later apologized, Ang Lee expressed apathy about how the film might negatively affect his leading men's careers. "I only wanted to do a good movie. I didn't care if their careers were doomed after that." Quoted in Stein (2005).

18. Quoted in Kaufman (2005).

19. Mildly grating in its earnest plea for gay respectability, *The Wedding Banquet* is one in a series of painstakingly politically correct, feel-good gay films to have emerged in the early to mid-1990s. As mentioned in my introduction, such films typically operate by desexualizing and sanitizing their depiction of queer couples and thus are viewable as the mainstream's co-optation of New Queer Cinema's less commercially compliant fare.

20. Quoted in Smith (2005).

21. Ibid., 70.

22. While it is true that the film performed well in the heartland (though not so well as in the blue states), the deafening silence from the far right contingent was less likely due to lack of moral condemnation as it was a canny move to avoid drumming up publicity and hence ticket sales – indicating that evangelical groups' floundering attack on animated series *SpongeBob SquarePants* earlier in 2005 was a lesson learned. In the April 10, 2006, edition of the *New York Times*, it was reported that Wal-Mart ignored an e-mail boycott campaign organized by the American Family Association to protest the corporation's prominently placed promotional materials advertising the sale of *Brokeback Mountain* DVDs. The AFA's director of special projects, Randy Sharp, claimed Wal-Mart was "trying to help normalize homosexuality in society." U.S. theater boycotts were limited to a lone instance in Salt Lake City, where Utah Jazz owner Larry Miller pulled the film from his megaplex hours before showtime. Overseas, the film was banned from theaters in the Bahamas (according to the April 1, 2006, edition of the *New York Times*) and in mainland China (as reported in the April 1, 2006, edition of the *Los Angeles Times*).

23. *Brokeback Mountain* press kit.

24. The term *melodrama* is derived in part from *melos* (music), and *Brokeback Mountain*'s instrumental score, composed and performed by Gustavo Santaolalla, is used to heart-wrenching effect to evoke the emotional somberness of the protagonists' doomed relationship. The film's other two key musical pieces are played back-to-back over the final credits and are an apt example of *Brokeback Mountain*'s aim to appeal to straight and queer viewers. The first, a folk song performed by country music icon Willie Nelson, croons

the gentlest of heteromasculine lyrics: "He was a friend of mine / Every time I think of him I just can't keep from crying." The second tune winks more cheekily at *Brokeback*'s queer Western conceit, with gay icon Rufus Wainwright performing an original song, "The Maker Makes," that includes the refrain "Get along, little doggies," an allusion to the traditional cowboy ballad "Git Along, Little Dogies."

25. Joyrich (1988), 147.
26. Quoted in Galloway (2006), S-14.
27. Quoted in *Brokeback Mountain* press kit.
28. Ibid.
29. See Winter (2005).
30. Quoted in Smith (2005), 68.
31. Turan (2005).
32. Smith (2005), 69.
33. Holden backs up this assertion by making mention of a line from Proulx's story that has Jack and Ennis locked in a "silent embrace satisfying some shared and sexless hunger." Holden (2005).
34. Lane (2005).
35. Quoted in *Brokeback Mountain* press kit.
36. Hoberman (2005).
37. Lane (2006).
38. Advertisements in some U.S. cities showed stills of the two married couples exclusively.
39. Carson (2005), 189–192.
40. Rich (2005).
41. French (2006).
42. Proulx (1997), 77.
43. For some critics this proved sufficient evidence; as Todd McCarthy wrote, "A quick sex scene in which Ennis flips his wife over on her stomach tells us all we need to know about his true preferences." McCarthy (2005).
44. Proulx (1997), 79.
45. According to the *Brokeback Mountain* press kit, members of the Calgary Gay Rodeo Association advised and consulted

with the production, and also appear in several sequences.
46. The film recreates the bathing scene from a reference in Proulx's story, which uses the line "no drawers, no socks, Jack noticed," but the scene of Jack tending Ennis after his fall was invented for the film. Proulx (1997), 75.
47. Schickel (2005), 68.
48. Keller (2002), 42–43.
49. Quoted in Lee (2006).
50. Quoted in Powers (2005).
51. Ramirez (2006).
52. Quoted in Peters (2005), 10–11.
53. Despite widespread press coverage of his relationships with actresses Kirsten Dunst and Reese Witherspoon and singer Taylor Swift, Gyllenhaal's sexuality has been the subject of speculation in fan communities since he first rose to prominence as sensitive teen Donnie Darko in the eponymous cult film (Richard Kelly, 2001).
54. *Brokeback Mountain* press kit. Quoted in Luscombe (2005).
55. Quoted in Ramirez (2007).
56. Quoted in Smith (2005), 70.
57. D'Angelo (2005), 72–74.
58. Keller (2005), 197.
59. Proulx made this statement at the Starz Denver International Film Festival in November 2005. Quoted in untitled article in *Screen International,* December 21, 2005 (no author named).
60. Proulx's story follows this line of dialogue with "though Jack had never asked him to swear anything and was himself not the swearing kind." Proulx (1997), 85.
61. *Brokeback Mountain* press kit.
62. Hoberman (2005).
63. Elsaesser (2004), 286. Ryan and Kellner (1988), 151.
64. Horton (1991), 5.
65. Fuchs (1993), 195.
66. Ibid., 202.
67. Wood (2003), 204–205. Wood traces the genre's trajectory to the explicitly gay films of the early 1980s (*Making Love,*

Victor Victoria [Blake Edwards, 1982]), at which point Reagan-era backlash compensated with the testosterone-fueled, competitive twosomes of action flicks such as *48 Hrs. (Walter Hill, 1982), Lethal Weapon* (Richard Donner, 1987), and *Top Gun.*

68. For example, Joseph McBride's interview with Hawks features the following exchange:

> McBride: What do you think when critics say, as some in fact have, that the male characters in your films border on homosexuality?
> Hawks: I'd say it's a goddamn silly statement to make. It sounds like a homosexual speaking.

Quoted in Breivold (2006), 70. See also McBride (1982).

69. Doty (2000a), 132, 149. I thank Alex for his comments on the *Wedding Crashers* portion of this chapter, and for the informing, inspiring influence his scholarship has had on my own.

70. Ibid., 140.

71. Arbuthnot and Seneca (1990), 121.

72. Wood (2003), 204.

73. See Paul (2002).

74. See for example Denby (2010).

75. Ibid., 204.

76. Doty (2000a), 136.

77. Cavell (1981), 31.

78. Wood clarifies that the "surreptitious gay text" designation problematically "rests on that strict division of heterosexual and homosexual which is one of the regulations on which patriarchy depends." Wood (2003), 204–205.

79. Ibid., 204.

80. Ibid., 260.

81. Cavell (1981), 17.

82. See Rubin (1997), 27–62.

83. Soanes (2001), 560.

84. A near-identical montage follows a short-term spat between Starsky (Ben Stiller) and Hutch (Owen Wilson) in the highly bromantic remake of the 1970s buddy cop television series.

85. Doty (2000a), 146.

86. Ibid., 134–135.

87. Another power player in the bromance game is Ivan Reitman's Montecito Picture Company, which produced *I Love You, Man, No Strings Attached* (Ivan Reitman, 2011), *Old School,* and *Road Trip.*

88. Bingham (2004), 217.

89. Cavell (1981), 31.

90. Benshoff and Griffin (2006), 275.

91. Shelton quoted in Howell (2009).

92. Savage quoted in Zak (2009).

93. Zak (2009); Howell (2009).

94. Holden (2009); Bunch (2009).

95. *Humpday*'s writer-director Shelton found limited theatrical distribution by, she confesses, playing up its "sexy hook" shamelessly. It went on to gross nearly $500,000 at the box office, by far the best performance by a mumblecore film up until that time, though still not sufficient to stay in theaters long, and likely affected negatively by the rival release of Kevin Smith's similarly themed *Zack and Miri Make a Porno* (2008). Shelton quoted in Zak (2009).

4. BISEXUALITY ON
THE BOOB TUBE

1. Torres (1993), 179. See also Kennedy (1997), 318–324.

2. Given the show's network home and primarily teen audience, eroticism between the two women remained strictly in the PG vein – even if they almost immediately set up domestic arrangements together, in an odd conflation of the "unthreatening girlfriends" trope and the joke about lesbians bringing a U-Haul on the second date.

3. Another preteen lesbian plotline, in the third season of *Once and Again* (Edward Zwick and Marshall Herskovitz, ABC, 1999–2002), may have continued had the show not been canceled at that season's conclusion. *The O.C.*'s Barton also plays one half of the couple (with Evan

Rachel Wood) in *Once and Again,* as well as stars in the lesbian teen drama *Lost and Delirious.* This sort of "incestuous" casting practice occurs often and signifies intent on the part of TV creators and filmmakers to play on name recognition among spectators in the know, further strengthening the intertextuality across the queer corpus. In *The L Word,* for example, several lead roles and cameo appearances are played by actors known for their previous work in lesbian films, including Leisha Hailey in *All Over Me,* Guinevere Turner in *Go Fish,* and Laurel Holloman in *The Incredibly True Adventures of Two Girls in Love.* It must be pointed out that *The L Word* also attempts to reach a crossover audience by giving central roles to actors with mainstream "straight" appeal, most notably Jennifer Beals (made famous in Adrian Lyne's 1983 *Flashdance*) as well as Pam Grier, blaxploitation icon and star of Quentin Tarantino's *Jackie Brown* (1997) – both of whom, as African Americans, are also clearly intended to encourage audience diversity. This point about casting raises a comparable example of how the contemporary industry also uses race and ethnicity (in addition to sexuality) as a crossover strategy. Increasingly frequently, both films and television series will assemble multi-ethnic casts as a means of attracting a wider and more diverse audience. My argument about crossover cinema's strategy of using sexuality relies on the same rules of attraction.

4. See Zeller-Jacques (2011), 103–120.

5. Two other of *The L Word*'s lead characters, Jenny Schecter (Mia Kirshner) and Tina Kennard (Laurel Holloman) are certainly readable as bisexual, though their characters do not use this precise term in self-identifying. Early in the series' run, Jenny is depicted experiencing her first same-sex relationships and thereby begins to question her sexual identity. As the series and Jenny's identity evolve, her sub-

stantial relationships are with women and with transitioning FTM character Max (Daniela Sea). If pressed to ascribe an identity to Jenny, I would more accurately characterize her as queer. Tina begins and ends the series in domestic partnership with a woman, but during a two-season interlude in which they are broken up, Tina has a relationship with a man.

6. For a comprehensive assessment of bisexual discourse in all six seasons of *The L Word,* see Moorman (2012).

7. Chaiken made these remarks during an appearance at UCLA's LGBT Center on January 18, 2007.

8. For an engaging article on Karen Walker's bi-suggestibility, see Mitchell (2006), 85–98.

9. "Boy, Girl, Boy, Girl . . . ," 6/25/2000.

10. See McCarthy (2001), 593–620.

11. Queer counterpublics are alternative discursive realms constructed through queer subjects' participation in social and political life. See Warner (2005).

12. Upon its debut, *A Shot at Love* ranked first in its time slot among MTV's target demographic of viewers aged eighteen to thirty-four. The first-season finale was the most-watched series telecast in MTV history, with 6.2 million viewers, and audience share increased with *A Shot at Love 2.*

13. A Vietnamese-American born in Singapore and raised in Houston, Nguyen first gained cyber-celebrity in 2006 for acquiring over one million friends on social networking site MySpace.

14. MTV also made episodes available for delayed free viewing on its website.

15. As billed on MTV's official website: http://www.mtv.com/ontv/dyn/tila_tequila_1/series.jhtml.

16. Julia Horncastle uses the term *queer bisexuality* to describe how contemporary scholars have construed bisexuality as a pluralistic construct rather than as a unitary or totalizing essence. See Horncastle (2008), 25–49; Genz (2006).

17. Tasker and Negra (2007), 22.

18. Litwoman (1991), 4–5.

19. Tasker and Negra (2007), 3.

20. Tasker and Negra (2007), 3, 19.

21. Genz (2006), 338, 345. See also Gill (2003), 100–106.

22. LeBesco (2004), 271.

23. Tila has been linked publicly with both men and women, and in December 2009 announced her engagement to Johnson & Johnson heiress Casey Johnson; the engagement was reportedly still on at the untimely instant of Johnson's death from drug overdose soon thereafter.

24. Tasker and Negra (2007), 21.

25. As billed on MTV's official website: http://www.mtv.com/ontv/dyn/a_double_shot_at_love/series.jhtml.

26. In a charming homage to her groundbreaking role on *Roseanne*, Bernhard appears coupled with Laura San Giacomo in an ironic "very special lesbian episode" ("Beards," 12/7/2011) of *Hot in Cleveland* (Suzanne Martin, TV Land, 2010–present).

27. See St. John (2005).

28. See Becker (2006).

29. FX continues to maintain its "straight dude" brand of irreverent original programming with such series as *It's Always Sunny in Philadelphia* (Rob McElhenney, 2005–present), *Justified* (Graham Yost, 2010–present), *Louie* (Louis C.K., 2010–present), and *Sons of Anarchy* (Kurt Sutter, 2008–present).

30. See Faludi (2007). See also Puar (2007).

31. Tyler May (1989), 159.

32. Hark (2004), 128, 135.

33. "Bitch," 8/30/2005.

34. Wood (2003), 204.

35. Farr (1998), 403.

36. See Sedgwick (1985).

37. Torres (1989), 102.

38. "Beached," 8/29/2006.

39. An October 2008 issue of *TV Guide* displayed a cover photograph of Laurie and Leonard with the headline "Isn't It Bromantic?" For an excellent discussion of *Boston Legal*'s best buds, who close the series with one proposing marriage to the other (that he accepts only necessitates the show's ending), see Marshall (2011). In advance of the March 2012 premiere of *Mad Men*'s fifth season, fan site Vulture posted a mash-up montage celebrating the bromantic bond between that show's male leads, Don Draper (Jon Hamm) and Roger Sterling (John Slattery). Accessed March 22, 2012, http://www.vulture.com/2012/03/roger-and-don-outed-gay-lovers.html?mid=twitter_vulture.

40. Episode aired 4/8/2010.

41. For a thorough and illuminating examination of representations of sexual identity in *Grey's Anatomy*, see Durden (2010).

42. Thomas (2012).

43. Panjabi won an Emmy Award for her performance in *The Good Wife* in 2010, and was nominated again in 2011.

44. Showrunner/producer Robert King made the prediction following season two's end, claiming the rationale to be the disproportionate number of female to male partners Kalinda has had on the show up to now, and citing her intense but short-lived relationship with a character played by Kelli Giddish (cut short when she left for a recurring role on *Law & Order: SVU*) as one they "can't do better than." Quoted in Bendix (2012).

CONCLUSION

1. *Tinker Tailor Soldier Spy* depicts Bill Haydon's male lover as a devoted British agent turned schoolmaster, while another equally honorable agent is revealed to be living with his male lover; their monosexual monogamy stands in sharp contrast to Bill's wolfish, duplicitous bisexuality.

2. Quoted in Angelides (2001), 172.

3. See Kahn (2011).

Bibliography

Andrews, David. "An Oneiric Fugue: The Various Logics of *Mulholland Drive.*" *Journal of Film and Video* 56, no. 1 (Spring 2004): 25–40. Accessed January 20, 2012. http://www.jstor.org/stable/20688441.

———. *Soft in the Middle: The Contemporary Soft Core Feature in Its Contexts.* Columbus: Ohio State University Press, 2006.

Angelides, Steven. *A History of Bisexuality.* Chicago: University of Chicago Press, 2001.

Arbuthnot, Lucie, and Gail Seneca. "Pre-Text and Text in *Gentlemen Prefer Blondes.*" In *Issues in Feminist Film Criticism*, edited by Patricia Erens, 112–125. Bloomington: Indiana University Press, 1990.

Austin, Guy. *Claude Chabrol.* Manchester, UK: Manchester University Press, 1999.

Austin, Thomas. "Gendered (Dis)pleasures: *Basic Instinct* and Female Viewers." *Journal of Popular British Cinema* 2 (1999): 4–21.

Becker, Ron. *Gay TV and Straight America.* New Brunswick, NJ: Rutgers University Press, 2006.

Bendix, Trish. "Kalinda Might Commit to Someone This Year on *The Good Wife.*" *AfterEllen*, January 13, 2012. Accessed January 20, 2012. http://www.afterellen.com/TV/kalinda-might-commit-to-someone-this-year-on-the-good-wife.

Bennett, Kathleen. "Feminist Bisexuality: A Both/And Option for an Either/Or World." In *Closer to Home: Bisexuality and Feminism*, edited by Elizabeth Reba Weise, 205–231. Seattle: Seal Press, 1992.

Benshoff, Harry M., and Sean Griffin. *Queer Images: A History of Gay and Lesbian Film in America.* Oxford, UK: Rowman & Littlefield, 2006.

Betz, Mark. "Art, Exploitation, Underground." In *Defining Cult Movies: The Cultural Politics of Oppositional Taste*, edited by Mark Jancovich, Antonio Lázaro Reboli, Julian Stringer, and Andrew Willis, 202–222. Manchester, UK: Manchester University Press, 2003.

Bingham, Dennis. "I'm Not Really a Man, But I Play One in the Movies." In *Hollywood: Critical Concepts in Media and Cultural Studies*, edited by Thomas Schatz, 214–232. New York: Routledge, 2004.

Bordwell, David. "The Art Cinema as a Mode of Film Practice." In *The European Cinema Reader*, edited by Catherine Fowler, 94–102. New York: Routledge, 2002.

Breivold, Scott, ed. *Howard Hawks: Interviews.* Jackson: University Press of Mississippi, 2006.

Brinks, Ellen. "Who's Been in My Closet? Mimetic Identification and the Psychosis of Class Transvestism in *Single White Female.*" In *Cruising the Performative: Interventions into the Representation of Ethnicity, Nationality, and Sexuality,* edited by Sue-Ellen Case, Philip Brett, and Susan Leigh Foster, 3–12. Bloomington: Indiana University Press, 1995.

Bunch, Sonny. "Bromance Plus: Two lifelong friends re-examine their man-love." *Washington Times,* July 24, 2009.

Burston, Paul. "Just a Gigolo? Narcissism, Nellyism, and the 'New Man' Theme." In *A Queer Romance: Lesbians, Gay Men and Popular Culture,* edited by Paul Burston and Colin Richardson, 111–122. New York: Routledge, 1995.

Butler, Judith. "Imitation and Gender In-subordination." in *Inside/Out: Lesbian Theories, Gay Theories,* edited by Diana Fuss, 13–31. New York: Routledge, 1991.

———. *Gender Trouble: Feminism and the Subversion of Identity.* Rev. ed. New York: Routledge, 1999.

Cagle, Chris. "Rough Trade: Sexual Taxonomy in Postwar America." In *RePresenting Bisexualities: Subjects and Cultures of Fluid Desire,* edited by Donald E. Hall and Maria Pramaggiore, 234–252. New York: NYU Press, 1996.

Cairns, Lucille. *Sapphism on Screen: Lesbian Desire in French and Francophone Cinema.* Edinburgh: Edinburgh University Press, 2006.

Carey, Benedict. "Straight, Gay, or Lying? Bisexuality Revisited." *New York Times,* July 5, 2005. Accessed July 31, 2010. http://www.nytimes.com/2005/07/05/health/05sex.html?_r=1&page wanted=2.

Carson, Tom. "Howdy, Life Pardner." *GQ.* December 5, 2005, 189–192.

Case, Sue-Ellen. "Tracking the Vampire." *differences* 3, no. 2 (1991): 1–20.

Castle, Terry. *The Apparitional Lesbian: Female Homosexuality and Modern Culture.* New York: Columbia University Press, 1993.

Cavell, Stanley. *Pursuits of Happiness: The Hollywood Comedy of Remarriage.* Cambridge, MA: Harvard University Press, 1981.

Chauncey, George. "Christian Brother-hood or Sexual Perversion? Homosexual Identities and the Construction of Sexual Boundaries in the World War I Era." *Journal of Social History* 19 (1985): 189–212.

———. *Gay New York: Gender, Urban Culture, and the Makings of the Gay Male World, 1890–1940.* New York: Basic Books, 1994.

Clark, Danae. "Commodity Lesbianism." In *The Lesbian and Gay Studies Reader,* edited by Henry Abelove, Michèle Aina Barale, and David M. Halperin, 186–201. New York: Routledge, 1993.

Clark-Flory, Tracy. "When gay is a choice." *Salon,* January 24, 2012. Accessed March 22, 2012. http://www.salon.com/2012/01/24/when_gay_is_a_choice/.

Clover, Carol. *Men, Women and Chainsaws: Gender in the Modern Horror Film.* London: British Film Institute, 1992.

Coffman, Christine E. *Insane Passions: Lesbianism and Psychosis in Literature and Film.* Middletown, CT: Wesleyan University Press, 2006.

Cohan, Steven. "Censorship and Narrative Indeterminacy in *Basic Instinct:* 'You won't learn anything from me I don't want you to know.'" In *Contemporary Hollywood Cinema,* edited by Steve Neale and Murray Smith, 263–279. New York: Routledge, 1998.

Cohen, Ed. "Are We (Not) What We Are Becoming?: 'Gay,' 'Identity,' 'Gay Studies,' and the Disciplining of Knowledge." In *Engendering Men: The Question of Male Feminist Criticism,* edited by Joseph A. Boone and Michael Cadden, 161–175. New York: Routledge, 1988.

Couldry, Nick. *Media Rituals: A Critical Approach.* New York: Routledge, 2003.

Crouch, David. "Tourist Practices and Performances." In *A Companion to Tourism*, edited by Alan L. Lew, C. Michael Hall, and Allan M. Williams, 85–95. Malden, MA: Blackwell, 2004.

Creed, Barbara. *The Monstrous-Feminine: Film, Feminism, Psychoanalysis.* New York: Routledge, 1993.

D'Angelo, Mike. "Life Pardners." *Esquire.* December 1, 2005, 72–74.

Däumer, Elisabeth D. "Queer Ethics: Or, The Challenge of Bisexuality to Lesbian Ethics." *Hypatia* 7, no. 4 (Autumn 1992): 91–105.

David, Larry. "Cowboys Are My Weakness." *New York Times,* January 1, 2006. Accessed January 19, 2012. http://www .nytimes.com/2006/01/01/opinion/01 david.html.

DeAngelis, Michael. *Gay Fandom and Crossover Stardom: James Dean, Mel Gibson, and Keanu Reeves.* Durham, NC: Duke University Press, 2001.

Deleyto, Celestino. "The Margins of Pleasure: Female Monstrosity and Male Paranoia in 'Basic Instinct.'" *Film Criticism* 21, no. 3 (Spring 1997): 20–43. Accessed January 10, 2006. Thomson Gale (A19618031).

D'Emilio, John. "Capitalism and Gay Identity." In *The Material Queer: A Les-BiGay Cultural Studies Reader,* edited by Donald Morton, 39–47. Boulder, CO: Westview, 1996.

de Lauretis, Teresa. "Queer Texts, Bad Habits, and the Issue of a Future." GLQ 17, no. 2–3 (2011): 243–263.

Denby, David. "A Fine Romance: the new comedy of the sexes." *New Yorker.* July 23, 2007. Accessed June 8, 2010. http://www.newyorker.com/ reporting/2007/07/23/070723fa_fact _denby.

Denizet-Lewis, Benoit. "Coming Out in Middle School." *New York Times,* September 23, 2009. Accessed April 28, 2010. http://www.nytimes.com/2009/

09/27/magazine/27out-=t.html?scp=4 &sq=youth%20sexual%20identity&st =cse.

d'Hauteserre, Anne-Marie. "Post-colonialism, Colonialism, and Tourism." In *A Companion to Tourism,* edited by Alan L. Lew, C. Michael Hall, and Allan M. Williams, 235–245. Malden, MA: Blackwell, 2004.

Doty, Alexander. *Flaming Classics: Queering the Film Canon.* New York: Routledge, 2000.

———. "Queer Theory." In *Film Studies: Critical Approaches,* edited by John Hill and Pamela Church Gibson, 148–149. New York: Oxford University Press, 2000.

Duggan, Lisa. "The New Homonormativity: The Sexual Politics of Neoliberalism." In *Materializing Democracy: Toward a Revitalized Cultural Politics,* edited by Russ Castronovo and Dana D. Nelson, 175–194. Durham, NC: Duke University Press, 2002.

Duggan, Lisa, and Richard Kim. "Beyond Gay Marriage." *Nation.* July 18, 2005. Accessed November 11, 2005. http://www .thenation.com/doc/20050718/kim.

du Plessis, Michael. "Blatantly Bisexual; or, Unthinking Queer Theory." in *Re-Presenting Bisexualities: Subjects and Cultures of Fluid Desire,* edited by Donald E. Hall and Maria Pramaggiore, 19–54. New York: NYU Press, 1996.

Durbin, Karen. "Cowboys in Love . . . With Each Other." *New York Times,* September 4, 2005.

Durden, Mary. "Lesbian Discretion is Advised: Negotiating Lesbian Desire in *Grey's Anatomy.*" Unpublished essay, Wellesley College, 2010.

Dyer, Richard. *The Culture of Queers.* New York: Routledge, 2002.

Elsaesser, Thomas. "The Pathos of Failure: American Films in the 1970s: Notes on the Unmotivated Hero." In *The Last Great American Picture Show:*

New Hollywood Cinema in the 1970s, edited by Thomas Elsaesser, Alexander Horwath, and Noel King, 279–292. Amsterdam: Amsterdam University Press, 2004.

———. *European Cinema: Face to Face with Hollywood*. Amsterdam: Amsterdam University Press, 2005.

Empson, William. *Some Versions of Pastoral*. Freeport, NY: Books for Libraries Press, 1972.

Erickson-Schroth, Laura, and Jennifer Mitchell. "Queering Queer Theory, or Why Bisexuality Matters." *Journal of Bisexuality* 9, no. 3–4 (2009): 297–315.

Faderman, Lillian. *Surpassing the Love of Men: Romantic Friendship and Love Between Women from the Renaissance to the Present*. New York: Morrow, 1981.

Faludi, Susan. *The Terror Dream: Fear and Fantasy in Post-9/11 America*. New York: Metropolitan, 2007.

Le Fanu, Sheridan. "Carmilla." In *In a Glass Darkly*, 243–319. New York: Oxford University Press, 1999.

Farr, Kathryn Ann. "Dominance through the Good Old Boys Sociability Group." In *Men's Lives*, edited by Michael S. Kimmel and Michael A. Messner, 403–418. New York: Macmillan, 1998.

Feyerabend, Paul. *Against Method*. 3rd ed. New York: Verso, 1993.

Fink, Bruce. *The Lacanian Subject: Between Language and Jouissance*. Princeton, NJ: Princeton University Press, 1995.

Fraser, Miriam. "Framing Contention: Bisexuality Displaced." In *RePresenting Bisexualities: Subjects and Cultures of Fluid Desire*, edited by Donald E. Hall and Maria Pramaggiore, 253–271. New York: NYU Press, 1996.

French, Philip. *"Brokeback Mountain." Observer*, January 8, 2006. Accessed November 25, 2007. http://film.guardian .co.uk/News_Story/Critic_Review/ Observer_Film_of_the_week/ 0,,1681373,00.html.

Freud, Sigmund. *The Standard Edition of the Complete Psychological Works of Sigmund Freud*. Translated and edited by James Strachey. 24 vols. London: Hogarth, 1953–1974.

———. *Three Essays on the Theory of Sexuality*. Translated and edited by James Strachey. New York: Basic Books, 1962.

Fuchs, Cynthia J. "The Buddy Politic." In *Screening the Male: Exploring Masculinities in Hollywood Cinema*, edited by Steven Cohan and Ina Rae Hark, 194–210. New York: Routledge, 1993.

Gabbard, Krin. "Altman's *3 Women*: Sanctuary in the Dream World." *Literature/ Film Quarterly* 8, no. 4 (1980): 258–264.

Galloway, Ron. "Wal-Mart Won't Quit Brokeback." *Huffington Post*, April 4, 2006. Accessed January 17, 2002. http:// www.huffingtonpost.com/rongalloway/ walmart-wont-quit-brokeba_b_18444 .html.

Galt, Rosalind, and Karl Schoonover, eds. *Global Art Cinema*. New York: Oxford University Press, 2010.

Garber, Marjorie. *Bisexuality and the Eroticism of Everyday Life*. Rev. ed. New York: Simon & Schuster, 2000.

Genz, Stéphanie. "Third Way/ve: The Politics of Postfeminism." *Feminist Theory* 7, no. 3 (2006): 33–53.

Gill, Rosalind. "From Sexual Objectification to Sexual Subjectification: The Resexualisation of Women's Bodies in the Media." *Feminist Media Studies* 3, no. 1 (2003): 100–106.

Girard, René. *Deceit, Desire, and the Novel: Self and Other in Literary Structure*. Translated by Yvonne Freccero. Baltimore, MD: Johns Hopkins University Press, 1990.

Gledhill, Christine. "Pleasurable Negotiations." In *Feminist Film Theory: A Reader*, edited by Sue Thornham, 166–179. New York: NYU Press, 1999.

Gomez, Jewelle. *The Gilda Stories: A Novel*. Ithaca, NY: Firebrand, 1991.

Graham, Paula. "Girl's Camp? The Politics of Parody." In *Immortal, Invisible: Lesbians and the Moving Image,* edited by Tamsin Wilton, 163–181. New York: Routledge, 1995.

Hain, Mark. "Explicit Ambiguity: Sexual Identity, Hitchcockian Criticism, and the Films of François Ozon." *Quarterly Review of Film and Video* 24 (2007): 277–288.

Hall, Donald E., and Maria Pramaggiore, eds. *RePresenting Bisexualities: Subjects and Cultures of Fluid Desire.* New York: NYU Press, 1996.

Hansen, Miriam. *Babel and Babylon: Spectatorship in American Silent Film.* Cambridge, MA: Harvard University Press, 1994.

Hanson, Ellis. "Undead." In *Inside/Out: Lesbian Theories, Gay Theories,* edited by Diana Fuss, 324–340. New York: Routledge, 1991.

———. "Lesbians Who Bite." In *Out Takes: Essays on Queer Theory and Film,* edited by Ellis Hanson, 183–222. Durham, NC: Duke University Press, 1999.

Hark, Ina Rae. "'Today Is the Longest Day of My Life': 24 as Mirror Narrative of 9/11." In *Film and Television After 9/11,* edited by Wheeler Winston Dixon, 121–141. Carbondale, IL: Southern Illinois University Press, 2004.

Hart, Lynda. *Fatal Women: Lesbian Sexuality and the Mark of Aggression.* Princeton, NJ: Princeton University Press, 1994.

Hemmings, Clare. "Resituating the Bisexual Body: From Identity to Difference." In *Activating Theory: Lesbian, Gay, Bisexual Politics,* edited by Joseph Bristow and Angelia R. Wilson, 118–138. London: Lawrence & Wishart, 1993.

———. "Bisexual Theoretical Perspectives: Emergent and Contingent Relationships." In *The Bisexual Imaginary: Representation, Identity, and Desire,* edited by Bi Academic Intervention, 14–37. London: Cassell, 1997.

———. *Bisexual Spaces: A Geography of Sexuality and Gender.* New York: Routledge, 2002.

Henderson, Lisa. "Simple Pleasures: Lesbian Community and Go Fish." In *Chick Flicks: Contemporary Women at the Movies,* edited by Suzanne Ferriss and Mallory Young, 132–157. New York: Routledge, 2008.

Hennessey, Rosemary. *Profit and Pleasure: Sexual Identities in Late Capitalism.* New York: Routledge, 2000.

Heung, Marina. "Black Widow." *Film Quarterly* 41, no. 1 (Autumn 1987): 54–58.

Higgins, Bill. "Cowboy Love Song." *Variety.* December 1, 2005. Accessed November 24, 2007. http://www.variety.com/vstory/VR1117933777.html?categoryid=38&cs=1.

Hoberman, J. "Blazing Saddles." *Village Voice,* November 30–December 6, 2005.

Holden, Stephen. "Riding the High Country, Finding and Losing Love." *New York Times,* December 9, 2005. Accessed November 23, 2007. http://movies.nytimes.com/2005/12/09/movies/09brok.html.

———. "Putting a Bromance to an Erotic Test." *New York Times,* July 10, 2009.

Hollinger, Karen. *In the Company of Women: Contemporary Female Friendship Films.* Minneapolis: University of Minnesota Press, 1998.

———. "Theorizing Mainstream Female Spectatorship: The Case of the Popular Lesbian Film." *Cinema Journal* 37, no. 2 (Winter 1998): 3–17.

Holmlund, Chris. "When is a Lesbian Not a Lesbian?": The Lesbian Continuum and the Mainstream Femme Film." *Camera Obscura* 25–26 (January–May 1991): 144–180.

———. "Cruisin' for a Bruisin': Hollywood's Deadly (Lesbian) Dolls." *Cinema Journal* 34, no. 1 (Fall 1994): 31–51.

Horncastle, Julia. "Queer Bisexuality: Perceptions of Bisexual Existence, Distinctions and Challenges." *Journal of Bisexuality* 8, no. 1–2 (2008): 25–49.

Horton, Andrew S. Introduction to *Comedy/Cinema/Theory*, edited by Andrew S. Horton, 1–24. Berkeley: University of California Press, 1991.

Howell, Peter. "Going 'beyond gay'; Sundance hit takes 'bromance' to new level." *Toronto Star*, January 24, 2009.

Hudson, Jennifer A. "'No Hay Banda, and Yet We Hear a Band': David Lynch's Reversal of Coherence in *Mulholland Drive*." *Journal of Film and Video* 56, no. 1 (Spring 2004): 17–24. Accessed January 20, 2012. http://www.jstor.org/stable/20688440.

Irigaray, Luce. *This Sex Which Is Not One*. Translated by Catherine Porter and Carolyn Burke. Ithaca, NY: Cornell University Press, 1985.

James, Christopher. "Denying Complexity: The Dismissal and Appropriation of Bisexuality in Queer, Lesbian, and Gay Theory." In *Queer Studies: A Lesbian, Gay, Bisexual & Transgender Anthology*, edited by Brett Beemyn and Mickey Eliason, 217–240. New York: NYU Press, 1996.

Joyrich, Lynne. "All That Television Allows: TV Melodrama, Postmodernism and Consumer Culture." *Camera Obscura* 16 (January 1988): 141–147.

Kahn, Vali Dagmar. "The Social Negotiation of Ambiguous In-Between Stigmatized Identities: Investigating Identity Processes in Multiracial and Bisexual People." PhD diss., University of Massachusetts Boston, 2011. Accessed January 20, 2012. http://scholarworks.umb.edu/doctoral_dissertations/59.

Kaufman, Anthony. "Range Rovers." *Variety*, October 27, 2005. Accessed November 25, 2007. http://www.variety.com/awardcentral_article/VR1117931754.html.

Kaysen, Susanna. *Girl, Interrupted*. New York: Random House, 1993.

Keller, James R. *Queer (Un)Friendly Film and Television*. Jefferson, NC: McFarland, 2002.

Kennedy, Roseanne. "The Gorgeous Lesbian in *L.A. Law:* The Present Absence?" In *Feminist Television Criticism: A Reader*, edited by Charlotte Brunsdon, Julie D'Acci, and Lynn Spigel, 318–324. New York: Oxford University Press, 1997.

King, Barry. "Embodying An Elastic Self: The Parametrics of Contemporary Stardom." In *Contemporary Hollywood Stardom*, edited by Thomas Austin and Martin Barker, 43–61. New York: Oxford University Press, 2003.

King, Katie. "There Are No Lesbians Here: Lesbianisms, Feminisms, and Global Gay Formations." In *Queer Globalizations: Citizenship and the Afterlife of Colonialism*, edited by Arnaldo Cruz-Malavé and Martin F. Manalansan IV, 33–48. New York: NYU Press, 2002.

Kinsey, Alfred C., Wardell B. Pomeroy, and Clyde E. Martin. *Sexual Behavior in the Human Male*. Philadelphia: W. B. Saunders, 1948.

Kinsey, Alfred C., Wardell B. Pomeroy, Clyde E. Martin, and Paul H. Gebhard. *Sexual Behavior in the Human Female*. Philadelphia: W. B. Saunders, 1953.

Knopf, Marcy Jane. "Bi-nary Bi-sexuality: Jane Bowles's *Two Serious Ladies*." In *RePresenting Bisexualities: Subjects and Cultures of Fluid Desire*. edited Donald E. Hall and Maria Pramaggiore, 142–164. New York: NYU Press, 1996.

Kristal, Nicole, and Mike Szymanski. *The Bisexual's Guide to the Universe*. New York: Alyson Books, 2006.

Lacan, Jacques. *Écrits: A Selection*. Translated by Alan Sheridan. New York: Norton, 1977.

Lane, Anthony. "New Frontiers." *New Yorker*. December 12, 2005. Accessed June 27, 2006. http://www.newyorker.com/printables/critics/051212crci_cinema.

———. "Chill: The Year of Living Strenuously." *New Yorker,* January 16, 2006. Accessed June 27, 2006. http://www.newyorker.com/printables/critics/060116crci_cinema.

Laplanche, Jean, and Jean-Bertrand Pontalis. *The Language of Psychoanalysis.* New York: W. W. Norton, 1973.

———. "Fantasy and the Origins of Sexuality." In *Formations of Fantasy,* edited by Victor Burgin, James Donald, and Cora Kaplan, 5–34. New York: Methuen, 1986.

LeBesco, Kathleen. "Got to Be Real: Mediating Gayness on *Survivor.*" In *Reality TV: Remaking Television Culture,* edited by Susan Murray and Laurie Ouellette, 271–287. New York: NYU Press, 2004.

Lee, Ryan. "Probing the 'Brokeback Syndrome.'" *Southern Voice,* January 13, 2006. Accessed January 19, 2006. http://www.southernvoice.com/print.cfm?content_id=4805.

Litwoman, Jane. "Some Thoughts on Bisexuality." In *Bi Any Other Name: Bisexual People Speak Out,* edited by Loraine Hutchins and Lani Kaahumanu, 4–5. Boston: Alyson Books, 1991.

Love, Heather K. "Spectacular Failure: The Figure of the Lesbian in *Mulholland Drive.*" *New Literary History* 35, no. 1 (2004): 117–132.

Luscombe, Belinda. "Heath Turns It Around." *Time,* November 20, 2005. Accessed November 25, 2007. http://www.time.com/time/magazine/article/0,9171,1132822-2,00.html.

Maltby, Richard. "'A Brief Romantic Interlude': Dick and Jane go to 3½ Seconds of the Classical Hollywood Cinema." In *Post-Theory: Reconstructing Film Studies,* edited by David Bordwell and Noël Carroll, 434–459. Madison: University of Wisconsin Press.

Martin, Biddy. *Femininity Played Straight: The Significance of Being Lesbian.* New York: Routledge, 1996.

Marshall, Kelli. "Bromance and the Boys of *Boston Legal.*" *FLOW,* May 19, 2011. Accessed January 20, 2012. http://flowtv.org/2011/05/flow-favorites-bromance-and-boston-legal/.

May, Elaine Tyler. "Explosive Issues: Sex, Women, and the Bomb." In *Recasting America: Culture and Politics of the Cold War,* edited by Lary May, 154–170. Chicago: University of Chicago Press, 1989.

McBride, Joseph. *Hawks on Hawks.* Berkeley: University of California Press, 1982.

McCarthy, Anna. "*Ellen:* Making Queer Television History." *GLQ* 7, no. 4 (2001): 593–620.

McCarthy, Todd. "*Brokeback Mountain.*" *Variety,* September 6, 2005. Accessed November 25, 2007. http://www.variety.com/review/VE1117928059.html.

McGowan, Todd. "Lost on *Mulholland Drive:* Navigating David Lynch's Panegyric to Hollywood." *Cinema Journal* 43, no. 2 (2004): 67–89.

McHugh, Kathleen. "'Sounds That Creep Inside You': Female Narration and Voiceover in the Films of Jane Campion." *Style* 35, no. 2 (Summer 2001): 193–228. Accessed April 23, 2004. Expanded Academic ASAP (A97074180).

McLean, Adrienne L. *Being Rita Hayworth: Labor, Identity, and Hollywood Stardom.* New Brunswick, NJ: Rutgers University Press, 2004.

Mead, Margaret. "Bisexuality: What's It All About?" *Redbook.* January 1975, 29, 31.

Michel, Frann. "Do Bats Eat Cats? Reading What Bisexuality Does." In *RePresenting Bisexualities: Subjects and Cultures of Fluid Desire,* edited by Donald E. Hall and Maria Pramaggiore, 55–69. New York: NYU Press, 1996.

Minkowitz, Donna. "How to have our family and smash it too (Wedding Vows)." *The Nation,* July 5, 2004. Accessed November 24, 2005. Expanded Academic ASAP (A118670299).

Mitchell, Danielle. "Straight and Crazy? Bisexual and Easy? Or Drunken Floozy? The Queer Politics of Karen Walker." In *The New Queer Aesthetic on Television,* edited by James R. Keller and Leslie Stratyner, 85–98. Jefferson, NC: McFarland, 2006.

Moorman, Jennifer. "'Shades of Grey': Articulations of Bisexuality in *The L Word.*" In *Televising Queer Women: A Reader,* rev. ed., edited by Rebecca Beirne, 119–134. New York: Palgrave Macmillan, 2012.

Morton, Donald. "Birth of the Cyberqueer." *PMLA* 110, no. 3 (May 1995): 369–381.

Mulvey, Laura. "Afterthoughts on 'Visual Pleasure and Narrative Cinema' Inspired by King Vidor's *Duel in the Sun.*" In *Visual and Other Pleasures,* 29–37. Bloomington: Indiana University Press, 1989.

Munn, Michael. *The Sharon Stone Story.* London: Robson Books, 1997.

Neale, Steve. "Art Cinema as Institution." In *The European Cinema Reader,* edited by Catherine Fowler, 103–120. New York: Routledge, 2002.

Neroni, Hillary. "Jane Campion's Jouissance: *Holy Smoke* and Feminist Film Theory." In *Lacan and Contemporary Film,* edited by Todd McGowan and Sheila Kunkle, 209–232. New York: Other Press, 2004.

Nochimson, Martha. "'All I Need is the Girl': The Life and Death of Creativity in *Mulholland Drive.*" In *American Dreams, Nightmare Visions: The Cinema of David Lynch,* edited by Erica Sheen and Annette Davison, 165–181. New York: Wallflower, 2004.

Paul, William. "The Impossibility of Romance: Hollywood Comedy, 1978–99." In *Genre and Contemporary Hollywood,* edited by Steve Neale, 117–129. London: British Film Institute, 2002.

Paulin, Scott. "Sex and the Singled Girl: Queer Representation and Containment in *Single White Female.*" *Camera Obscura* 37 (January 1996): 33–68.

Perlmutter, Ruth. "Memories, Dreams, Screens." *Quarterly Review of Film and Video* 22 (2005): 125–134.

Powers, John. "Lonesome Cowboys." *Vogue,* December 2005. Accessed January 22, 2012. http://www.accessmy library.com/coms2/summary_0286 -12163320_ITM.

Pramaggiore, Maria. "BI-ntroduction I: Epistemologies of the Fence." In *RePresenting Bisexualities: Subjects and Cultures of Fluid Desire,* edited by Donald E. Hall and Maria Pramaggiore, 1–7. New York: NYU Press, 1996.

———. "Straddling the Screen: Bisexual Spectatorship and Contemporary Narrative Film." In *RePresenting Bisexualities: Subjects and Cultures of Fluid Desire,* edited by Donald E. Hall and Maria Pramaggiore, 272–300. New York: NYU Press, 1996.

Proulx, Annie. "Brokeback Mountain." *New Yorker.* October 13, 1997, 74–85.

Puar, Jasbir K. *Terrorist Assemblages: Homonationalism in Queer Times.* Durham, NC: Duke University Press, 2007.

Ramirez, Anthony. "You Can Leave Your Hat On." *New York Times,* January 4, 2006. Accessed November 23, 2007. http://www.nytimes.com/2006/01/04/ nyregion/04bold.html.

Rich, Adrienne. "Compulsory Heterosexuality and Lesbian Existence." In *The Lesbian and Gay Studies Reader,* edited by Henry Abelove, Michèle Aina Barale, and David M. Halperin, 227–254. New York: Routledge, 1993.

Rich, Frank. "Two Gay Cowboys Hit a Home Run." *New York Times,* December 18, 2005.

Rubin, Gayle. "The Traffic in Women: Notes on the 'Political Economy' of Sex." In *The Second Wave: A Reader in Feminist Theory,* edited by Linda Nicholson, 27–62. New York: Routledge, 1997.

Rust, Paula C. *Bisexuality and the Challenge to Lesbian Politics: Sex, Loyalty, and Revolution.* New York: NYU Press, 1995.

Ryan, Michael, and Douglas Kellner. *Camera Politica: The Politics and Ideology of Contemporary Hollywood Film.* Bloomington: Indiana University Press, 1988.

Samuels, Robert. *Hitchcock's Bi-Textuality: Lacan, Feminisms, and Queer Theory.* Albany, NY: SUNY Press, 1998.

Schickel, Richard. "A Tender Cowpoke Love Story." *Time.* November 28, 2005, 68.

Sedgwick, Eve Kosofsky. *Between Men: English Literature and Male Homosocial Desire.* New York: Columbia University Press, 1985.

Self, Robert T. *Robert Altman's Subliminal Reality.* Minneapolis: University of Minnesota Press, 2002.

Shetley, Vernon. "The Presence of the Past: *Mulholland Drive* against *Vertigo.*" *Raritan* 25, no. 3 (2006): 112–128.

Simpson, Mark. *It's a Queer World.* London: Vintage, 1996.

Smith, Sean. "Forbidden Territory." *Newsweek.* November 21, 2005, 70.

Smyth, Cherry. "The Transgressive Sexual Subject." In *A Queer Romance: Lesbians, Gay Men and Popular Culture,* edited by Paul Burston and Colin Richardon, 123–143. New York: Routledge, 1995.

Soanes, Catherine, ed. *Oxford Dictionary of Contemporary English.* 3rd ed. New York: Oxford University Press, 2001.

Sontag, Susan. *Styles of Radical Free Will.* New York: Farrar, Straus and Giroux, 1967.

———. *Reborn: Journals and Notebooks, 1947–1963.* Edited by David Rieff. New York: Farrar, Strauss and Giroux, 2008.

St. John, Warren. "What Men Want: Neanderthal TV." *New York Times,* December 11, 2005. Accessed December 18, 2009. http://www.nytimes.com/2005/12/11/fashion/sundaystyles/11MEN.html?_r=1&scp=1&sq=neanderthal%20TV&st=cse.

Stacey, Jackie. *Star Gazing: Hollywood Cinema and Female Spectatorship.* New York: Routledge, 1994.

Stamp, Shelley. *Movie-Struck Girls.* Princeton, NJ: Princeton University Press, 2000.

Stasia, Cristina. "Butch-Femme Interrupted: Angelina Jolie, Bisexuality and the New Butch Femme." In *Bisexuality and Transgenderism: InterSEXions of the Others,* edited by Jonathan Alexander and Karen Yescavage, 181–201. Boston: Harrington Park Press, 2003.

Stein, Ruthe. "Ang Lee Reworks the Classic Western and Gives 'Pardners' a New Meaning – Two Straight Actors Learn to Be Lovers." *San Francisco Chronicle,* November 30, 2005. Accessed November 25, 2007. http://www.sfgate.com/cgibin/article.cgi?f=/c/a/2005/11/30/DDGACFVDLE1.DTL.

Strain, Ellen. *Public Places, Private Journeys: Ethnography, Entertainment, and the Tourist Gaze.* New Brunswick, NJ: Rutgers University Press, 2003.

Tasker, Yvonne, and Diane Negra. "Introduction: Feminist Politics and Postfeminist Culture." In *Interrogating Post-feminism: Gender and the Politics of Popular Culture,* edited by Yvonne Tasker and Diane Negra, 1–26. Durham, NC: Duke University Press, 2007.

Taubin, Amy. "In Dreams." *Film Comment.* September–October 2001, 51–54.

Thomas, June. "Why Bisexual Women are TV's New Hot Thing." *Slate,* March 8, 2012, Accessed March 22, 2012. http://www.slate.com/blogs/browbeat/2012/03/08/bisexual_women_are_tv_s_hot_new_thing.html.

Toles, George. "Auditioning Betty in *Mulholland Drive.*" *Film Quarterly* 58, no. 1 (Fall 2004): 2–13.

Torres, Sasha. "Melodrama, Masculinity, and the Family: *thirtysomething* as Therapy." *Camera Obscura* 19 (January 1989): 86–107.

———. "Television/Feminism: *Heart-Beat* and Prime Time Lesbianism." In *The Lesbian and Gay Studies Reader*, edited by Henry Abelove, Michèle Aina Barale, and David M. Halperin, 176–185. New York: Routledge, 1993.

Traub, Valerie. "The Ambiguities of 'Lesbian' Viewing Pleasure: The (Dis)articulations of *Black Widow*." In *Out in Culture: Gay, Lesbian, and Queer Essays on Popular Culture*, edited by Corey K. Creekmur and Alexander Doty, 115–136. Durham, NC: Duke University Press, 1995.

Tuller, David. "No Surprise for Bisexual Men: Report Indicates They Exist." *New York Times*, August 23, 2011.

Turan, Kenneth. "*Brokeback Mountain*." *Los Angeles Times*, December 9, 2005. Accessed November 23, 2007. http://www.calendarlive.com/movies/turan/cletbrokeback9dec09,0,186375.story.

Turner, Victor. *The Ritual Process*. Ithaca, NY: Cornell University Press, 1977.

Tyler, Carole-Anne. "Boys Will Be Girls: The Politics of Gay Drag." In *Inside/Out: Lesbian Theories, Gay Theories*, edited by Diana Fuss, 32–70. New York: Routledge, 1991.

van Gennep, Arnold. *The Rites of Passage*. London: Routledge Kegan Paul, 1977.

Warner, Michael. *Publics and Counterpublics*. New York: Zone, 2005.

Weiss, Andrea. *Vampires and Violets: Lesbians in Film*. New York: Penguin, 1993.

———. "'A Queer Feeling When I Look at You': Hollywood Stars and Lesbian Spectatorship in the 1930s." In *Multiple Voices in Feminist Film Criticism*, edited by Diane Carson, Linda Dittmar, and Janice R. Welsch, 330–342. Minneapolis: University of Minnesota Press, 1994.

White, Patricia. *UnInvited: Classical Hollywood Cinema and Lesbian Representability*. Bloomington: Indiana University Press, 1990.

Williams, Linda. *Hard Core: Power, Pleasure, and the "Frenzy of the Visible."* Berkeley: University of California Press, 1989.

Willis, Ellen, Martha Fineman, Patricia Hill Collins, Judith Butler, Susan Brownmiller, E. J. Graff, Michael Eric Dyson, and Judith Stacey. "Can Marriage Be Saved? A Forum." *Nation*, July 14, 2004. Accessed November 23, 2007. http://www.thenation.com/doc/20040705/forum2.

Willis, Sharon. "Hardware and Hardbodies, What Do Women Want?: A Reading of *Thelma and Louise*." In *Film Theory Goes to the Movies*, edited by Jim Collins, Hilary Radner, and Ava Preacher Collins, 120–128. New York: Routledge, 1993.

Wilton, Tamsin, ed. *Immortal, Invisible: Lesbians and the Moving Image*. New York: Routledge, 1995.

Winokur, Mark. "Body and Soul: Identifying (with) the Black Lesbian Body in Cheryl Dunye's *The Watermelon Woman*." In *Recovering the Black Female Body: Self-Representations by African American Women*, edited by Michael Bennett and Vanessa D. Dickerson, 231–252. New Brunswick, NJ: Rutgers University Press, 2001.

Winter, Jessica. "The Scripting News." *Village Voice*, November 30–December 6, 2005. Accessed November 23, 2007. http://www.villagevoice.com/film/0548,winter,70454,20.html.

Wood, Robin, and Michael Walker. *Claude Chabrol*. New York: Praeger, 1970.

Wood, Robin. *Hollywood from Vietnam to Reagan . . . and Beyond*, rev. ed. New York: Columbia University Press, 2003.

Yescavage, Karen, and Jonathan Alexander. "Seeing What We Want to See: Searching for Bisexual Representation in 'Threesome' Films." *Journal of Bisexuality* 3, no. 2 (2003): 109–127.

Yukman, Lidia. "Loving Dora: Rereading Freud Through H.D.'s *Her.*" In *RePresenting Bisexualities: Subjects and Cultures of Fluid Desire,* edited by Donald E. Hall and Maria Pramaggiore, 124–141. New York: NYU Press, 1996.

Zak, Dan. "Isn't It Bromantic? Arriving at 'Humpday'" *Washington Post,* July 19, 2009.

Zeller-Jacques, Martin. "'Challenging and Alternative': Screening Queer Girls on Channel 4." In *Women on Screen,* edited by Melanie Waters. New York: Palgrave Macmillan, 2011.

Žižek, Slavoj. *The Art of the Ridiculous Sublime: On David Lynch's Lost Highway.* Seattle: University of Washington Press, 2000.

Index

MARIA SAN FILIPPO has taught film and television studies and gender and sexuality studies at Harvard University, MIT, UCLA, and Wellesley College, where she was the 2008–2010 Mellon Postdoctoral Fellow in Cinema and Media Studies. Her work has appeared in the journals *Cine-Action*, *Cineaste*, *English Language Notes*, *Film History*, *In Media Res*, the *Journal of Bisexuality*, the *Quarterly Review of Film and Video*, and *Senses of Cinema*, and the anthologies *Global Art Cinema* (2010) and *Millennial Masculinity: Men in Contemporary American Cinema* (2012). She is a 2012–2013 research associate in feminist approaches to new media at the Five College Women's Studies Research Center.

CPSIA information can be obtained at www.ICGtesting.com
Printed in the USA
LVOW12*1923221113

362499LV00001B/2/P